MADEIRA

June 2018.

Richard,
    A little light Reading to
Recall a lovely holiday in Madeira.
With love, Susan.

Dad,
"The world is a book and those who
do not travel only read one page"
                St. Augustine of Hippo

Thank you for sharing your chapter
on Madeira with me.
        Lots of love
                George xxx

THE CLASSIC WINE LIBRARY

Series editor: Richard Mayson

Cognac: The story of the world's greatest brandy, Nicholas Faith
Port and the Douro, Richard Mayson
Sherry, Julian Jeffs

MADEIRA

THE ISLANDS AND THEIR WINES

RICHARD MAYSON

The right of Richard Mayson to be identified as the author of this book has been asserted in accordance with the Copyright, Designs and Patents Act 1988.

First published in 2015 by
Infinite Ideas Limited
36 St Giles
Oxford
OX1 3LD
United Kingdom
www.infideas.com

A CIP catalogue record for this book is available from the British Library

ISBN 978–1–908984–30–2

Wine labels on pages 5, 41, 111, 112, 116, 123, 136, 148, 174, 193 and 195 from author's own collection.
Illustrations on pages 16, 41, 67, 70, 71, 76, 149, 167, 191 and 199 from Henry Vizetelly, *Facts About Port and Madeira* (1880).
Photograph on page 81 and plate pages 1, 3, 4, 6 (top right) and 8 (bottom) courtesy of Ricardo Diogo Freitas of Barbeito.
Photographs on page 67 and plate pages 2, 5, 6 (top left and bottom), 7 and 8 (top) courtesy of Christopher Blandy of the Madeira Wine Company.

Text designed and typeset by Nicki Averill

Printed and bound in Great Britain by TJ International Ltd, Padstow, Cornwall

To Richard Francis Blandy, my late father-in-law,
who helped to introduce me to madeira wine.

CONTENTS

ACKNOWLEDGEMENTS

This book is the result of many informative visits to Madeira over a period of thirty-five years. There are many individuals who have been generous with their time, wines and knowledge of the island. I should first acknowledge my debt of gratitude to my late father-in-law, Richard Blandy. I met him a decade before I met my future wife, his daughter Katrina. At the time Richard Blandy was the Honorary British Consul on the island. I recall being unforgivably late for a meeting with him in his office one Friday afternoon at the end of a fact-finding week in Madeira researching my first book, *Portugal's Wines and Wine Makers*. The conversation that I had with him that day helped to explain the complexities of these isolated islands, their ways, the local economy and the way the wine trade worked, so much so that it all slipped into place. His commitment to Madeira, along with his passion for the island's wines, was always evident at subsequent tastings in London. In conversation he was never short of wise words of advice. Richard Blandy died in 2002, aged 55, having been my father-in-law for just four weeks. This book is dedicated in fond memory of him.

I must go on to thank the other members of the Blandy family for their cooperation and support during the time I have been writing this book, Michael Blandy and Christopher Blandy in particular. I am also grateful for help from both James Symington and Dominic Symington, business partners with the Blandys until 2011. Francisco Albuquerque, wine maker for the Madeira Wine Company, has been an enormous help over many years, having patiently answered technical questions and shared his enthusiasm for madeira wine, both past and present.

But in case you think this book is all about my extended Madeira family, there are many others who have been very open in sharing their knowledge of the island. I am especially grateful to Ricardo Diogo

Freitas of Barbeito whose passion for madeira wine is infectious and who has spent many hours with me tasting and talking, sharing his thoughts and opinions on the past, present and future. The late John Cossart of Henriques & Henriques will also be fondly remembered for the time he spent in conversation with anyone prepared to listen to his strongly expressed opinions. I am grateful to him, and to his colleague and successor Humberto Jardim.

There are many others in the madeira trade who have been very generous with their time and, in alphabetical order, I am grateful to Artur and Edmundo Barros e Sousa (Barros e Sousa), Isabel and Helena Borges (H. M. Borges), the late Siegfredo Costa Campos, Juan Teixiera and Júlio Fernandes, all from Justino Henriques, Jacques Faro da Silva (Madeira Wine Company) and Luís d'Oliveira (Pereira D'Oliveira). Andrew Blandy and Pedro Diniz have both been very helpful with their first-hand knowledge of planting and managing a vineyard in Madeira.

In addition I am very grateful to Adam Blandy, Anthony Miles, Dr Francis Zino and the late Ferdinando Bianchi for imparting their deep historical knowledge of the island. I must also acknowledge the research of Emanuel 'Mannie' Berk, which he has willingly shared with fellow madeira wine *aficionados* at two superb themed tastings jointly organised with Roy Hersh in New York in 2012 and 2013. Patrick Grubb M.W. has been unstintingly generous at his annual tastings in London and I am grateful to him for his guidance over many years. Geoff and Pam Cole, representing D'Oliveira in the UK, are always present at tastings and trade fairs and are always willing to share an interesting wine.

Although I have endeavoured to be scrupulously independent of any family ties whilst writing this book, I must thank Valerie Blandy for agreeing to read through the first draft. I must also acknowledge the help of my assistant Diana Burgess in this task. My publisher Infinite Ideas has been supportive throughout and I especially wish to acknowledge the hard work and patient co-operation of Rebecca Clare and Kate Santon in editing this book. Finally I would like to thank my immediate family, my wife Katrina and my children, Edward, Jamie and Isabella, who have stood patiently by me through the many difficult times when I thought this book would never be finished.

PREFACE

Those who know me well can confirm that this book has been a long time in the making. I was fortunate to start writing it when I was spending some time living on the island of Madeira. My office at the time was directly above a madeira wine store. It was high summer and with the window open, I could just glimpse the Atlantic. Every so often, and completely unheralded, the most wonderful, ethereal vapours would waft in through the window on the warm breeze. I occasionally had to stop writing to savour these aromas and the flow of words would temporarily dry up.

Madeira is a wine like no other. It is fine wine in *extremis*. Heat and air, both the sworn enemies of most wines and wine makers, conspire to turn madeira into one of the most enthralling of the world's wines as well as the most resilient. Wines from the nineteenth and even the eighteenth centuries still retain an ethereal, youthful gloss, even after spending what is, in wine terms, an aeon in cask and bottle. Having gone through this extreme and often extensive ageing process, madeira is virtually indestructible. Once the cork is removed, the wine comes to no harm, even if the bottle is left on ullage for months, even for years on end. If ever there was a wine to take away with you to a desert island, this is it.

Madeira is sometimes described as an 'ageless' wine. This is misleading because Madeira *needs* age to taste the way it should. This was clearly observed as far back as 1841 by Bruno Perestrelo da Câmara, who wrote of a Sercial wine that 'no less than ten years are needed for this liquid to acquire the flavour, aroma and hint of burnt toffee which characterises it'. There are no shortcuts, although it is not for want of trying that the shippers have long used artificial heating to obtain that maderised taste in a wine that is no more than two or three years of age. This is something of a handicap for madeira in the realm of fortified wine. A young ruby port may not have complexity but it still tastes like ruby port and a young fino tastes like sherry, but in madeira there is really no substitute for cask age. As a result there is a considerable difference between these cheaper, younger wines and those which have extended ageing in cask. For this reason I make no apologies for focusing in this book on older wines, even though they account for perhaps 10 per cent of the current madeira trade.

Madeira, the islands and the wines, can be impenetrable even for those deeply involved in the wine trade. In the past, trade visitors have often left the island feeling more confounded than when they arrived. Witness wine writer Margaret Rand, writing in the UK wine trade weekly *Harpers* in 2000, who expressed her frustration thus: 'Newton's First Law of Motion states that for every action there is an equal and opposite reaction. Madeira is like that: for every answer to a question there is an equal and opposite answer.' After giving examples she continued: 'I say this to give an idea of the feeling of helplessness that is apt to creep up on one on the island, as hard facts soften and dissolve like clouds over the mountains'. I sympathise as I have also experienced a similar feeling of obstruction at times in the past. But the reason for this apparent evasiveness was either because there were few hard facts (official statistics being hard to come by) or that the truth was too unpalatable to be made public. In order to interpret what was really going on, you spent your time reading between the lines.

Thankfully, over the past fifteen years, this obfuscation has diminished. Helped by investment and, dare I say, regulation from the EU, and with a younger generation in charge, Madeira is both more obedient and open. This book marshals information from my many visits to the island going back to 1990, as well as those earlier visitors who have documented their experiences. It seeks to present the island as it is today as well as to record the changes that have transformed the wine landscape, both literally and figuratively.

A great madeira wine is, without doubt, one of the most difficult wines to describe but it is certainly the most uplifting to taste. In this book on the islands and the wines I endeavour to describe what makes madeira wine unique. This is not a history book: it is intended to be about contemporary Madeira, the islands and their wines. A number of excellent books have been written on the history of madeira wine, not least Alberto Vieira's comprehensive *A Vinha e O Vinho na História da*

Madeira – Séculos XV a XX. (And in the English language, over a third of Alex Liddell's book, *Madeira, the Mid-Atlantic Wine* is devoted to the history of the wine trade.) For although Madeira was discovered by the Portuguese in the fifteenth century (when Bordeaux, Burgundy and the vineyards of northern Portugal were already well established), wine has been an essential and integral part of the island's history ever since. Wine was dominant through much of the eighteenth and nineteenth centuries, and remained an important part of the economy until mass tourism began to take pole position from the 1970s onwards.

Chapter 1 sets out to explain the origins of the industry, its steady growth and sharp reversals of fortune. It is far from exhaustive but it sets the scene for the madeira wine trade as it is in the early twenty-first century. I have quoted extensively throughout this book from Henry Vizetelly's *Facts About Port and Madeira*, written after a visit to the island during the vintage of 1877. This may seem like a long time ago, but Vizetelly's writing shows a real understanding of Madeira at the time. As many of the old wines still available on the market date from this period and earlier, I have taken selective passages from his book which describe the vineyards, the wine making and the wine stores (*armazens*) at this time. Another observer who visited Madeira at a time of profound change was Rupert Croft-Cooke, whose book *Madeira* was published in 1961. I have quoted from this where it helps to explain the way wine was handled as recently as the 1950s. On Madeira the not too distant past really was a foreign country – they did things very differently there.

The remainder of the book rounds more firmly on the present. Chapter 2 describes the physical character of the archipelago as it is today. The state of the vines and vineyards and the way in which the wines are made are covered in Chapters 3 and 4 respectively. In the latter chapter I make no apologies for exploring the way in which wines were made until the rapid changes of the 1960s and 1970s, especially as many of the wines from these vintages are only now being bottled. I have also included short vintage reports covering the last twenty years, which give an indication of the wines that lie ahead. The shippers (producers) of madeira wine are profiled in Chapter 5, together with short tasting notes on some of their most representative wines. Chapter 6 provides a compendium of some of the historic wines that have made Madeira so famous. It is very far from being exhaustive but it is a comprehensive assessment of the wines that I have tasted over a period of nearly thirty years (often more than once) together with as much of the relevant contextual information as I have been able to find. There are sections on buying, keeping, serving and tasting madeira wine in Chapter 7, followed by a short guide for anyone visiting the islands. Finally, I have assembled my own thoughts on the future for Madeira wine in a Postscript. A number of authoritative and scholarly books have been written on different aspects of madeira and the Portuguese wine trade. These and other documentary sources are listed in the bibliography on page 243.

Madeira is a passion and without a number of passionate individuals the industry would not have survived. Some of these are profiled in Chapter 1 while others are mentioned in Chapters 5 and 6, among them the individuals who have amassed fine collections of old dated wines. To this I add my own passion for one of the world's most mystical and miraculous wines. I hope that some of this passion rubs off on readers of this book. Above all this book is intended to be a contemporary guide for those visiting Madeira as well as a manageable and easy armchair read, preferably accompanied by a glass of madeira wine.

As I was concluding the first draft of this book in early September, the aromas wafting into my office window suddenly changed. Over the top of the ethereal smell of wine ageing in wood came the fresh aroma of fermenting grape must. A new vintage was on the way. Unlike most wines which are made for drinking within four or five years, I felt myself writing with the near certain knowledge that the fruits of this vintage and future vintages will be appreciated by my children, grandchildren, great-grandchildren and even great-great-grandchildren.

Such is the nature of madeira wine.

Richard Mayson
Funchal, 2015

1

MADEIRA WINE: AN INTRODUCTORY HISTORY

THE MOUTH OF HELL?

It is probable that the Moors knew of a group of islands off the coast of North Africa when they invaded the Iberian Peninsula in the eighth century. The early 'flat earth' navigators gave the islands a wide berth. This forbidding mass of rock, capped by steaming clouds, was thought by many to be 'the mouth of hell'. If anyone sailed too close they ran the risk of falling off the edge of the earth into a bottomless pit, to be consumed by serpents and monsters. Madeira is shown as the *Isola de Lolegname* ('the island of wood') on the Medici Map of Africa (*Portulano Medicio*) dated 1351, although it is possible that it was added on at a later date. But other fourteenth-century maps also show an archipelago north of the Canaries fifty years before they were officially discovered and colonised by the Portuguese.

An early legend with perhaps an element of truth tells of an Englishman named Robert Machin who fell madly in love with a young noblewoman, Anna d'Arfet. Unable to marry at home, they eloped to sea intending to reach the Mediterranean but were driven out into the Atlantic by a north-easterly gale. After thirteen days at sea they landed on a deserted island. Anna died on arrival and Robert perished a few days later, but some members of the crew survived and set sail once more. They were captured by the Moors but a fellow prisoner, a Spaniard named Juan de Morales, heard of the island they had found. He was subsequently captured by the Portuguese who were at war with Spain and told his story to the sea

1

captain, João Gonçalves 'O Zarco'. Zarco, meaning 'the blue eyed', was a disciple of Infante Dom Henrique (Prince Henry the Navigator) and he set sail with Tristão Vaz Teixeira and Bartolomeu Perestrello, landing on Porto Santo in 1418. Zarco and Teixeira returned to Sagres in the Algarve leaving Perestrello and some of the crew to occupy the island. Prince Henry ordered Zarco and Teixeira back to Porto Santo to discover what lay under the dense mound of cloud to the south-west. In July 1420 they found a densely forested island and named it *Ilha da Madeira* ('Island of the Woods' in Portuguese).

THE FIRST WINES

Madeira officially became a part of Portugal by order of King João I in 1425 who donated it to his son, Prince Henry. Henry raised funds to colonise the island, a mission led by Zarco and Teixeira. Zarco took command of the south and west of the island and Teixeira took control of the east with Perestrello left in charge of Porto Santo. The first settlers were mostly scions of noble families from mainland Portugal who were able to lease land rent free from the governors provided it was put to productive use. With them came labourers, mainly from the north of Portugal. Forests had to be cleared to provide space for agricultural land and Zarco agreed to set fire to them. The fire apparently burned for seven years, destroying most of Madeira's native forest but greatly enriching the soil with ash and embers.

The first crops to be planted were for subsistence and almost certainly would have included vines. These originated in the Portuguese mainland. Prince Henry introduced sugar cane which flourished on the island, and is reputed to have brought more vines from the Mediterranean. Among these was a variety known as Malvasia that had been sent from Candia in Crete but which may have already been established in mainland Portugal. By 1450, just twenty-five years after the colony was first established, wine was already being exported. In 1455 a Venetian navigator named Alvise de Cà da Mosto told of 'very good wines, really exceptionally good … in such quantity that they suffice for the islanders and many are exported'. He makes special mention of Malvasia.

Madeira's first capital was Machico, supposedly named after the ill-fated Robert Machin. As the island was colonised the narrow valley and shallow bay became inadequate and the capital moved along the coast to a broad protective bay to the west. Funchal, named after the *funcho* or fennel found growing there, graduated to the rank of a city in 1508 when the building of the cathedral began. The first bishop was appointed on its completion in 1514, by which time the population of the island had reached 5,000. The five loaves of sugar in Funchal's coat of arms represent the importance of sugar cane to the island's economy.

In 1498 foreign settlers were granted permanent right of residence on the island. The first foreign merchants were mostly Italians and included the Lomelinos and Acciaiolis, both of which subsequently became important shippers of Madeira wine (see Chapter 6). Simon Acciaioli, who landed on Madeira in 1515, is credited with introducing the Malvasia Babosa grape to the island. Sugar cane, still the most important crop on the island at the beginning of the sixteenth century, declined in importance after 1570 when Brazil (discovered by the Portuguese in 1500) became a cheaper source. As sugar's importance declined, vines took the place of sugar cane as the principal crop and madeira wine was exported to France and England.

The vineyards were irrigated, and by all accounts they were extremely productive, (just as they are today). They were confined to the lower reaches of the narrow river valleys, mostly along the south coast. There were no interconnecting roads and the only communication between one vineyard area and another was by sea. In 1530 an Italian named Giulio Landi stated that the island 'produces a large quantity of wine of all kinds but most are fortified white wines … as well as Malmsey, but in lesser quantities which is reputed to be better than that from Candia'. In his book *A Vinho e O Vinho na Historia da Madeira,* Alberto Vieira estimates that in the 1560s Madeira was exporting around a million litres of wine annually. These early wines were almost certainly dry, may have been fortified and were produced from white grape varieties brought to the island by the early settlers from the north of Portugal. The only exception was the highly prized Malvasia which already had a reputation for richness, possibly derived from raisinised grapes.

LANDLORDS AND PEASANTS: *MORGADOS* AND THE *CONTRATO DE COLÓNIA*

From the time of its colonisation, Madeiran society became starkly divided. The landowners and merchants lived in Funchal while the countryside was farmed by the peasants. The landowners established *morgados* or entails whereby estates were inherited by primogeniture. A feudal contract, termed the *colónia,* was made between the landowner and the tenant who was obliged to give the landlord half of the harvest. All improvements to the land (known as *bemfeitorias*) became the property of the tenant and if the owner wanted to reclaim the land, he was obliged to pay an indemnity. Government officials leant to the side of the tenant, and so the result was that the so-called 'improvements' eventually became worth more than the value of the land itself. The *contracto de colónia* was hereditary and the land and any improvements became sub-divided between the tenant's heirs.

As a consequence, although property ownership in Madeira was concentrated in the hands of a few powerful landowners, the holdings became increasingly fragmented. Rupert Croft-Cooke, visiting the islands in the late 1950s, described the system of landholding thus: 'Very little about it has changed since William Bolton bought wine from Portuguese landowners who made it nearly three hundred years ago. Now, as then, the land is held under the old feudal system of *caseiros*. The caseiro is a smallholder who cultivates his land and pays for it by giving half its produce to the landowner though everything on it, house, walls even trees remain his own. This system, it can be well understood, discourages capricious changes on both sides.' The system of *morgados* continued until 1863 but the *contracto de colonia* was only abolished in 1977 (after the 1974 revolution - see page 23). Tenants were given the right to buy their freeholds leading to the spread of housing on what had been prime agricultural land. Famous estates were broken up (see Torre Bella on page 205 as an example) and many of the best vineyards on the outskirts of Funchal were consequently lost.

MADEIRA: WINE OF THE AMERICAS

In 1478 Christopher Columbus visited Funchal and married Filipa Perestello e Moniz, daughter of the first governor of Porto Santo. Columbus studied his father-in-law's maps and concluded that there was a route across the western ocean to Japan. He submitted his plans to the King João II of Portugal who turned them down; he then spent the next five years trawling the courts of Europe until he was finally accepted by Isabella I of Spain. His discovery of the West Indies in 1492 and the subsequent colonisation of the North American continent proved very beneficial to Madeira, which became an important victualling port for ships crossing the Atlantic.

Madeira's wine trade suffered when Portugal fell into the hands of the Spanish House of Habsburg after 1581. In 1590 the first recorded British trader, named Robert Willoughby, arrived on the island. He was followed by other British merchants during the first half of the sixteenth century and by 1658 they had their own consul in Funchal. The British prospered from their colonial markets in America and, Portugal having regained her independence from 1640 onwards, the British mercantile strength was considerably reinforced by the Staple Act of 1663. This exempted both Madeira and the Azores from an earlier Act prohibiting the export of goods to the English colonies other than from English ports. The

merchants in Funchal were thereby handed a virtual monopoly in the shipment of wine between the West Indies and the English plantations in North America. A lucrative trading triangle formed as produce and products from Britain and the new colonies were traded for madeira wine. Christopher Jefferson from St Kitts visited Madeira in 1676 and wrote 'There is no commoditie better in these parts than Madeira Wines. They are soe generally and soe plentifully drunk, being the only drink that is naturale here, except brandy and rum, which are too hott'. In his book *Madeira, the Island Vineyard*, Noel Cossart records that by 1680 there were as many as thirty wine shippers on Madeira, seven or eight of them being Portuguese, ten British and about ten of other European nationalities. At the end of the century annual exports of madeira were esstimated to be in the order of 4 million litres.

There is no evidence to suggest that the madeira shipped overseas at this time was anything other than young wine from the previous vintage. Malvasia, although highly prized for its rich flavour, is known to have been spoiled easily and was not made in large quantities; however, it commanded a significant premium in price over other wines. The bulk of madeira wine was made from unnamed white grape varieties. Red wines (*Tinto*), often referred to as 'Tento' or 'Tent' and later as 'Madeira Burgundy', were considered to be inferior in quality although red was often mixed with white wine. This apparently gave the wines greater longevity. Sir Hans Sloane, who visited Madeira in 1689, described white wine mixed with a little *tinto* 'expos'd to Sun-beams and heat' adding 'the better it is, and instead of putting it in a cool Cellar they expose it to the Sun'. He goes on to compare the wine to sherry. As a result of such treatment these wines were clearly 'maderised' and able to withstand the heat of the American plantations and the West Indies.

Towards the end of the seventeenth century it was found, almost certainly by accident, that madeira wine was much improved after pitching and rolling in the hold of a ship as it sailed across the tropics. William Bolton (below) describes in his letters the process of 'back-loading' where wines were shipped to the tropics and back to Madeira with the intention of improving and developing it in cask. It led to a fashion developed for *vinho da roda* or *tornaviagem* (literally 'return journey'). These became increasingly sought after in fashionable markets during the eighteenth century.

MEN WHO SHAPED MADEIRA

William Bolton (unknown: fl. late C17–early C18)

Much information on the madeira wine trade at the turn of the eighteenth century is contained within the Bolton letters which were uncovered and published by André Simon, a bookseller from Leicester, England in 1926. William Bolton was a merchant in Warwickshire, England who took advantage of the Staple Act. He was a merchant ship owner and banker who first came to Madeira in 1695. His correspondence (which was never intended for publication) begins shortly after his arrival on the island, when Bolton was acting for Robert Heysham, and continues for nearly twenty years. William Bolton shipped wine from Madeira to the West Indies, New York and Boston, England and Ireland, and supplied wine to ships calling at Funchal on their way to South America, St. Helena, Madagascar, India and Java. Although wine was his staple commodity, like many merchants at the time he imported food, raw materials and manufactured items both for the island and for shipping to other parts of the world. Among these imports were wheat from Devon and Cornwall in England, meat, butter and cheese from Ireland, fish from Newfoundland, whale oil and timber from New York, rice and maize from Carolina and Virginia, sugar from the West Indies and textiles from London. The Bolton letters provide some fascinating detail on the wine trade at the time. For instance, there is a letter from 30 June 1709: 'tho' we find the wines of the last Vintage does not prove soe stronge as in some other yeares, we likewise observe yr order to us for 6 hogsheads of Rich Malmsey, which, at present is not to be had in the whole island having 3 vessells this yeare loaded for England which Drained the Country of all. We showed Captain Bulcock a sample of what there was to be gott: we told him we thought it not att all fitting to send you.' The Bolton letters also illustrate the strategic importance of Madeira for Atlantic shipping.

Although England itself remained a relatively small market, British merchants grew in importance and were helped by the Methuen Treaty of 1703 which granted preferential rates of duty to Portuguese wines. A British factory[1] or *feitoria,* similar to those operating in Oporto and Lisbon, was well established in Funchal by the 1720s. There was a Factory House on the Ribeira de Santa Luzia and an English church. The burial ground for non-Catholics lay next to the present-day British Cemetery in the centre of Funchal. A number of subsequently famous shippers arrived around the middle of the century, including John Leacock, Thomas Gordon and Francis Newton (later Cossart Gordon). North America, the West Indies and, increasingly, the East Indies were to be the main markets for madeira wine throughout the eighteenth century. America was the principal customer, continuing to buy wine even during the War of Independence (1777–82). There are few reliable figures of total exports, but it is thought that shipments more than doubled during the second half of the century, reaching nearly seven million litres in 1800. The American market accounted for between 50 and 80 per cent of total production. Such was madeira's reputation in America that it was reputedly used by Thomas Jefferson to toast the Declaration of Independence in 1776 and George Washington's inauguration in 1789 was similarly toasted with madeira wine. The history of Madeira's trade with America between 1640 and 1815, and its impact on American society, is covered in detail in David Hancock's scholarly book *Oceans of Wine.*

OVERPRODUCTION AND 'MOCK MADEIRA'

During the eighteenth century, in parallel with the port wine industry on the Portuguese mainland, demand for madeira increased faster than supply. This led to considerable fraud and adulteration. Wines from the Canaries, the Azores and the Portuguese mainland were imported into Funchal and then re-exported as madeira. Perhaps following on from the example of the Marquês de Pombal who legislated to control port wine on the mainland, in 1768 the governor of Madeira initiated a series of

---

1   The term 'factory' means a body of factors or merchants carrying out business in a foreign country. The Portuguese established *feitorias* in India at the end of the fifteenth century and it is possible that the English usage of the term derives from the Portuguese.

GEORGE WASHINGTON'S WINES

George Washington, the first President of the United States of America, ordered prodigious quantities of madeira. Washington's correspondence and order books are full of references to pipes of madeira wine. As early as 1760 there is record of a letter from Hill, Lamar & Hill in Madeira describing 'a pipe of wine which altho' very dear we hope will prove satisfactory after standing a summer to show its quality in which as well as the colour we have carefully endeavoured to please you.' In 1768, writing from his family estate Mount Vernon, overlooking the Potomac River, Washington wrote to his agents 'I should be obliged to you for sending me a Butt (of about One hundred and fifty Gall'ns) of your choicest Madeira Wine' and requested 'cuttings of the Madeira Grape (that kind I mean of which the Wine is made) but if ... there be any sort of Impropriety I beg that no notice be taken of it'. It seems that the latter part of this request was ignored. Washington continued to be supplied with madeira throughout the War of Independence, presumably from English shippers. His chief concern in later life seems to be that of the adulteration of the wine when it reached America. In 1785 he wrote 'as I have been very unlucky hitherto, in the transportation of Wine (in the common Craft of the Country) from one Port, or from one river to another, I had rather the old Madeira ordered ... for my use should remain with you (as I am not in immediate want) until a conveyance may offer to Alexandria.' Alexandria was Washington's favoured, most trusted port. Washington continued to serve and drink Madeira until the end of his life. In 1795 there is an order for two pipes of the best Madeira for the President to be picked up by a ship called the *Ganges* sailing from Madeira via the East Indies, thereby exposing the wine to a long, hot sea voyage.

measures to regulate the wine trade. This included an attempt to demarcate the island, separating inferior wines from the north from the better wines in the south. There was even a proposal to create a monopoly company along the lines of the *Companhia Geral da Agicultura das Vinhas do Alto Douro*. The legislation seemingly had little effect and was insufficient to prevent a sharp fall in the price of madeira wine and a slump in sales in the early nineteenth century. Fraudulent madeira continued to be an issue throughout the next century. As Charles Tovey writes in *Poole's Tales* (quoted at length in Julian Jeff's book *Sherry*) a publican near Cambridge recounted that he had but two sorts of wine in his cellar, port and sherry: 'if anyone ordered Madeira:- From one bottle of Sherry take two glasses of wine, which replace by two glasses of Brandy, and add thereto a squeeze of lemon; and this I find to give general satisfaction, especially to the young gentlemen from Cambridge.' I found the same rather casual approach to madeira when I visited Rutherglen, Australia in the 1991. When a respected fortified wine producer there asked me if I would like to taste his 'madeira' he said 'it's just the same wine as my "sherry", but this cask has gone volatile!'

FORTIFICATION AND HEATING

There is no record of precisely when madeira first became a fortified wine, its natural alcohol bolstered by the addition of grape spirit or brandy, although fortification is mentioned as early as 1530 (we cannot be certain of this). Suffice to say that madeira probably followed the same trajectory as port, which gradually evolved into a sweet, fortified wine from the end of the seventeenth century onwards. Certainly by the middle of the eighteenth century it had become commonplace to add 'a bucket or two of brandy in each pipe' according to the madeira shipper Francis Newton. In 1756 a Mr Burgess wrote from London to Michael Nowlan, an associate of John Leacock, 'some Gentlemen here that are knowing in the Wine Trade assure me that if a couple of gallons of fine clear Brandy was put into each pipe of our best wines twill improve them greatly'. I have certainly tasted wines claiming to be prior to this which were fully fortified although they may have been bolstered subsequently (see Chapter 6). The brandy was initially French and was added to wines that had already fermented and were consequently dry; it would have helped to stabilise and preserve the wine for shipment. But, just as with port, there were detractors. The same Francis Newton, writing in 1753, took pride in the fact that his wines were 'fresh and full flavoured unlike the ones laced with Brandy'. Captain Cook called at Madeira en route to the south Pacific in 1768 and took over 3,000 gallons of wine on board *Endeavour* to combat scurvy among his crew. A contemporary chronicler states that 'it is commonly reported that no distilled spirit is added to these wines, but I have been well assured of the contrary, and have seen spirit used for that purpose'. Until the middle of the nineteenth century most madeira wine was only fortified immediately prior to shipment. With the exception of the highly-prized Malmseys, which were still produced in tiny quantities, most madeira wines were dry. The best wines continued to be fortified with French brandy until its use was prohibited in 1822, and thereafter distilled spirit from the north of the island and Porto Santo was used. Inexpensive wines were fortified with *aguardente de cana*, spirit distilled from the cane sugar grown on the island.

The term *vinho do sol* (wine heated by the sun) was in common use by 1730 but the first artificial heating of madeira wine only took place towards the end of the eighteenth century. The rapid expansion of the English market meant that there was an insufficient quantity of mature wine to fulfil orders and the shippers looked for a short cut. In 1794 Sr. Pantelão Fernandes built the first *armazém de calor* (artificially heated warehouse) on the island and, judging it a success, others followed building themselves stoves or boilers (*estufas*) in which to heat large volumes of wine. A contemporary shipper, John Leacock, summed up its effects: 'to those who are not good judges, the new wine with three months *Estufa* imitates wine of 4 or 5 years old, & we don't think that the deception will be easily discovered ...'. But the 'deception' was discovered and much abused, with wines being heated to boiling point. It was also reported that bottles of Madeira wine were 'plunged into a trench filled with fermenting horse manure ... and in a few months the maturity of a voyage is gained'. *Estufagem*, as the process of artificial heating became known, was consequently banned in the early part of the nineteenth century but in 1835, following lobbying by an influential shipper, a royal decree regulated the temperature to which the wine could be heated. In 1847 it is recorded that there were thirty-nine *estufas* in Funchal.

Genuine *vinho da roda* continued to command a high price in England where East Indies and West Indies madeiras were among the most fashionable of wines. Malvasia was still the most prestigious wine and although other varietals were shipped, most wines were named after their destination. The names of generic madeiras like 'London Particular' or 'India Market' originated at wine auctions held in London in the 1760s and some of these names survived as brands well into the twentieth century. 'Rainwater' was the exception. At the end of the eighteenth century some pipes of Verdelho were left unstopped and rainwater seeped in, diluting the wine. This style of wine found favour in Virginia and thereafter a paler more delicate blend of madeira named 'Rainwater' was made up specifically for the American market. André Simon (who represented the Madeira Wine Association in London in the 1930s and worked briefly in Madeira) records that Rainwater madeira deserved to be called a gentleman: 'one that will never remind you tomorrow of the favour he did you last night'.

MEN WHO SHAPED MADEIRA

Henry Veitch (1782–1857)

In 1809, during the British occupation of Madeira (see below), a Scotsman named Henry Veitch was appointed as His Majesty's Consul in Funchal. A wealthy and forceful man, Veitch was a bon-viveur with a fondness for madeira parties. He built a number of large houses, the most notable of which are the former Consulate in the centre of Funchal, Quinta Calça (now the Clube Naval) and Quinta do Jardim da Serra in the Sercial vineyards above Estreito de Câmara de Lobos. Veitch travelled the island and, it is fair to say, enjoyed the company of the local women, leaving a large number of fair-haired children 'whose descendents are distinguishable to this day' according to Noel Cossart, writing in the early 1980s. In August 1815 Napoleon stopped at Funchal whilst en route to exile in St Helena. Henry Veitch visited him on board ship and Napoleon received a cask of 1792 madeira. A man of liberal sympathies, Veitch was removed from office in 1828 with the outbreak of the civil war in Portugal between the Constitutionalists and Absolutists. He was reinstated in 1831 but lost office again shortly afterwards. Veitch was buried in a mausoleum at Jardim da Serra and his house there is now a hotel. His house on the Rua 5 de Outubro in the centre of Funchal is used by IVBAM and, until recently, housed a museum of wine. The story of Napoleon's wine is told on page 197.

CRISIS, AFTER CRISIS, AFTER CRISIS

The popularity of madeira continued into the early nineteenth century with total shipments exceeding 20,000 pipes in some years prior to 1815. The British, who continued to dominate the trade, made themselves unpopular with the islanders by treating Madeira like a colony of their own. Cited in the *Elucidário Madeirense* (published in 1921), a local historian named Dr Azevedo wrote in 1873: 'Madeira is largely anglicized in race, costume, ownership of land, as well as in its trade and money; English (after Portuguese) is the language spoken most frequently… it is only national pride which contrives to keep us Portuguese.' Writing after a visit four years later, Henry Vizetelly describes how the British exercised a virtual monopoly of the wine trade on the island and, by levying a tax on every pipe of wine shipped, they built themselves a cemetery where British subjects could be interned rather than having their bodies being flung out to sea 'furnishing food for the fishes'. Established in the 1770s, the British Cemetery on the Rua da Carreira is still in use and remains a quiet oasis in the centre of Funchal where the graves of many prominent British families can be seen.

In order to protect their interests from the French during the Peninsular Wars, the British Army occupied the island in 1801–02 and again from 1807 to 1814. The boom in wine shipments that accompanied the wars proved short lived. Faced with some poor vintages and competition from the Azores, Sicily, Tenerife and the Cape, all of which produced their own so-called 'madeira' wines, exports of true madeira fell significantly after 1815, inflicting hardship on many of the island's inhabitants. Even the American market, so important in the eighteenth century, proved unsustainable. With the cellars full of unwanted wine, by 1824 the growers had 40,000 pipes of mature wine seeking a market. The British shippers took much of the blame but the situation was complicated by discrimination from the mainland, which saddled the island with high taxation on imported goods at the same time as prohibiting the export of wine to Brazil (previously a lucrative market for cheaper wines) due to the War of Two Brothers (1825–34). With the islands having come to rely almost exclusively on wine, the trade was insufficient to support a population of over 100,000 when exports fell to 2.2 million litres in 1830. The potato crop failed in 1846 and there was an outbreak of cholera in 1850 when 10,000 people died.

Although the islands received significant humanitarian support, most of the peasants were destitute. Emigration was the only solution and, between 1835 and 1855, an estimated 40,000 people left Madeira.

In 1851 *Oidium tuckeri* made its first appearance on the island. Better known as powdery mildew (and on Madeira as *mangara*), it was transferred from North America to England where it was first detected in the garden of a Mr Tucker in Margate, Kent in 1845. This disease initially manifests itself as a white fungus on vine leaves before spreading to bunches of grapes, reducing both yield and quality. Greatly aided by Madeira's warm, humid, breezy climate, oidium took little over a year to spread round the island and by 1855 production had fallen to just 36 pipes (about 15,000 litres). Robert White writing in a contemporary guide book, *Madeira – Its Climate and Scenery,* declared 'the wine of Madeira which has acquired worldwide celebrity, will soon be no more than a thing of the past'. With no cure available and the economy in total ruin, Madeira was reduced to accepting foreign aid. To help alleviate hardship, a number of public works were initiated including the construction of the first road to link Funchal with Câmara de Lobos, the *Estrada Monumental.* The women were greatly helped by the philanthropy of Elizabeth Phelps (the daughter of a wine shipper) who introduced them to the intricate embroidery that is still a signature industry on the island today. A number of British shippers left, but those with the tenacity to remain bought up large quantities of mature wine from the ones who had abandoned the island. By 1861–2 exports had fallen to less than 1,000 pipes (418,000 litres). This considerably outstripped production which had not exceeded 200 pipes (83,600 litres) for most of the 1850s.

Oidium was eventually brought under control by dusting the leaves of the vines with sulphur (a practice which is carried out by spraying through the growing season today). But with large swathes of vines having been uprooted and replanted with sugar cane, it took time for the island's vineyards to recover. The highly prized Terrantez (a grape variety susceptible to oidium) was nearly lost altogether and the productive American Isabella vine, which is resistant to the fungus, became widely planted on the island. A decade after oidium first appeared on Madeira there were 2,500 hectares of vineyard on the island, and by the end of the 1860s production had risen once more.

MEN WHO SHAPED MADEIRA

Charles Ridpath Blandy 1812–79

Son of John Blandy (1783–1855, see page 115), the founding father of the Blandy dynasty, Charles Ridpath is credited with building the firm into the company it remains today. Charles Ridpath came to know Madeira well. The family had a house at Santo António and Charles would ride back and forth to town each day. For three years they took a house in the midst of the vineyards at Campanário to the west of Câmara de Lobos. Charles Ridpath was 32 when his father died, and took charge of the family firm which already had an office in London as well as the wine business in Funchal. With the outbreak of oidium in the 1850s many British merchants decided to leave the island and Charles Ridpath bought up their stocks. According to Graham Blandy, who was to head the family firm a century later, Charles Ridpath 'was intent on purchasing large stocks of wine for which he had no regular market of any magnitude and was doing so by borrowing monies at interest to make this for investment in doubtful transactions'. He evidently took the most enormous risks and his sons Graham John Blandy and John Burden Blandy viewed their father's reckless behaviour as the road to ruin. By 1862 his position became so dangerous that his two elder sons formed their own firm. Charles Ridpath was persuaded to retire from parts of the business, including the wine trade, in 1868 – but he continued trading nonetheless. With commercial dexterity he traded with both sides during the American Civil War (1861–65). His position was vindicated when phylloxera reached Madeira a decade later and Blandy's, with their considerable stocks of old wine, were able to prosper from the general shortage of madeira. At the time of his death in 1879, however, the company's financial position was still precarious and he died a lonely death at the Great Western Hotel in Paddington, London. Many of the great pre-phylloxera wines amassed by Charles Ridpath Blandy are still available to taste today (see pages 147–59).

THE ARMAZENS OF MESSRS. BLANDY BROTHERS AT FUNCHAL, MADEIRA.

Yet more setbacks followed. The American Civil War (1861–65) temporarily closed a lucrative market, and the opening of the Suez Canal in November 1869 diverted shipping routes away from Madeira. But a minute louse named *Phylloxera vastarix* had the greatest effect on the island, with an impact that is still felt today.

Phylloxera had been identified in a greenhouse in Hammersmith, London in 1863. It completes part of its life cycle underground, feeding on vine roots and sapping the strength from the plant. With the ability to reproduce rapidly, it spread quickly through Europe in the 1860s, reaching Madeira, it is thought, on some cuttings of Isabella brought directly from North America. It was first noticed on the island in 1872 (four years after it had reached mainland Portugal) and spread slowly but steadily through the island's vineyards, initially reducing yields but eventually causing the affected vines to wither and die. At first the effect of phylloxera was localised, and it took eleven years to reach Porto Moniz on the northwest tip of the island. Luckily it did not thrive in the dry sandy soils of Porto Santo and the island remained relatively immune.

Growers went to extraordinary lengths to protect themselves from attack. Henry Vizetelly, who visited Madeira at the height of the epidemic in 1877, describes the measures that some growers took in an effort to save their vineyards. He found Thomas Slapp Leacock (see page 41), owner of the São João vineyard in Funchal, painting the roots of his vines with 'a kind of varnish' and using tar he eventually managed to protect his vines. Such treatments were much too laborious for general use and vineyards that had died were being replaced with sugar cane.

Ironically the solution (there is still no cure) came from America, the original source of the phylloxera plague. European vines (*Vitis vinifera*) were grafted onto rootstock from American vine species, *Vitis labrusca*, *riparia* and *rupestris*, which were found to resist phylloxera. However a ban on the import of American vines, imposed when the cause of phylloxera was first ascertained, was only lifted by the Portuguese government in 1883. Seeking a quick return to full production, many of Madeira's growers planted American vines without grafting. This led to a debate that has taken well over a century to resolve. Varieties like Jacquet, Isabella, Cunningham and Herbremont, known collectively as the *produtores diretos* or 'direct producers' because they grow on their own roots, took the place of Madeira's traditional *vinifera* varieties in many vineyards. The white Verdelho grape which, prior to phylloxera, had made up two thirds of the vineyards on the island, was largely supplanted by the red Tinta Negra (Mole) and direct producers. It is estimated that by the 1920s the high yielding but inferior direct producers accounted for as much as 80 per cent of all madeira wine.

MEN WHO SHAPED MADEIRA

Harry Hinton

The son of William Hinton, Harry Hinton was educated in England and as an 18-year-old student, brought the first football to Madeira in 1875. The first game of football in Portugal was played at the Hinton family *quinta* in Camacha in the same year. Harry Hinton became Honorary President of the Marítimo football team. Harry Hinton went on to be a successful but controversial businessman and built up a hugely successful sugar business in Madeira and Africa. The company secured a monopoly supplying all the fortifying *aguardente de cana* for madeira wine until the end of the 1960s. Harry Hinton also entered the wine trade and was one of the first members of the Madeira Wine Association when it was formed in 1913, but was forced to leave in 1917 when he married Isabel Welsh after a love affair that was the talk of the island. The Welsh family ultimately inherited Hinton's assets.

Although the immediate impact of phylloxera was by no means as devastating to Madeira as that of oidium twenty years earlier, a number of famous families left, including Osborne, Duff and Gordon, who re-established themselves as successful wine shippers in Jerez. Production rose to 8,000 pipes (3.3 million litres) in 1895, with annual exports averaging between 2.5 million litres by the turn of the twentieth century. Although Madeira had lost important markets to Malaga and Jerez as well as to counterfeit madeiras, it also captured new markets. In his family memoir Cecil Miles records that 'the wine trade had by this time [the turn of the twentieth century] got over the phylloxera scare, contrary to the expectations of those who had left the island, and was once more flourishing, sending its finest wines to the Russian court where the Tsar much appreciated it and set the fashion'. The Grand Duke of St Petersburg apparently took over 76,000 bottles in one year! Nonetheless the twin plagues of oidium and phylloxera changed Madeira forever and still have a bearing on the island's vineyards (see Chapter 3).

WAR AND SOCIAL CHANGE

By the turn of the twentieth century *Vinho da Roda* ceased to be viable although as late as 1907 Cossart, Gordon & Co. advertised '1,000 pipes of the finest Madeira for shipment to India and back for the express purpose of benefiting from the sea voyage'.

In 1908, Madeira was officially demarcated for the first time (alongside two other fortified-wine producing areas on the mainland, Carcavelos and Setúbal). 'Madeira' finally won recognition in the Anglo-Portuguese treaty of 1914, bringing an end to much of the trade in fraudulent wines that had damaged the island's wine industry over the previous century. From the 1880s until the First World War, the Germans established a strong foothold in Madeira, threatening the hegemony of the still unpopular British, with the connivance of the Portuguese authorities. In return for improving the sanitary conditions in Funchal, a German syndicate planned to build a new resort (William Reid's famous hotel was briefly under threat of expropriation). However, when Portugal joined in the war on the side of the allies in 1916, all German property on the island was expropriated. Funchal was shelled by the Germans in December 1917 and, threatened by submarines, shipments of wine, embroidery and wicker virtually ceased for the second half of the war. Following the October Revolution of 1917, the lucrative Russian market abruptly collapsed. This was a great loss to Krohn, a shipper which in 1900 was the second largest after Cossart Gordon based on its trade with Germany and Russia. The company went out of business. In the same year, owing to an absence of sulphur on the island, nearly every bunch of grapes was subject to oidium and the harvest was a disaster.

Alongside port, madeira enjoyed a minor boom after the First World War with annual shipments rising to over 8 million litres in 1919, the highest for over a century. But at the end of the war there was an acute shortage of alcohol to fortify the wine. This was caused by a ruling in the Portuguese parliament forbidding the use of grape spirit and requiring that alcohol distilled from cane sugar be used in its place. The supply of *aguardente de cana* was controlled by Hinton's sugar factory who refused to pay the price demanded by the sugar producers.

The burgeoning Scandinavian market partly made up for the abrupt loss of the Russian market, but madeira was hit again by American prohibition and the Volstead Act of 1920. Sales were erratic, falling to 1.6 million litres in 1921 but rising again to exceed 4 million litres from 1923 to 1925. The shippers were forced into making economies, and in 1925 a number of leading shippers – including Wm. Hinton, Welsh and Cunha, Blandy Bros. and Leacock & Co. – pooled their resources to form the Madeira Wine Association (MWA – see page 111). When prohibition was lifted in 1934, Americans turned to the newly fashionable cocktail rather than madeira wine, and the US market for madeira has never fully recovered. Other firms joined the MWA which became known locally and rather cruelly as the 'shipper's cemetery'. The MWA had seventeen members by the end of the 1930s.

The labelling and marketing of madeira changed profoundly during the inter-war period with new brand names being accompanied by the use of varietals – Sercial, Verdelho, Bual and Malvasia or Malmsey. This was well short of the truth. Most of these wines were not in fact made from the specified grapes but from the direct producers and/or Tinta Negra Mole that had taken their place following phylloxera. By the 1950s the traditional *vinifera* grape varieties (including Tinta Negra) accounted for little more that a quarter of production. It became the accepted practice to sell varietal wines as no more than an indication of the style of the wine. Thus Sercial was a euphemism for a dry wine,

Verdelho for medium dry, Bual/Boal for medium sweet and Malvazia/
Malmsey for rich. This misleading use of Madeira's varietals continued
until it was prohibited by the EEC (now the EU) in 1990.

Although Portugal remained neutral throughout, the Second World War
was more damaging to Madeira than the first. Shipping declined, prohibiting
both imports and exports. A number of significant construction projects
undertaken during the war helped to reduce unemployment, including
the construction of the Avenida do Mar in Funchal and the Mercado
dos Lavradores; the latter is still one of Funchal's best modern buildings.
Although wine continued to be shipped in reduced quantities during the
war, profound social changes meant that markets collapsed and annual
shipments fell below 3 million litres in the later 1940s and early 1950s.
Scandinavia remained the leading market for premium-quality Madeira
while France grew into the largest market in volume terms for bulk (*granel*),
used mainly in cooking and flavouring. In 1957 new legislation was enacted
to regulate the production of madeira. Following the political line of the
authoritarian Salazar regime on the mainland, cooperative wineries were
established in the 1950s at Porto Santo, Câmara de Lobos and later at São
Vicente. These were not widely embraced by Madeira's fiercely individual
growers and no longer exist. Although export volumes rose in the 1960s,
peaking at over 5 million litres in 1972, the number of shippers continued
to diminish. From sixty registered madeira shippers at the time of the
Second World War, the number fell to twenty-three in 1973.

THE GROWTH OF TOURISM

Madeira has long been a tourist destination, with visitors from northern
Europe attracted all year round by the island's amenable climate. The first
travel guides written in the early nineteenth century focus on medical and
climatic conditions. In 1840 there were two hotels in Funchal and by 1891
there were seventeen. In the mid-twentieth century ships en route to South
Africa made frequent calls at Funchal bringing visitors to stay at fashionable
hotels like Reid's and the Savoy. Among the many famous visitors were
David Lloyd George, George Bernard Shaw, President Baptista of Cuba
and Sir Winston and Lady Churchill. The Churchills' visit in 1950 helped
to put Madeira back on the tourist map after the Second World War, and
Dennis and Margaret Thatcher honeymooned at the Savoy Hotel in 1951.

MEN WHO SHAPED MADEIRA

Mario Barbeito (1905–1985)

It must have taken considerable chutzpah to set up as a new madeira shipper in the lean years that followed the Second World War. Mario Barbeito trained as an accountant and began working for the now defunct Companhia Vitícola da Madeira (CVM). But, with capital of his own and access to wine stocks, he started producing and selling madeira under his own name in 1948. Barbeito rented an old cane sugar factory situated rather incongruously next to Reid's Hotel as well as a vineyard in Caniço (Jardim do Sol – 'sun garden'). Like the other major shippers in the post-war period, Barbeito made money mostly from selling bulk wines for export, building up markets in Scandinavia in the 1950s and Japan in the mid-1960s. He revolutionised the labelling of bottled wine and created brands like Delvino and Veramar. During his lifetime Mario Barbeito was an enthusiastic collector of books and built up a collection of 23,000 volumes. He maintained a special interest in Christopher Columbus and had a collection of memorabilia which was kept latterly in a small museum below the family's wine shop on the Praça do Infante in the centre of Funchal. When the Ribeira de São João overflowed in February 2010 (see page 28) the shop was inundated and 22,000 volumes were destroyed. Mario Barbeito died in 1985, leaving the business with his daughter Manuela de Freitas, the first woman to head up a madeira wine shipper and, apart from D. Antónia Ferreira, one of the first women in Portugal to lead a wine business. The company is now run by Mario Barbeito's grandsons and is one of the most dynamic shippers on the island (see page 93).

A contemporary guide book used by my parents on their own honeymoon to Madeira a year later describes the island much as it had been a century earlier. There were still very few cars on the cobbled roads: 'the roar and rattle of the motor bus and tearing taxi do not vex us … the old world town [Funchal] is full of charm with its grass-grown, cobbled streets, its *carros* [carriages] and *corças* (sledges) and its sense of abundant leisure.' Photographs from the era show fields of sugar cane growing near the Convento de Santa Clara close to the centre of modern-day Funchal and an ox cart parked up on the Estrada Monumental outside Reid's. A chapter on the wine trade describes the vintage, 'treading out the grapes – in *lagars* (sic) by the feet of men. The method is the same today as in Bible times...'

In 1949 Aquila Airways began a seaplane service from England, taking nine hours to fly from Southampton to Funchal, but the service was suspended after a serious accident in 1958. In 1960 an airport was built on Porto Santo, sweeping away much of the island's vineyard but bringing tourists in steadily greater numbers. Four years later the first commercial flight landed at Sta. Catarina airport near Santa Cruz on Madeira island itself. Just over 11,000 people used the airport in 1964 and this rapidly increased until over a million passengers a year were using the much extended runway in 2005. Tourism has had a greater impact on Madeira than anything since the legendary seven-year fire in the fifteenth century. The number of hotel rooms grew from 2,295 in 1967 to 12,244 in 1982, and to well over 20,000 today. As Funchal has expanded westwards up the mountain sides, prime vineyards in areas like Santo António and São Martinho have been lost to real estate. Old photographs show that vines once grew where the giant Carlton Hotel (ex-Sheraton) now stands and Thomas Slapp Leacock's famous São João vineyard (see page 41), which used to be behind where the Hotel Four Views Baía now stands, succumbed to apartment blocks as recently as the 1990s. Although tourism has undoubtedly brought huge economic benefits to Madeira (not least a greatly expanded local market for wine) it has been at considerable environmental cost. Tourism has long overtaken agriculture as Madeira's most important source of income.

EXPATRIATE LIFE IN FUNCHAL IN THE EARLY 1960s

Social life for expats and Anglo-Madeiran families centred on the British Country Club for tennis, squash, snooker and afternoon teas. The English Rooms offered a library, snooker table and bar. Reid's, the Savoy and Miramar hotels all had a dance band playing after dinner while the English Church held an annual fund-raising fete. There was just one restaurant in town, the *Combatentes*, which still flourishes, overlooking the public gardens. As Adam Blandy recalled in *The Blandys of Madeira, 1811–2011*, 'life in Madeira in the 1960s was good'. This charmed and rather isolated life would all be blown apart by the Revolution a decade later (see page 23). The British Club (now Quinta Magnolia) was taken over by the Regional Government in 1980.

REVOLUTION AND AUTONOMY

On the morning of 25 April 1974 the Armed Forces Movement (MFA) took control of the streets of Lisbon and overthrew the *Estado Novo* (New State), better known as the Salazar regime, which was established in 1932. Portugal's President Américo Tomás and Prime Minister Marcello Caetano were briefly held at the São Lourenço fort in Funchal before being sent to exile in Brazil. The austere Salazar dictatorship had never been popular in Madeira and the military coup was generally welcomed with as much enthusiasm on the island as it was throughout mainland Portugal. However, the revolution soon ran out of control and, when a pro-Communist government took over in Lisbon in the summer of 1975, Madeira threatened to secede and proclaim its independence. Large sections of the economy (including banks and insurance companies) were nationalised in March 1975 and many companies, wine shippers included, struggled to survive the upheaval. The island's anti-Communist resistance was led by Dr Alberto João Jardim, then Director of the newspaper *Jornal de Madeira*. When the island was granted autonomy in the post-revolutionary constitution of 1976, Alberto João Jardim was elected President of the Autonomous Regional Government. He is stepping down in 2015 after thirty-seven years, having been in power for a year longer than Salazar.

In 1979 the Regional Government created the Instituto do Vinho da Madeira (IVM) to regulate the production of grapes and wine on the islands. Housed in Consul Veitch's house on the Rua 5 de Outubro, the IVM had a wide ranging brief covering viticulture, vinification, chemical analysis and promotion. All wines leaving the island are tasted by a panel, and a seal of guarantee is granted once the wines have met the required standard. In 2006 the IVM was supplanted by the *Instituto do Vinho, do Bordado e do Artesanato* (IVBAM) which took embroidery and handicraft under its wing as well as wine. IVBAM's responsibilites with respect to wine are outlined in Appendix I.

One far-reaching consequence of the 1974–5 revolution was the end of the almost feudal system of land holding, the *contrato de colónia*. Tenants were given the right to buy the freehold of their properties and those who did so quickly made profits selling on their small plots for real estate. Large areas of prime vineyard around São Martinho and Câmara de Lobos have consequently been lost to piecemeal development over

MEN WHO SHAPED MADEIRA

Noel Cossart (1907–1987)

Noel Cossart was the author of what was for many years the main work of reference on madeira wine. Published by Christie's in 1984 at the instigation of Michael Broadbent, it was a record of a lifetime spent in the madeira wine trade. Noel joined his family firm Cossart Gordon in 1925 at the age of eighteen. At the time it was the island's largest shipper but in post-war years it fell on hard times and in 1953 joined the Madeira Wine Association (see page 111). Noel had an independent spirit and struggled for many years to keep his firm solvent, holding on to his small family shareholding until his death in 1987. A sociable man who enjoyed entertaining, his later life was something of disappointment as he was sidelined in the business that he felt so passionately about. In 1976, two years after the revolution in Portugal, he returned to England and – following his retirement 'for the third and last time' – set about writing about madeira wine. When his book *Madeira, the Island Vineyard* was finally published Noel assumed the role of Madeira's leading historian. The book is full of historical nuggets including a fascinating appendix of madeira vintages from 1774 to 1956, from which I have included some observations in Chapter 6 of this book. But Cossart's book is as remarkable for what it doesn't say as what it does. Perhaps because of his distance from the trade or due to the poor state of the madeira wine industry at the time, he says frustratingly little about the vineyards, grapes and wine production as it was in the 1970s and early 1980s. When I joined the wine trade from university in 1984 Noel Cossart's book was the standard reference work for students and yet it only told only half the story. The real story, as I found when I first visited Madeira six years after the book's first publication in 1984, was rather different (see page 73).

the past thirty years. Once a rural village, São Martinho has now been completely consumed by Funchal.

Portugal became a member of the European Economic Community (subsequently the European Union or EU) in 1986, bringing huge economic benefits to the then-impoverished regions like Madeira. From 1992 onwards the POSEIMA (*Programa de Opções Específicas*

para fazer face o Afastamento e a Insularidade da Madeira e dos Açores)
brought money directly to improve the archipelago's infrastructure
and wine industry. As recently as the mid-1990s it took half a day to
drive from Funchal to the vineyards at São Vicente on the north side
of the island, whereas today – with an impressive network of tunnels
and expressways – they can be reached in as little as forty minutes. The
acronym POSEIMA can be found written on the side of casks in the
wine stores indicating that the shipper has received support from the
EU. Six shippers – Henriques & Henriques, Justinos, Barbeito, and
the Madeira Wine Company as well as the now defunct Silva Vinho –
benefitted directly from EU funding, which helped them to build new
premises outside the cramped centre of Funchal.

European Union legislation had a direct and ultimately beneficial impact
on the island's wine industry, effectively enforcing the ban on the export of
wine made from direct producers and/or hybrid vines from the mid-1980s
onwards. Sales immediately fell by 30 per cent but this was accompanied by
an EU-funded campaign to convert the island's vineyards back to European,
vitis vinifera, grape varieties. By 2006, an estimated 150 hectares had been
replanted, mostly with Tinta Negra Mole but the planting of the classic
white varieties has also increased although these grapes still only account
for less than 10 per cent of total production. Through the *Direcção Regional
da Agricultura,* the Regional Government has established four experimental
vineyards on Madeira and one on Porto Santo which have helped to save
some of Madeira's historic grape varieties from near extinction (see Chapter
3). Although progress has been slow compared to some other regions, it
would still be true to say that Madeira's vineyards are now in a better state
than at any time for the past hundred and fifty years.

MADEIRA IN THE TWENTY-FIRST CENTURY

With worldwide shipments of Madeira having averaged 3.66 million litres
a year during the 1990s, in 2001 sales peaked at 4.71 million litres. This
figure is distorted by the announcement that bulk shipments of madeira
would be suspended on 1 January 2002 (following on from a similar
move by sherry and port in 1996). Exports initially suffered a sharp drop

MEN WHO SHAPED MADEIRA

Richard Blandy (1947–2002)

This book is dedicated to my late father-in-law Richard Blandy. He died, aged 55, shortly after my wife Katrina and I were married on the island in 2002. His all-too-short life was remarkable for his many achievements. During a time of considerable turbulence for Portugal and Madeira, Richard Blandy effectively reinvented the family company, steering it into the twenty-first century. His obituary, published in the *Daily Telegraph,* summed it up: 'a clear-thinking strategist, he realised that Blandy's could no longer afford to own "trophy" assets...' The most prominent of these assets were Reid's Hotel (which the Blandy family had taken on as a bad debt in 1936 and was sold to Orient Express Hotels in 1996) and the Madeira Wine Company (MWC), half of which was sold to the Symington family of Oporto in 1988; two years later they took the controlling interest. The Symingtons were brought in help with the distribution of Blandy's, Cossart Gordon, Leacock and Miles – the four best-known brands of madeira all under the MWC umbrella at the time. But they were shocked by the prevailing standards of vinification, *estufagem* and ageing and began to shake up the company's wine making. During the 1990s with the board of the MWC still chaired by Richard Blandy, the Symington family transformed the wine-making process. The unpleasant 'synthetic cheese ball' character that was the buzzword for standard madeira when I joined the wine trade in the mid-1980s gradually faded from the wines. Without this thorough cleaning up (at a time when global standards in the wine industry had already dramatically improved) it seems unlikely that the Madeira Wine Company would have survived. In 2011 when the Blandy family was celebrating its bicentenary on the island (and when Richard Blandy would have been approaching retirement) the Symingtons sold most of their shares in the MWC back to the Blandys. It was a company anew. Richard Blandy enjoyed his wines but you would never describe him as a 'wine man'. He was a calm and astute businessman who made many friends and very few enemies.

to 2.8 million litres (and some companies were hit more severely than others) but have recovered slowly to average 3.37 million litres in the decade to 2013. The average price has risen steadily over the past decade from €4.05 to €5.28 per litre.

Total sales in 2014 were 3.37 million litres, with the trade currently shared between seven registered shippers: Justino's, The Madeira Wine Company, Henriques & Henriques, Barbeito, J. Faria, H.M. Borges and Pereira d'Oliveira (in order of sales volume). These companies are profiled individually in Chapter 5.

Wines produced from the traditional grape varieties (Sercial, Verdelho, Bual, Malvasia, Terrantez and Bastardo) accounted for just under 230,000 litres of sales in 2014 (representing just 6.2 per cent of the total). With sales totalling just over 90,000 litres, Malvasia/ Malmsey is much the most popular of the classic varietals, followed by Boal (66,000 litres).

Sales of wines with an indication of age (five years old and above, including *colheita* and *frasqueira,* a.k.a 'vintage') amounted to 470,000 litres in 2014 (12.7 per cent of the total). In 2014 the top five markets were as follows: France (1.01 million litres), Portugal (0.59 million litres), UK (0.31 million litres), Japan (0.28 million litres) and Germany (0.27 million litres). Sales in Portugal are mostly to tourists visiting Madeira (0.53 million litres). There is a surprisingly poor local market for Madeira wine on the Portuguese mainland. The average price per litre sold in France is €3.36, compared with €6.60 in the United Kingdom and €7.00 in the USA.

These global figures mask some interesting and encouraging trends which can be seen in the figures reproduced in Appendices II and III. Sales of older wine, namely twenty- and forty-year-old blends, have increased significantly over the past five years and the colheita category has grown to represent over 20,000 litres of sales in 2014 since the first wines were launched in the early 2000s. There has also been a small but significant revival of the Terrantez grape, particularly at the twenty year old and *frasqueira* (vintage) levels. These and other trends are discussed in more detail in the Postscript at the end of the book.

A full breakdown of sales by country, grape variety and age can be found in the appendices on pages 245–50.

In February 2015, just as this book was at its final proof stage, a long awaited new law was published covering DO Madeira (i.e. fortified wine), DO Madeirense and IG Terras Madeirenses. The main changes include the reclassification of the grape varieties in Chapter 3, the use of Tinta Negra as a permitted varietal on labels, the addition of more age categories and mandatory bottling dates on the labels of dated wines. These and other more minor changes in the legislation have been incorporated into the book.

FLOODS: DEATH AND DESTRUCTION

Madeira has long been prone to flash floods. With torrential autumn and winter rain the narrow river valleys quickly become conduits for boulders and debris from the mountains, sometimes with catastrophic consequences. The worst recorded floods occurred on 9 October 1803. After several days of heavy rain the rivers burst their banks and in the centre of Funchal; Santa Maria parish was especially badly affected with whole buildings washed out to sea. Over 600 people are estimated to have died.

Cossart Gordon, whose *armazens* used to sit on the edge of the Ribeira de Santa Luzia, lost an entire store together with several hundred pipes of wine. In the wake of this tragedy, a French engineer named Brigadier Oudinot ordered the building of high walls to contain the Ribeira de Santa Luzia and Ribeira de João Gomes, which converge in the centre of Funchal. These flood defences, along with those along the Ribeira de São João, were spectacularly breached on 20 February 2010 when a torrential downpour on already saturated land caused mud and boulders to be swept into Funchal. The urbanisation of the slopes above the city served to accelerate the run off. There were over forty deaths, houses were swept away and the damage to the centre of the city was considerable, with two large subterranean shopping centres and car parks filling up with water. Two wine shippers were also directly affected. Pereira D'Oliveira's wine store in the Rua Visconde de Anadia and Barbeito's wine shop on the Avenida Arriaga were inundated, with the loss of valuable stock and artefacts. At the time of writing, the centre of Funchal is once more subject to significant flood alleviation measures.

2

THE ISLANDS OF MADEIRA
AND PORTO SANTO

Madeira is a long-extinct volcanic hotspot lying on the African tectonic plate, 978 kilometres southwest of Lisbon, Portugal, and 700 kilometres off the coast of Morocco. Eruptions began around 20 million years ago, forming a chain of mostly submerged mountain peaks in the Atlantic parallel to the North African coast. There are some who believe this to be part of the lost continent of Atlantis.

At 33 degrees north, Madeira is the principal island (740.7 km²) and gives its name to the larger but lesser known archipelago. This includes the islands of Porto Santo, 40 kilometres north east; the Desertas, 18 kilometres south east and the Selvagens, 275 kilometres due south towards the Canary Islands. Both the Desertas and the Selvagens islands are uninhabited. Porto Santo was the first to erupt from the ocean around 14 million years ago followed by Madeira itself, at the start of the Pliocene, approximately 5.2 million years ago. Unlike the Azores to the north west, which are still volcanically active, there has been no major volcanic activity recorded in the Madeiran archipelago for around 6,000 years.

With the exception of two isolated outcrops of calcareous rock, the islands are entirely volcanic and are made up of basalt interspersed with red and yellow tufa (solidified volcanic mud). This has weathered to give a huge variety of different soils. The best for grape growing tend to be the looser, less fertile, gravelly soils which have been banked up to form *poios*, small step-like terraces rising up from the ocean to about

700 metres above sea level. Due to erosion and centuries of working the earth, the soils in the most intensively cultivated parts of Madeira island are frequently mixed; consequently no single grape variety or style of wine is identified with a particular soil type. The soils have a naturally high pH and this is always said to contribute to the high natural acidity in madeira wines.

Madeira is much the most dramatic of the islands, rising to a height of 1,862 metres at Pico Ruivo. Measuring 58 kilometres from east to west and 23 kilometres in width at its widest point, the island can be divided into three distinct zones. We walked the island from east to west over a period of three days in 2003, starting out from the narrow windswept peninsula of Ponta de São Lourenço. For most visitors arriving either by sea or by air from mainland Europe, this is their first view of the island. It was for Rupert Croft-Cooke, who arrived by sea before the airport was built in 1960: 'My first view of it was in the chill light of daybreak after two days at sea. Looking across the grey water I saw the lighthouse on the Ponta de São Lourenço in the extreme east and thereafter the slopes and villages as we came along the coast towards Funchal. Not only was there no sign of the vine; there seemed no-where it could grow.' There are now a few scattered vineyards in the eastern part of the island including one at Caniçal which is very visible from the plane shortly before landing. But the eastern section of Madeira, made up of smaller plateaux at Chão de Lagoa and Santo da Serra as well as the broad Machico valley, has never been important for viticulture.

The central section of the island is the most vertiginous (as I can vouch for, by my attacks of vertigo) with the sharp peaks of Ruivo, Torres, Arieiro and Cidrão, all in excess of 1,800 metres, divided from each other by deeply incised valleys. The landscape here is breathtakingly beautiful and resembles the much photographed peaks of Java. Ribeira Brava (the 'wild stream') flows south, forming an unpredictable seasonal torrent. The wider valley of São Vicente runs north and, although mostly shaped by lava flows, there is a small calcareous outcrop at Lameiros. The north coast is steeper and much less easy to cultivate than the south. However Cabo Girão, west of Câmara de Lobos, rises 589 metres out of the Atlantic and ranks as the second highest cliff face in the world.

A high plateau, known as Paúl da Serra, occupies much of the western section of the island. At a height of between 1,400 and 1,500 metres, it serves as a natural water reserve and is the source of many of the *levadas* (irrigation channels) that traverse the island. There are no large rivers on Madeira but the Paúl da Serra is the source of several significant streams. Ribeira da Janela flows down to the north coast and a number of smaller *ribeiras,* running parallel to each other, drain towards the south coast creating so-called *lombos* (shoulders or headlands) in between. This is where some of the best vineyards are now located (see Chapter 3). The western most point on the island is Ponta do Pargo where a small vineyard had been planted the last time I visited.

A distinctive feature of the Madeiran coastline is the so-called *fajã*. These are fertile coastal platforms formed by rock falls from the cliffs above. The most famous is Fajã dos Padres at the foot of Cabo Girão, traditionally the source of some of the best Malvasia grapes. In 1930, on the day of the carnival celebrations, a huge section of Cabo Girão fell into the sea producing a wave that killed seventeen people standing on the shore at nearby Câmara de Lobos. More recently another *fajã* was formed at the foot of Penha de Aguiar on the north side of the island, fortunately without loss of life.

The island of Porto Santo is just 12 kilometres long and 6 kilometres wide (47.17 km²) but rises to 516 metres at Pico do Facho on the west side of the island. Most of the island is volcanic but the flatter central section is composed of calcareous sandstone and clays – hence the broad, golden sandy beach. This extends 9 kilometres along the south coast of the island and is responsible for the huge increase in population in the summer months when Madeira decamps to Porto Santo.

CLIMATE

For an island of its size, Madeira has an extraordinarily diverse climate. The predominantly humid, west-north-westerly winds are forced to rise and condense over the island. This produces Madeira's so-called *capacete* or 'helmet' of cloud, which often leaves the middle altitudes (600–1400 metres) shrouded in mist. Annual average rainfall varies greatly according to altitude and aspect. Much the driest part of the island is the easterly Ponta de São Lourenço with rainfall of less than 500 mm per annum. The mountain peaks of the interior are wettest, with average annual rainfall reaching nearly 3,000 mm at Pico do Arieiro. Funchal itself averages 640 mm, whereas Ponta Delgada over on the north coast receives an average of over 1,100 mm a year. Most rain falls from October to March, usually in torrential downpours (see note on flooding on page 28). July and August are the driest months, with little or no rain at all.

Temperatures also vary greatly with altitude, although the annual range between February (the coldest month) and August (the warmest) is no more than 10°C anywhere on the island. With an August mean of 22.3°C and a January mean of 16.1°C, Funchal enjoys an equable climate where the thermometer rarely rises above 30°C. Relative humidity is normally around 80 per cent. The exception to this is when the wind veers round to the east and brings with it a burning, dust-carrying wind known as the *leste*. This usually only lasts a few days at a time but, as it is accompanied by very low levels of humidity, it can be very damaging to the vines (as well as people's patience!).

As well as being considerably wetter, the north side of the island is also cooler with less sunlight and is frequently buffeted by northerly winds. Much the coolest areas of Madeira are the high mountains at the centre of the island where seasonal differences are most marked. The mean temperature at Pico do Arieiro in January is just 5.5°C. Frost is commonplace and snow is far from unknown. Before the advent of refrigeration there was an icehouse on the way up to Pico Arieiro, which once kept the guests at Reid's Hotel supplied with ice during the summer months.

Although humidity varies greatly on the island, the humid, subtropical climate is a paradise for pests and diseases. Oidium (powdery mildew), which arrived from North America in the mid-nineteenth century (see page 14), is an enduring problem and growers have to spray regularly during the growing season to keep it under control. It is particularly virulent during May and June, two months which can be fairly wet, at altitudes over 150 metres. Likewise rain just before or during harvest can be disastrous, causing grey rot to spread through the vineyard prior to picking.

Porto Santo receives much less rain than Madeira with an annual average of just 386 mm a year. In recent years there has been a serious drought on the island, the water shortage exacerbated by the increase in tourism and the construction of a golf course. Although there is a desalination plant at Vila Baleira, water frequently has to be shipped from Madeira in the summer months. Long-term lack of water has been partly responsible for the decline in the island's agriculture, particularly viticulture.

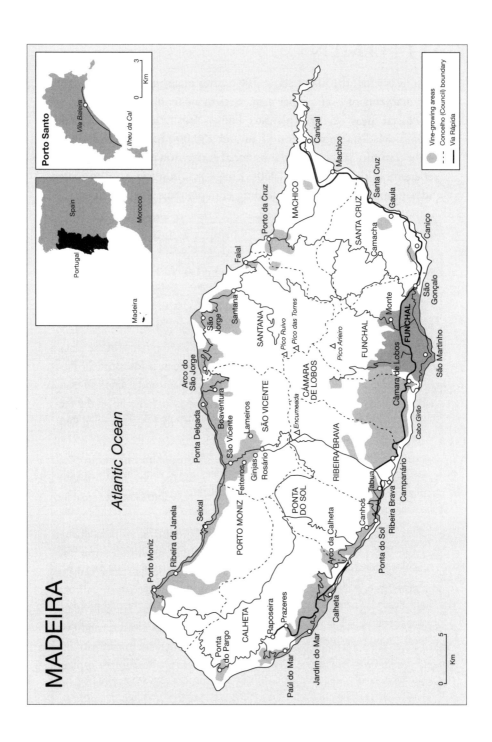

MADEIRA

Atlantic Ocean

Porto Santo

Via Baleira
Ilheu da Cal

0   3
Km

Spain

Portugal

Madeira

Morocco

Vine-growing areas
Concelho (Council) boundary
Via Rápida

Caniçal
Machico
Santa Cruz
MACHICO
Porto da Cruz
Gaula
Faial
Caniço
SANTA CRUZ
Camacha
Santana
SANTANA
São Gonçalo
São Jorge
Pico Ruivo
Pico das Torres
Monte
FUNCHAL
Arco do
São Jorge
FUNCHAL
Pico Arieiro
São Martinho
Boaventura
CÂMARA
DE LOBOS
Câmara de Lobos
Ponta Delgada
Lameiros
Encumeada
São Vicente
SÃO VICENTE
Cabo Girão
Seixal
Ginjas
Rosário
RIBEIRA BRAVA
Campanário
Ribeira da Janela
Feiteiros
Tabua
Porto Moniz
PONTA
DO SOL
Ribeira Brava
Canhas
Ponta do Sol
PORTO MONIZ
Arco da Calheta
Prazeres
Raposeira
CALHETA
Canhos
Ponta
do Pargo
Calheta
Paúl do Mar
Jardim do Mar

0   5
Km

SETTLEMENT

With nearly half the island above 700 metres in altitude and 66 per cent with gradients of over 25 per cent, settlement tends to be confined to the coastal areas or small plateaux known locally as *achadas* (literally 'found'). Madeira's population of around 250,000 has been fairly stable for the past fifty years, despite substantial emigration to South Africa and Venezuela in the 1950s and 1960s. Emigrants, however, tend to return and a number of the island's leading entrepreneurs made their way in

FUNCHAL IN THE NINETEENTH CENTURY, AND TODAY

The city of Funchal has long dominated Madeira's economy, serving as the main port and the capital. Today it spreads up the hillsides from the small historic downtown area clustered around two of the oldest buildings on the island, the cathedral and the Palaçio de São Lourenço. There is still not much in the way of good architecture but there is an elegance about the Avenida de Arriaga with its wide pavements, theatre and sub-tropical gardens. In the mid-nineteenth century, with much of the island suffering from grinding poverty caused by oidium and phylloxera, Funchal was by all accounts down at heel. Vizetelly, writing in the late 1870s, describes it as 'one of the most disappointing things in Madeira'. He writes that the main praça is 'a shabby affair' and states that the theatre has been converted into a wine store. Vizetelly describes the shops as 'dingy' and goes on to say that 'as for *articles de luxe*, one never sees them displayed; and the only shops boasting of embellishment are those of the chemists.' With the commercial district having been badly hit by the recent recession, the *pharmácias* are still some of the best-stocked shops in the city today. 'The Funchal streets are invariably narrow and paved with small round stones, most difficult to walk upon: how English and Portuguese ladies in fashionable high-healed shoes manage to accomplish it is a mystery'. Most of the city's streets are still cobbled, now polished by generations of sledges and wheels. When stepping out of a shipper's wine store on the Rua dos Ferreiros I once took a bad tumble on the cobbles; it wasn't the effect of the wine, but my leather soles. When walking in Funchal, be warned: wear soft shoes!

South Africa before returning to invest in Madeira. The city of Funchal, capital of the archipelago, has around half Madeira's population and has grown rapidly, with families moving in from the outlying countryside. However, the construction of new roads and tunnels linking Funchal with outlying parts of the island should slow down or even reverse this pattern of internal migration. The construction boom to the east and west of the city is partly due to tourism but has been exacerbated by the breakdown of the extended family as young couples clamour for their own apartments.

Porto Santo has a permanent population of around 5,000 which more than triples in the summer months. The island's population is clustered round the only town on the island, Vila Baleira.

AGRICULTURE

Until tourism began to take over in the 1970s (see page 22), agriculture was the mainstay of the Madeiran economy. On the south side of Madeira up to around 600 metres above sea level, nearly every patch of land was cultivated – making the island almost self-sufficient in fruit, vegetables and flowers. To make the most of the land available, much of the island has been carved into the tiny terraces called *poios*. There is more to this than meets the eye; it has much to do with the so-called *contracto de colónia*. Henry Vizetelly, writing in the 1870s explains the *raison d'être* behind these terraces:

'The system was originally adopted as a precaution against the periodical rains which wash the soil away down the precipitous mountain slopes. Today whenever it is possible to accumulate soil and raise a wall it is certain to be done by the occupier of the land, even though the land is unlikely to be commensurate with the time and toil expended. But then, according to the system of tenure universal in the island, a landlord is unable to eject a tenant without first compensating him for all the so-called improvements – which do not, by the way, include actual buildings erected – that the tenant has made to the land. The bemfeitorias or improvements are valued by government officials who invariably lean to the side of the tenant and estimate them at a high value. The consequence is that the more soil a tenant heaps up and the

more walls he raises on a small plot, the more certain he is of never being turned off it, for in time these erections, to which the peasant and his family devote all their leisure … often exceed the value of the land itself.'

This system of tenure is explained in more detail on page 4 and lasted more or less unchanged until after the revolution of 1974, when tenants were able to buy their own land. Subsequently large amounts of agricultural land on the south coast have been lost to piecemeal residential development and many of the more inaccessible *poios* have been abandoned.

Vines and grapes vie with bananas as Madeira's most important single crop, with both taking up around 20 per cent of the cultivatable area (see section on vineyards in Chapter 3). Banana plantations have colonised most of the *poios* on the south coast, up to about 300 metres above sea level. Other sub-tropical crops that also flourish at lower altitudes include mangos, *annona* (custard apple), avocados and sugar cane. Potatoes (including sweet potatoes) and cabbages are also important, often growing beside or frequently underneath the canopy of vines. Cereals, vegetables, strawberries, apples, pears and peaches tend to be cultivated at an altitude of around 300 metres, and on the edge of the forests at around 600 metres, cherries and chestnuts are also grown. Cattle are kept, but tend to be smelled rather than seen as they are kept indoors. Sheep graze freely at high altitudes on the Paúl da Serra which, in the frequent mists, can resemble the moors of northern England.

Much of Madeira's produce is sold in local markets, especially at Funchal which is a riot of colour and aroma at all times of the year. It is sad, however, that the growing number of supermarkets on the island source most of their fresh produce abroad, often from Holland and Spain where agriculture is on a considerably larger scale and more efficient than on Madeira or the Portuguese mainland.

GOVERNMENT

Madeira, along with Porto Santo, is an autonomous region within the Republic of Portugal, with its own regional parliament and government based in Funchal and elected every four years. Since 1978, the regional President (effectively First Minister) has been Alberto João Jardim,

LEVADAS

Madeira's crops are irrigated by a remarkable labyrinth of water channels known as *levadas*. Construction began soon after the island was colonised in the fifteenth century and by 1452 the first water-powered mill was in use. Many *levadas* were privately owned, supplying water to agricultural estates. The Blandy family, for example, had their own *levada* rising on the south side of Pico Arieiro and supplying the fields and gardens of Quinta do Palheiro; it is still known as the 'Blandy *Levada*' today. At the start of the twentieth century there were 1,000 kilometres of *levadas*, which has subsequently doubled in extent to over 2,000 kilometres including around 40 kilometres of tunnels. Twentieth-century *levadas* include the Machico and Caniçal *levada* built in 1949 and the Levada do Norte built in 1952. As well as irrigating smallholdings all over the island, some of the newer *levadas* have also been harnessed to generate electricity. The system is generally well maintained and carefully regulated to ensure fair distribution of water. With a good supply of piped water, the island is less reliant on the *levada* system than it used to be. Rupert Croft-Cooke, writing in 1960, says: 'the water is managed by committees appointed by the people. A farmer may be entitled to so many hours of water every fifteen days, and he will be duly notified by the committee to be ready to receive this water at a given hour of the day or night; at the hour appointed the stream of water will be deflected to his farm. He may have to be ready to receive his allowance at two o'clock in the morning but if he is not there for it he will wait, perhaps for another fortnight.' The distribution of water on Madeira is now regulated by the *Instituto de Gestão de Água* (IGA). The more accessible *levadas* have become tourist attractions and there are some spectacular paths to be followed alongside the channels.

representing the PPD/PSD-M (Partido Social Democrata – Madeira), who have commanded a majority since the parliament's inception. Elections to the island's regional assembly are held every four years. Madeira and Porto Santo are divided into eleven *concelhos* (municipalities): Funchal, Câmara de Lobos, Ribeira Brava, Ponta do Sol, Calheta, Porto Moniz, São Vicente, Santana, Machico, Santa Cruz and Porto Santo.

3

VINES AND VINEYARDS

Madeira can lay claim to the world's original varietal wines. The words 'Sercial', 'Verdelho', 'Bual' and 'Malvasia' (Malmsey) appeared stencilled on bottles long before Chardonnay or Cabernet Sauvignon entered the lexicon of the modern wine label. Madeira wine enthusiasts consequently have a longstanding interest in the make-up of the islands' vineyards, which have been in a state of constant flux ever since the early settlers planted the first vines in the fifteenth century.

THE VINES

The white Verdelho grape was the principal variety growing on the island before the twin plagues of oidium and phylloxera, with Terrantez and Malvasia planted in much smaller quantities but always the most highly prized. From the 1870s onwards there was a seismic shift with high-yielding, disease-resistant grape varieties largely ousting the classic varieties. A red grape called Tinta Negra Mole (now known officially as Tinta Negra) was the chief beneficiary of the upheaval but, until as recently as the early 1990s, over half the island's wine production came from so-called 'direct producer' and hybrid varieties introduced from North America. Imported as rootstock to protect the traditional European (*Vitis vinifera*) varieties from phylloxera (see page 16), the direct producers yield well and are disease resistant. Consequently they were popular with small growers looking to maximise their returns. Grapes from ungrafted *Vitis labrusca and Vitis riparia* (and the hybrids derived from them) are much less good for fortified wine than the European *vinifera* vines and were mostly used to make inexpensive madeiras and unfortified rustic table wines for local consumption. However, red hybrid varieties like Isabella, Jacquet, Cunningham (known locally as 'Canim') Hebremont, Isabella and Jacquet (sometimes spelt Jacquez), all extensively planted post-phylloxera, had some support among the shippers. Peter Cossart (the younger brother of Noel Cossart at Cossart Gordon who was responsible for the wines of Henriques & Henriques for over fifty years) always claimed he liked the direct producers and that they made some good wines. High yielding, sweet and probably naturally acidic, they were indeed capable of producing some reasonably good wines, particularly in years when the *vinifera* varieties were disease ridden. But there is no getting away from their so-called 'foxy', rustic character. There is no knowing how much of this wine entered into fortified madeira blends post-phylloxera, often masquerading as one of the so-called 'noble' varieties.

All grapes from direct producer and American hybrid vines contain a substance called anthocyanin diglucoside, known locally as *malvina*. This is thought to be carcinogenic and it is sometimes claimed that *malvina* causes mental disorders, although there is no proof of it leading to either condition. It was always technically illegal to produce madeira from the direct producers, but production figures show that from the 1950s through to the end of the 1970s between two-thirds and three-quarters of the island's grape production came from them. Most of these vineyards were on the north side of the island (although figures from the 1980s show that there was still plenty in Câmara de Lobos, Ribeira Brava and Calheta on the south coast and some of the Madeira Wine Company's vintage reports from the 1980s still smack of desperation at the lack of good quality grapes). At the end of the 1980s, Jacquet was fetching 40 escudos a kilo whereas Tinta Negra sold for 180 escudos a kilo. The ban on direct producers was only enforced following Portugal's accession to the then EEC in 1986. All wines were subsequently routinely tested for *malvina* by the Madeira Wine Institute (IVM) but apparently it is difficult to detect *malvina* in a wine that is more than ten years old. Although large areas of vineyard planted with hybrids and direct producers have since either been replanted or abandoned, according to current estimates there are still more non-*vinifera* vineyards (i.e. direct producers) on the island than *vinifera,* in a proportion of around 60:40 (see page 17). There is still a substantial local market for so-called *vinho seco* (also referred to as *vinho americano* or *morangeiro),* a light acidic red wine which smells alarmingly of synthetic strawberries.

MEN WHO SHAPED MADEIRA

Thomas Slapp Leacock (1817–1885?)

The grandson of John Leacock who founded the eponymous firm in 1758, Thomas Slapp Leacock was in charge of the business when phylloxera took hold on the island in the 1870s. He was one of the leading zoologists of his day (an authority on snails) and conducted experiments with electricity. But his fame comes from the work he undertook at the Alto do Pico de São João vineyard which is documented by Henry Vizetelly. Leacock was the first person on the island to identify phylloxera and in 1873 he was already experimenting with various treatments to combat the plague. He began by treating the roots of his vines with resin and essence of turpentine and later used tar to protect the roots from the phylloxera louse. He also used copper sulphate to combat the aerial form of the disease and, in his own vineyards, he had managed to control the disease by 1883. Thomas Slapp Leacock is credited with saving some of Madeira's traditional grape varieties from extinction, and his research was donated to Cambridge University.

THE VINTAGE AT MR. LEACOCK'S QUINTA AT SÃO JOÃO, NEAR FUNCHAL, MADEIRA.

(p. 159.)

The quality of Madeira's wine grapes has improved immeasurably since the 1990s, with large swathes of vineyard having been either abandoned or replanted. Under two EU-financed schemes dating from 2001 to 2011, 300 growers replanted 99 hectares of vines. Although smaller in area and fewer in number, the majority of vineyards are now better tended than at any time since the mid-nineteenth century. The legal minimum ripeness for grapes destined to produce madeira wine is a mere 9° Baumé (roughly equivalent to 9% abv, or alcohol by volume), with an exemption for Sercial, even the best of which often struggles to reach this level of ripeness. In practice, the 9° Baumé minimum has only been rigorously enforced by the authorities since 2004. It means that there is now more of an incentive for growers to produce a smaller but better quality crop.

Once categorised as *nobre* ('noble'), *boa* ('good') or merely 'authorised', the official classification of Madeira's *vinifera* grapes has now been simplified into two categories: recommended and authorised. The traditional grape varieties that predate phylloxera (Sercial, Verdelho, Bual, Malvasia and Terrantez) are the most highly valued and still produce the best and most sought-after wines. The following grape varieties are currently permitted for the production of madeira wine:

Recommended varieties (Castas recomendadas)

White (brancas): Sercial, Verdelho, Malvasia Fina (Boal), Malvasia Cândida, Malvasia de São Jorge, Moscatel Graúdo, Folgosão (Terrantez), Listrão
Red (tintas): Tinta Negra, Bastardo, Tinta, Malvasia Candida Roxa, Verdelho Tinto

Authorised varieties (Castas autorizadas)

White (brancas): Caracol, Rio Grande, Valveirinho
Red (tintas): Complexa, Deliciosa and Triunfo.

Recommended varieties

The following varieties are currently (February 2015) 'recommended' by IVBAM. In the profiles that follow I am grateful for first-hand information from Andrew Blandy at Quinta de Santa Luzia, Funchal, and his consultant viticulturalist Eng. Gonçalo Caldeira of the Madeira

Wine Company. The varieties below are listed in order of the area they cover on the island.

Tinta Negra

This red grape is the most planted grape variety on the island by far, with 277 hectares in 2010. Also planted on the Canaries, it is by no means the oldest variety and was probably introduced to Madeira from mainland Portugal in the eighteenth century. Red grapes being much less common at the time, it simply went under the name 'Tinta' (although wines may also have included the poorer quality red Maroto) until the early nineteenth century, when the name Negra Mole ('soft black') was added. Occasionally bottles of madeira labelled *Tinta* can still be found. The name was officially truncated to Tinta Negra by the *Instituto da Vinha e do Vinho* in Lisbon in 2000.

It has been frequently stated that the variety was developed from the Pinot Noir and Grenache grapes (perhaps this is due to an eighteenth-century wine called 'Madeira Burgundy'), but this does not stand up to any scientific scrutiny. Recent DNA testing has identified that Tinta Negra equates to Molar, a variety grown in Estremadura (Lisboa) and Colares on the Portuguese mainland (although I have never come across it in any quantity). This name derives from the Latin *mollis* (meaning 'soft'). Known at one time in Spain as Mollar, it probably originated from Andalucía, and has also been cultivated in South America where it is also known as Negramoll. In Portugal Tinta Negra is also known as Saborinho (meaning 'small and flavoursome' which somehow seems a misnomer).

The area of vineyard planted with Tinta Negra increased exponentially after phylloxera. It is a very productive variety and relatively easy to grow, hence its popularity with small growers. More has been planted since the early 1990s to replace the direct producers (see above). Until 1993, when the legislation was altered, much of the madeira wine masquerading under the names of the traditional varieties was made from Tinta Negra (often blended with the now illegal direct producers). Such is its acceptance by both growers and wine-makers that this chameleon of a grape now accounts for nearly 90 per cent of all Madeira wine, ranging in style from dry through medium dry and medium sweet to rich. Under the old grape classification system, Tinta Negra was classified as merely 'good' with the term 'noble' reserved for the traditional varieties. It is now officially 'recommended' but the name 'Tinta Negra' was prohibited from appearing on a label until 2015. This versatile grape variety is nonetheless capable of producing some very good wine. Starting out purple-pink in colour, the wines quickly turn amber with *estufagem* and/or ageing in cask. Tinta Negra grapes are soft and fleshy (hence '*mole*') and ripen to between 9° and 12° Baumé depending on yield and where they are grown. Tinta Negra is grown all over Madeira (with a small quantity on Porto Santo) but the greatest concentration is at Estreito de Câmara de Lobos (160 hectares) on the south side of the island and at São Vicente on the north (109 hectares).

Verdelho

With 46 hectares growing on the island, the white Verdelho grape is the second most planted *vinifera* variety on Madeira. Until phylloxera, it was the single most planted grape and Vizetelly describes it as accounting for as much as two-thirds of the island's vines. Verdelho was not particularly highly regarded until early in the twentieth century when it was promoted under the old classification system from being merely 'good' (*boa*) to 'noble' (*nobre*). It is currently one of the five white varieties to be 'recommended' (as opposed to 'authorised'). It is uncertain as to where Verdelho originated. It may have been brought from mainland Portugal where, until very recently, it was confused with Gouveio which grows widely in the Douro and is used for white port. It has also been identified erroneously as being the same as Verdejo in Spain and Verdicchio in Sicily. Given that most of the world's Verdelho vineyards originated from Madeira – there is a tiny amount growing in France (the Loire), California and rather more in Australia – it is possible that Madeira can lay claim to Verdelho as its own grape.

Verdelho produces small, closed bunches of grapes. Consequently it is rather susceptible to bunch rot and *coulure* and very susceptible to downy and powdery mildew (oidium). It performs at its best on the island in cooler conditions, either at higher altitudes on the south side of the island (there is some particularly good Verdelho grown at Raposeira) or on the north side at Ribeira de Janela/Porto Moniz (9.8 hectares), São Vicente (16 hectares) and Ponta Delgada/Santana (6.27 hectares). Verdelho is a moderately productive variety. Planted in the right place, the grapes rarely struggle to ripen producing moderate levels of sugar (10–12° Baumé) and have characteristically high levels of acidity. It is therefore well suited to producing medium dry wines, in between Sercial and Boal in style (see below). Verdelho is also used occasionally to produce dry table wines under the Terras Madeirenses designation; it has to be said with limited success. There is also a red variant of Verdelho (Verdelho Roxo) which is still found in the north west of Portugal but appears to be extinct on Madeira.

Malvasia

The best known of all Madeira's grapes, the name 'Malvasia' (and its English corruption 'Malmsey') is in fact an umbrella for a number of different grape varieties. Historically, much the most highly prized is the **Malvasia Cândida**. Recent DNA profiling has revealed that this is the same as Malvasia di Lipari, grown in Italy, Greece, Spain and Croatia. Its origin is uncertain but it was purportedly brought to Madeira from Crete (Candia) in the fifteenth century either by Venetian traders or by the Infante Dom Henrique (Prince Henry the Navigator) himself. Malvasia Cândida was always in short supply. During the second half of the eighteenth century Francis Newton (erstwhile partner in Cossart Gordon) wrote frequently to his London partners lamenting the lack of Malvasia wine. Decimated by oidium and not widely replanted after phylloxera, by the mid-twentieth century Malvasia Cândida was almost extinct. It is very difficult to grow and production varies alarmingly from year to year. It is so tetchy that at Quinta de Santa Luzia in Funchal the Malvasia Cândida planted there in 2005 was regrafted in 2014 to Malvasia Fina (Boal). Malvasia Candida is very prone to attack by oidium and needs a well-exposed site at low altitudes to flourish. It also needs to be trained on *latadas* (see below) as it has to be pruned with at least eight buds to produce a commercial crop. It is subject to apical growth with the flowering tending to be towards the end of the cane. Traditionally Malvasia Cândida grapes were only picked when they began to shrivel or raisinise on the vine, so concentrating the natural sugars to produce the sweetest and most concentrated of wines. Only about 4 hectares of Malvasia Cândida is currently grown on Madeira at Jardim do Mar and on Fajã dos Padres, both at sea level on the south side of the island, as well as in the Government's experimental vineyards.

Most wine bottled under the name Malvasia/Malmsey is in fact made from a grape known locally as **Malvasia de São Jorge**. Until 2015 Malvasia de São Jorge was no more than 'authorised' by IVBAM but is now officially 'recommended'. It is a modern variety that was introduced from Bairrada by Professor Leão Ferreira de Almeida of the Estação Agronómica Nacional in Lisbon and came to be planted on Madeira from the late 1970s onwards. Named after the parish of São Jorge on the north side of the island, the area of production expanded rapidly in the replanting programme that took place from the 1990s onwards, and there are now 36 hectares, mostly around Santana on the north coast. This productive variety nonetheless has its drawbacks as it is highly susceptible to bunch rot. But it is aromatic when young and well liked by all the shippers.

A number of other so-called 'Malvasias' are found growing on Madeira. In his book *Madeira, the Island Vineyard*, Noel Cossart mentions the **Malvasia Babosa** ('Lazy Malmsey'). This variety was supposedly introduced to Madeira by the Genoese nobleman Simon Accaioli in 1515 but it is not clear what this variety equates to, other than being known just as Babosa on the Portuguese mainland. It seems that this sub-variety no longer exists on the island. There is also **Malvasia Fina** (see under Boal below), and **Malvasia Roxa** ('Purple Malvasia'). In the winery no distinction is made between the different types of Malvasia and, when it comes to vinifying the grapes, all the above varieties are pressed and fermented together. Malmsey should therefore be thought of as a style of wine rather than a varietal.

Boal (Bual)

Like Malvasia, Boal (Bual in English) is a name that covers not one but a number of grape varieties in Portugal. Professor Cincinnato da Costa, writing in his tome *O Portugal Viticola / Le Portugal Vinicole* at the turn of the twentieth century lists no less than sixteen sub-varieties. These include tantalising names like Boal carrasquenho, Boal de Alicante, Boal pardo ('grey' Boal) Boal Calhariz, Boal desembargador ('unembargoed' Boal), Boal roxo (purple Boal), Boal frio ('cold' Boal), Boal liso ('smooth' Boal) Boal ratinho ('small mouse' Boal), Boal ramilhete (floral 'nosegay' Boal) and Boal Bonifácio.

The Boal growing on Madeira, also known as the Boal Cachudo (*cacho* meaning 'bunch'), has had the official and rather confusing official title of Malvasia Fina since 2000. It almost certainly originated on the Portuguese mainland (or *continente* as it is referred to on Madeira) having been planted in the Douro and Dão for centuries. In *Wine Grapes* (Robinson et al.), viticulturalist Rolando Faustino suggests that due to its wide genetic diversity it is probably from the Douro but neither Dão nor the Lisbon region can be ruled out. Interestingly, Cincinnato da Costa distinguishes Boal Cachudo and Malvasia Fina as separate grape varieties, placing the first in the Lisbon region (as well as Madeira) and the second in the Douro. Such was the confusion in nomenclature at the time.

Under the name Malvasia Fina it is the second most planted white grape in the Douro and therefore ends up in almost all white port. Rebello de Fonseca heaped praise on the grape in the nineteenth century saying 'you can eat it, make raisins from it as well as wonderful wine. Among white grapes only Moscatel is better'. In fact in the Douro it was sometimes known by farmers as the Malvasia de Passa because of its tendency to raisinise and shrivel on the vine. From my experience in Portugal (and elsewhere) grapes that are good to eat rarely make the best wine. In Portugal this variety is also known by the local names Arinto do Dão and Assário. Boal is also grown on the Azores. In most of the places where Malvasia Fina is grown it would be stretching it to call this grape 'fine'.

Malvasia Fina is a relatively easy grape to grow. It buds late and ripens early and it is relatively resistant to oidium and mildew. Boal produces large bunches (hence the name) and is consistently the most productive of the white grapes, making it popular with growers. The only significant drawback is that it is very susceptible to drought and therefore needs plenty of groundwater to flourish. On the *continente* it is not especially prized as a variety and rarely appears as a varietal wine; on Madeira, Boal is the third most planted of all the white grape varieties. Boal is traditionally found growing on warmer sites on the south side of the island, usually at 100 to 300 metres above sea level. Today, the best wines originate from small plots in Campanário, Calheta, Arco de Calheta and Ponta do Pargo to the west of Funchal. It does not perform well on the cooler and damper north side of the island and there is very little planted there as a result. Unlike some of the other white grapes (e.g. Terrantez and Sercial) there is seemingly no shortage of Boal even though the total registered area is no more than 18.2 hectares (8.8 hectares in Calheta, 6.6 hectares in Camara de Lobos and 3.6 hectares in Ribeira Brava). Boal is capable of ripening to between 11 and 13° Baumé but the average Baumé in recent years has been less than 10°, more a reflection of high yields. Nevertheless it produces wines that are medium sweet or medium rich in style.

In his book, *Madeira, the Island Vineyard,* Noel Cossart says little about Boal as a grape but writes of the wine that 'Bual was a great favourite in officers' messes and clubs in India, being lighter than Malmsey or Port'. My late father-in-law, Richard Blandy (who chaired Blandy's from 1986 to 2001) always professed that Bual was his favourite style of Madeira wine and advocated drinking it with curry – 'like chutney', he would exclaim. I have tried this and the combination really works!

Sercial

Known officially on the Portuguese mainland as Esgana Cão ('dog strangler'), Sercial is characterised by ferociously high levels of natural acidity. Perhaps for this reason it was often said to be related to Rhine Riesling but in fact it has no connection at all. Sercial probably originates from the Bucelas region just outside Lisbon where, with the slightly less acidic Arinto, it produces crisp dry white wines. Very occasionally it is referred to on Madeira as Esgana, Esganinho, Esganiso or Esganacão. *Esgana* means 'strangle' or 'choke' in Portuguese, a reference to the high natural acidity that this grape retains almost wherever it is grown, even in relatively warm conditions. Sercial on Madeira should not be confused with Cerceal or Sercialinho which grow in the Dão and Bairrada regions respectively and are different varieties.

Vizetelly describes Sercial as 'now exceedingly rare' and describes the wine as 'strong, dry … with an exquisite bouquet'. He goes on to observe with accuracy that 'when young … this wine is harsh to the palate, age being requisite to bring it to perfection and develop that nutty flavour for which it is distinguished'. Sercial is still very rare, with just 17.8 hectares of vineyard on the island, mostly to be found growing at the highest altitudes (up to 800 metres at Jardim da Serra – 8.6 hectares) or close to sea level around Porto Moniz / Seixal (6.4 hectares) on the cool north coast. At high altitudes Sercial is usually trained close to the ground to gain the maximum amount of heat from the volcanic soil. There is also some Sercial planted at Quinta de Santa Luzia, approximately 145 metres above sea level where bud burst is very variable: on some canes a few buds would burst in spring whilst others remained latent, only to burst later in the year. Resistant to oidium, Sercial is generally the last grape to be harvested, ripening with some difficulty to 11° Baumé. The large bunches of grapes are thin skinned and prone to rot. Apart from Terrantez (below), Sercial is the least productive of the traditional white grape varieties. But Sercial produces some of the most enduring Madeira wine, kept alive for decades by searing levels of acidity (up to 12 g/l in some wines). Sadly this is the least appreciated style of madeira, and production of Sercial continues to decline with few new vineyards having been planted in recent years.

SERCIAL AND MALMSEY IN 1841

The following description of two of Madeira's most prized styles of wine by Paulo Perestrelo da Câmara in the *Breve Noticia Sobre a Madeira*, written in 1841, could apply almost equally today: 'Let us begin with Sercial which, in my view, is the most exquisite of all grapes not least because of its expense and rarity and because it takes so long to meet perfection. The grapes seldom reach a perfect ripeness, always maintain a slight tartness and, being grown on the coast are scorched by the sea air and southern sun. No less than ten years are needed for this liquid to acquire the flavour, aroma and hint of burnt toffee which characterises it. Sercial is closely followed by Malmsey, a sweet beverage that many prefer to Sercial and consider equal in superiority and value. The comparison is valid, given that the best Malmsey grapes make only 200 pipes a year. This fabulous nectar, with its mellifluous flavour, has the pungent aroma of a posy of sweet-smelling flowers. This precious beverage is ready to drink after eight years, but is even better left longer, but even at only a year old it is agreeable, giving off its perfume and full flavour of the grape.' Tasting notes on wines made in the 1840s and earlier may be found in Chapter 6.

Terrantez

Alongside the fabled Malvasia Cândida, Terrantez is the most highly prized of all Madeira's grapes. It produces wonderfully aromatic wines that are at once both sweet and astringent and have a capacity to evolve well in cask. In fact Terrantez is so well regarded that a short rhyming ditty was written in its praise:

> *As uvas de Terrantez,*
> *Não as coma nem as dês,*
> *Para vinho Deus as fez.*[2]

It was thought that Terrantez came from the Portuguese mainland and was the same variety as the port grape by the name of Folgosão; however, DNA testing has proved that the latter is a different variety from Terrantez. It is still referred to as Folgosão in the 2015 legislation. The Terrantez grown on the Azores is also distinct. In the eighteenth and early nineteenth centuries Terrantez was relatively widely planted but its susceptibility to oidium meant that it was all but wiped out in the 1850s. Known for its miniscule yield, following phylloxera little or no Terrantez was replanted. By the 1920s it was reported as being almost extinct although a small quantity was still cultivated on Porto Santo. Terrantez has now made a modest recovery and total production has risen sharply to 7,500 kilos a year. There is a small quantity in Calheta and it is encouraging to find that Henriques & Henriques have planted Terrantez at Ribeira de Caixa. A small plot of it has been planted at Quinta de Santa Luzia, close to the centre of Funchal, and another on the north side of the island at São Jorge. Altogether, this takes the total to just over 2 hectares.

Terrantez is relatively easy to train and needs a vertical cordon. It is a variety that continues to be very susceptible to oidium but is much more resistant to downy mildew. Terrantez ripens late but the small berries in compact bunches make it very susceptible to botrytis (bunch rot). For this reason it is always picked when it reaches 9–9.5° Baumé. At Quinta da Santa Luzia it is always the first grape to be harvested. In short, Terrantez is an extremely tetchy variety and the only reason that a handful of growers persist with it is due to the quality of the wine it produces.

Bastardo

The same grape variety as Trousseau, cultivated in the Jura in France, this early ripening red grape is planted fairly extensively in northern Portugal

---

2 'Terrantez grapes, neither eat or give them away, for God made them to produce wine.'

but was all but extinguished from Madeira by phylloxera. Occasionally called Bastardinho ('Little Bastard') it is found in tiny quantities, mostly in the government's experimental vineyards. The fact that Bastardo is low yielding with small bunches and very susceptible to disease may account for the name! Officially 1.61 hectares exists but there is, in fact, much less than this growing on the island. Although old varietal Bastardo wines can still be found, they are very much a rarity (the most recent I have tasted was a 1954 from Blandy's). Bastardo produces pale, sweet wines with fairly low levels of natural acidity. Vizetelly describes it as having 'a very fine bouquet … sweet to the taste, leaving behind it, however, a not unpleasant astringency'. This I can vouch for as, since 2010, Barbeito have been producing a varietal Bastardo from a plot of vines at São Jorge belonging to the Mayor of Santana. The grapes are picked in early September and again with another pass through the vineyard later in the month. Ricardo Diogo found that he was unable to obtain sufficient colour from pneumatic pressing and since 2013 Barbeito have been treading Bastardo by foot in the old fashioned way. This produces a delicate pink, aromatic wine with a fruit character not unlike Pinot Noir. The wines are currently being aged in pipe and will be released as *colheitas* and/or *frasqueiras* in due course.

Moscatel

A number of different types of Muscat or Moscatel are still planted on Madeira, producing table grapes for the local market. There used to be a Moscatel wine. Noel Cossart recalls that 1900, 1903 and 1909 were notable Moscatel vintages but precious little has been produced in recent years. The grapes are high in sugar and low in acidity, producing wines that are rich and (atypically for Madeira) rather cloying. The Moscatel Graúdo recommended by IVBAM is Muscat of Alexandria, which is planted in a number of guises on mainland Portugal (e.g. Moscatel de Setúbal) and crops up in vineyards all around the Mediterranean.

Listrão

Once grown on Madeira as a white table grape, on the island of Porto Santo Listrão makes a flabby white and a soft dry fortified wine known as Listrão de Porto Santo. Listrão is the same variety as the Palomino Fino grape in Jerez and Malvasia Rei in mainland Portugal. In the semi-desert-like conditions on Porto Santo, Listrão reaches sugar levels in excess of 13° Baumé with a corresponding lack of acidity. It used to be fermented dry on the island then shipped to Madeira to be blended with Sercial or Verdelho. This practice has all but ended and most Listrão is now made into very ordinary dry white wine, sold off to visitors in the summer months; I found that one taste was enough. Barros e Sousa were the last to make a fortified varietal wine from Listrão.

Tinta (da Madeira)

Officially known just as 'Tinta' this grape produces wines similar in style to Tinta Negra. Tinta was often mixed with Verdelho to give colour and body. There is very little Tinta (da Madeira) planted on the island and it exists only in the government's experimental vineyards. It is a modern grape thought to be the same as Egiodola developed in Bordeaux in the 1950s. However, this is described in Robinson et al. as quite a tannic variety, which Tinta da Madeira is not.

Authorised varieties

Complexa

Developed in mainland Portugal in the 1960s, Complexa earns its name by being a tetrahybrid of three *vinifera* varieties: Castelão with Tintinha and Tintinha with Moscatel de Hamburgo. It was introduced to Madeira as an experimental alternative to Tinta Negra and, at the time, was classified as 'good' rather than 'noble'. Complexa produces a slightly less astringent wine than Negra Mole with higher alcohol levels. There are 38.7 hectares of Complexa vineyard planted mainly on the south side of the island around Calheta and in the north around São Jorge and Santana. It resists disease, making it popular with small growers but although the individual berries are large and weigh well, Complexa yields relatively little due to having relatively large pips. It is therefore much less popular with wine-makers than it is with growers!

Triunfo

Madeira's Triunfo is the result of a crossing between the Portuguese Castelão grape and Moscatel de Hamburgo and therefore has similar parentage to Complexa (above). Developed on mainland Portugal in the

1950s, it is planted on Madeira as an experimental variety. Triunfo yields grapes with reasonable levels of sugar but low acidity.

Caracol

The charmingly named white 'snail' grape is only found on the island of Porto Santo. It was supposedly introduced to the island in the 1930s by a Portuguese emigrant to South Africa and planted at Eiras by José da Silva. Originally known as Uva de Eiras, it was later renamed Caracol as this was Sr. Silva's nickname. It is cultivated as both a table and a wine grape.

Rio Grande

This white grape is a modern crossing of Diagalves and Fernão Pires. It is mostly found on the Azorean island of Pico but a few vines are found on Madeira, mostly in the regional government's experimental vineyards.

Deliciosa and **Valveirinha** are red and white grapes respectively which appear only to exist in the regional government's experimental vineyards.

VINEYARDS OLD AND NEW

There is, at long last, an official register or *cadastro* of vineyards on Madeira and Porto Santo. This has been a knotty problem ever since the *Instituto do Vinho da Madeira* (IVM) was established in 1979, but a visit to Madeira's vineyards will reveal just how intractable this problem is. It is now estimated that there are currently around 1,100 hectares of vineyard on the island, split between 1,755 growers. Of this, less than 500 hectares are given over to *Vitis vinifera* varieties. The average size of a vineyard holding is 0.3 of a hectare and, with a total of nearly 5,500 separate plots, the average area of each parcel of vineyard is just 0.095 hectares. Take a walk into the western suburbs of Funchal above Virtudes and São Martinho and you will find vines clambering up to houses with horticulture below. Instead of talking yields in international terms of hectolitres per hectare, individual growers often speak of kilos per square metre. Yields are high, the grapes swollen by irrigation. The maximum yield permitted under the 2015 law is high at 150 hl/ha. In practice yields are often considerably higher with some vineyards attaining yields of 200 hl/ha. Under the law, IVBAM is permitted to alter the maximum yield according to climatic conditions and the potential quality of the grape musts.

At just under 10 hectares in extent, much the largest vineyard on the island belongs to the shipper Henriques & Henriques (see page 103). Although many of the shippers owned their own vineyards in the nineteenth century (e.g. Leacock's São João) most subsequently disposed of their holdings and relied increasingly on an army of individual growers. With the grapes pressed in *lagares* on site and transported to Funchal as grape must, the shippers came to exercise very little control over the quality of the fruit. Today Justino's, the largest shipper in terms of volume, buys grapes from over 700 growers. For most of these farmers, grape growing is a secondary occupation. In recent years the shippers have been working much more closely with growers to improve the quality of their grapes. The shippers employ their own agents in the outlying villages to coordinate the harvest and help small farmers during the growing season. A computer system can trace the contents of any one wine back to the individual grower. In 2012 the Madeira Wine Company took another big step forward when they leased two vineyards (together amounting to nearly 7 hectares) on the north side of the island in order to secure more white grapes. They are also managing just under a hectare of vineyard now planted entirely with white grapes belonging to Andrew Blandy at Quinta da Santa Luzia in Funchal.

Vineyards on Madeira have been cultivated in much the same way for hundreds of years. Older vineyards are supported on *latadas*, low pergolas about a metre or so in height, under which other crops such as potatoes, cabbages and beans are frequently grown. Frequent summer irrigation and the application of fertilisers to the horticultural crops below the canopy serves to increase yields and debases the quality of the grapes. Apart from the fact that metal or timber supports have replaced bamboo, the following eighteenth-century description of a typical Madeiran vineyard would apply today: 'one or more walks a yard or two wide, intersect each vineyard … Along these walks, which are arched over by lathes about seven feet high, they erect wooden pillars at regular distances to support a lattice work of bamboos, which slopes down from both sides of the walk, till it is only a foot and a half or two feet high, in which elevation it extends over the whole vineyard. The vines are in this manner supported from the ground, and the people have room to root out the weeds which spring up between them. In the season of the vintage they creep under this lattice-work, cut off the grapes, and lay them into baskets: some of the bunches of these grapes that I saw weighed six pounds upwards.' On the north side of the island it used to be common to train vines up chestnut trees, just as in the Minho region of northern Portugal. On Madeira this practice died out with oidium in the mid-nineteenth century.

Most of Madeira's vineyards are planted on *poios*, the small terraces with retaining stone walls often constructed centuries ago. When the vines are in leaf, the terracing is hardly visible. Looking upwards at the huge slope of vines at Estreito de Câmara de Lobos, the houses appear to be surrounded by one giant canopy. Although the *latada* system seems to suit some varieties (Malvasia Cândida, for example) many of the vineyards planted since the 1990s are trained on to vertical cordons (referred to locally as *espaldeira*). These vineyards are laid out at a higher density (4,600–5,200 plants per hectares as opposed to 2,500–3,000 in traditional vineyards), tend to be larger in size and are much easier to cultivate. However the *latada* system helps to maximise exposure to the sun on the cooler north side of the island as well as increasing aeration and reducing erosion. On vertiginous slopes, some of which at Seixal (see below) have an inclination of 65 per cent, the *latada* is the only practical way to cultivate.

Where are the vineyards?

This is a question asked by many a visitor to Madeira. The answer is that until as recently as the 1960s, many of the finest wine grapes were grown in the western outskirts of Funchal and in nearby Câmara de Lobos. Pico de São João (St. John's Hill), São Martinho, Santo António and São Roque were all important grape producing areas, noted primarily for the quality of their predominantly sweet wines. Vizetelly describes Leacock's São João as being about 13 acres in extent in the late 1870s, and supported like modern vineyards on horizontal wires. He also describes São Martinho as 'an important viticultural district yielding a high class wine with a fine bouquet…'. São Martinho frequently appeared on bottles of fine nineteenth-century vintages. One of the island's leading nineteenth century vineyards was at Quinta Stanford, just above the modern day Pestana Miramar Hotel where the Rua Dr. Pitta now runs (see page 180). At nearby Ribeiro Secco, Vizetelly mentions a vineyard belonging to the sherry shippers Messrs. Davies planted with Palomino (Listrão). Richard Davies owned the famous Quinta Vigia most of which was demolished in the early 1970s to build the

Casino Park Hotel. As the city of Funchal has grown these vineyards have been taken over piecemeal by modern hotels, housing and warehousing. One of the last historic plots of Terrantez disappeared as recently as 1999 under Madeira Shopping, the island's largest shopping centre, close to São Martinho. Vizetelly states that the vineyards of Santo António 'usually yield a good wine'. Although a few small plots of vines can still be found cheek by jowl with houses around Santo António and Virtudes, at 0.89 hectares the largest vineyard in Funchal today is surprisingly close to the city centre at Quinta de Santa Luzia. The entire Funchal municipality now has just under 3 hectares of vineyard.

To the west of Funchal, the former fishing village of Câmara de Lobos (or Cama de Lobos as it was once known) is reputed to be the site of Madeira's first vineyards. The Pico de Torre above the town was once the centre of the huge Torre Bella estate, which once extended along the south coast as far as Arco de Calheta (see page 205). Vizetelly describes the scene as 'a fertile hollow, formerly covered with vines which yielded one of the finest and most robust Madeira growths' and goes on to say how phylloxera destroyed nearly all the vineyards and that they were replaced by sugar cane. The Torre Bella estate was broken up after the 1974 revolution and much of the best vineyard land around Câmara de Lobos has either been built on or given over to bananas. There are still one or two small plots of well-tended vineyard at the top of Pico da Torre (beside the *miradouro*) but banana plantations have largely colonised the agricultural *poios* above Câmara de Lobos up to about 200 metres above sea level.

Most of the island's vineyards (around 180 hectares) are now to be found at higher altitudes around Estreito de Câmara de Lobos. The principal grape variety here is Tinta Negra but there are small plots of Boal and Verdelho in the deep sheltered valleys of Marinheira, Vargem, and Jesus Maria José. Henriques & Henriques have some Terrantez and Malvasia Cândida visible from the *Via Rapida* (expressway) at Ribeira de Caixa below Estreito. Above Estreito, Quinta das Romeiras is one of the larger estates to remain intact, belonging to the Araújo family (see page 137). Vineyards on the south side of the island are found up to an altitude of 800 metres, some of the highest being at Jardim da Serra above Estreito where some of the best Sercial is still grown.

At the foot of Cabo Girão just to the west of Câmara de Lobos is one of Madeira's most historic vineyards, Fajã dos Padres. The result of a huge rock fall from a 300-metre cliff, the *fajã* was only accessible by sea until a rather precarious lift was built down the cliff side in 1984. It was once the property of the Jesuits and the chapel became the *adega*. The 9-hectare Fajã dos Padres is now a tourist destination in its own right with a beach bar and a cluster of self-catering holiday cottages. Tropical fruit is the principal crop but there is still a small vineyard capable of producing some of the best Malvasia Cândida on the island as well as a small quantity of Terrantez, both of which are bought by Barbeito.

Above Cabo Girão, Quinta Grande is one of the most fertile parts of the island, where vines mingle with vegetables and other crops. Above the old main road (EN 229) at Ribeira do Escrivão is Madeira's largest single vineyard with 10 hectares of vines belonging to wine shippers Henriques & Henriques. This looks very different to any other vineyard on the island, having been laid out by Miguel Corte Real, a viticulturalist working for the Port shipper Cockburn on the mainland. The terraces, which have been bulldozed from the hillside, resemble those of the Douro and are known as *patamares*. Rising up to 750 metres above sea level, the vineyard is mostly planted with Verdelho and Sercial, but in cool years even these varieties struggle to ripen. Henriques & Henriques have recently had more success with Terrantez.

Travelling west and staying above the jagged coastline is Campanário, described by Vizetelly as 'not so important as Cama de Lobos' but 'yielding a wine of even higher character – less powerful, but altogether more refined in flavour and bouquet'. He goes on to conclude that in 'our judgement the best Campanário growths surpass the more generally prized Cama de Lobos vintages by reason of their greater delicacy of flavour and more fragrant bouquet'. Despite this, I have come across very few wines with Campanário on the label. Today Campanário is home to a few good Boal vineyards; a plot can be seen below the church and immediately above the road tunnel that now takes the *via rapida* from Funchal to Ribeira Brava. Nearby Caldeira (meaning 'boiler') is, as its name suggests, very warm and productive. These are among the first vineyards to be harvested, usually in late August.

There are few vineyards on the south coast between Ribeira Brava and Ponta do Sol, much of which is too steep for agriculture, and the coastal zone around Lugar de Baixo and Madelena do Mar is mostly given over to bananas which are reputed to be the best on the island. At Arco de

Calheta, so called because of the natural amphitheatre facing southeast and out to sea, bananas form the dominant crop with just a few vineyards in between, and some very good Bual is grown here. Sadly, many of the growers around here are getting old and are not being succeeded, leading to a growing shortage of Bual. Above Calheta (between Arco de Calheta and Estreito de Calheta) are some of Madeira's best individual vineyards, planted on the well-exposed *lombos* (literally 'loins') or headlands that slope down from the south-easterly flank of the Paúl da Serra. Plots of vines on Lombo do Doutor, Lombo do Salão, Lombo das Laranjeiras, Lombo dos Reis and Lombo dos Serrões produce good grapes, particularly Bual. The narrow Santa Catarina valley nearby produces both grapes and sugar cane. There is a distillery on the coast at Calheta that still produces the *aguadente de cana* (sugarcane brandy) that used to fortify Madeira wine.

One of the five government-run experimental vineyards can be found at the appropriately named Quinta das Vinhas at Estreito de Calheta. Over a hundred grape varieties can be found here, including foreign varietals such as Cabernet Sauvignon, Merlot, Chardonnay and Chenin Blanc as well as indigenous Portuguese grapes and varieties from Madeira and the Canaries.

West of Jardim do Mar, the island is too cool and windswept for bananas but there are plots of cereals, vegetables and vines. Vineyards at Raposeira and Fajã de Ovelha, 400 to 600 metres or so above Paúl do Mar, produce some of the best Verdelho. Sercial used to be grown on Fajã Grande and Fajã Pequena but these narrow coastal platforms have now been abandoned. However the land around Ponta do Pargo is relatively level compared to the rest of the island and used to be valued for its Sercial. The area is still intensively cultivated, producing apples, sweet potatoes and cereals. There is a relatively new and well-tended vineyard, close to the lighthouse below Ponta do Pargo, that serves as a minor mecca for the tourists who make the two-hour journey from Funchal to visit the most westerly point on the island. Sadly, for those like me who enjoy the traditional Madeira countryside, work began on a huge golf course in this area, only to come to a halt following the financial crisis in 2008.

With the decline in viticulture on the south of the island, the valley of São Vicente, immediately north of Ribeira Brava, is now second only to Estreito de Câmara de Lobos as the main area for grape growing, with

140 hectares. This whole area has been given new economic impetus by the construction of a road tunnel under Encumeada linking the north coast with the south, which now puts São Vicente within a forty-minute drive of Funchal. Vineyards on the lava slopes around the communities of Ginjas, Feiteiras, Lameiros and Lanço above the town of São Vicente are extremely productive. Ninety-five per cent of the production is Tinta Negra but there is also a small and increasing quantity of Verdelho (14.57 hectares at the last count). Although sheltered from the northerly wind, the area is considerably cooler than on the south side of the island and there are few vineyards above 350 metres.

The village of Seixal, west of São Vicente on the north coast, has the steepest and most spectacular vineyards on the island, like hanging gardens cascading into the sea. Seixal is known for Sercial (7.03 hectares), whereas the adjacent communities of Ribeira da Janela and Porto Moniz traditionally grew Verdelho (11.1 hectares) although there now are much larger quantities of the direct producers (mostly Jacquet). The vineyards at Porto Moniz, the most north-westerly point on the island, are a patchwork of tiny plots sheltered from the north winds by windbreaks made from *urze* or brushwood.

The villages east of São Vicente towards Santana still produce large quantities of American hybrid grapes (again mostly Jacquet). With the exception of the steep sided and rather dank valley of Boaventura (still mostly planted with direct producers, mostly Herbremont), many of these vineyards have been either abandoned or replaced with European *vinifera* varieties. There is an impressive new 5-hectare vineyard on *patamares* at Ponta Delgada producing Verdelho and Arnsburger, as well as Cabernet Sauvignon and Merlot. At Arco de São Jorge there is an experimental vineyard with a number of different clones of Malvasia and Verdelho. There is also a small wine museum in the centre of the village next to the rose garden. Further west, the towns of São Jorge and Santana are the source of Malvasia de São Jorge (34.17 hectares), the principal variant of Malvasia growing on Madeira. The largest vineyard here is Quinta do Bispo, a property belonging to the church, at São Jorge. This has been leased by the Madeira Wine Company who have planted 4.5 hectares of Malvasia de São Jorge, Verdelho and Sercial, partly on newly constructed *patamares*. At nearby Achada do Gramacha between São Jorge and Santana the MWC have 2 hectares of organically grown Sercial and Verdelho at Quinta do Furão. This relatively flat cliff-top vineyard was initially developed by the MWC in the early 1980s but was sold off in 1993. A small hotel was subsequently developed on the site and the vineyard was leased back again in 2012, as the Blandy family took a strategic decision to take greater control from the grape to the bottle.

Historically there have been few vineyards east side of the island although Henry Vizetelly describes a visit to a 4-acre vineyard (mostly Verdelho) at Santa Cruz belonging to messrs. Krohn in the 1870s. Today the municipalities of Santa Cruz and Machico claim just 2 and 10 hectares of vineyard respectively. The climate becomes progressively arid as you near Ponta de São Lourenço and historically was much considered much less suitable for viticulture which explains Vizetelly's comment about the wines being 'light' an of 'fair quality'. However with the recent fashion for unfortified wines a number of new vineyards have been planted here. A 6-hectare vineyard at Caniçal in the Machico municipality (clearly visible from the plane shortly before landing at Santa Catarina airport) has been planted with Touriga Nacional, Touriga Franca, Trincadeira, Merlot and Cabernet Sauvignon, varieties which are better suited to the relatively warm, dry climate.

Grapes from the island of Porto Santo have always been included in Madeira wine and were once favoured by wine makers due to their high natural sugar content. But due to long-term shortage of water, coastal development and the cost of transport, vineyards have been largely abandoned. There are still a few vines growing in the sand at Vila Baleira and in the centre of the island where there is a government-funded experimental vineyard. A large area of vineyard was lost with the construction of the airport runway in 1960 which, having subsequently been extended, covers much of the central part of the island. Porto Santo is known for the white Listrão grape though it is unclear how much is still grown on the island. Official records show 0.2 hectares of Complexa and 0.3 hectares of Verdelho.

4

THE PRODUCTION OF MADEIRA WINE

VINTAGE: PRESENT AND PAST

Madeirans need few excuses for a celebration and the start of the grape harvest was always an important day in the local calendar. The traditional start was the day of *Nossa Senhora do Monte* (15 August) when the peaceful oasis above Funchal comes to life with the sound of music and rockets and the smell of *bolo do caco* (the local flat bread) and *espetada* (cubes of beef traditionally cooked on a laurel skewer). Apart from on the island of Porto Santo, the grapes are barely ripe at this stage and picking usually begins at least a week later (although grapes have been picked as early as the first week of August). The *Instituto do Vinho, Bordado e Artesanato da Madeira* (IVBAM) declares an official start to the harvest, usually 1 September, although in practice the vintage is already well under way by then.

The first grapes to be harvested are traditionally those from the warmest sites close to sea level on the south side of the island. With so much of this land having been given over to bananas or buildings, the first grapes (Tinta Negra) now tend to arrive from Estreito de Câmara de Lobos or São Vicente. Most of the traditional wine-producing towns and villages (and a number of former wine-producing villages) mark the beginning of the harvest with their own *Festa das Vindimas* (Vintage Festival). In Funchal the *Festa do Vinho da Madeira* is a week-long street party organised by the municipality that takes place at the start of September on the Avenida da Arriaga, but it is very much stage-managed for tourists.

Vintage on Madeira is a stop-start affair with dribs and drabs of grapes arriving from all over the island over a period of six weeks; the last grapes from Jardim da Serra sometimes arrive as late as mid-October. The same vineyards are often picked more than once with the picking of the so-called *netos* ('grandchildren') from the second flowering often giving the harvest renewed impetus in late September. It was ever thus. At Leacock's famous São João vineyard the grapes would be picked at no less than eight different times with only the perfectly ripe bunches being gathered on each occasion. Some growers still arrive at the *adega* with no more than a few buckets of grapes, which amounts to their entire annual production.

In theory the grapes should have a minimum sugar reading of 9° Baumé (roughly 9% potential alcohol by volume, abv). Sugar readings are never very high and most of the island's grapes are picked at between 8 and 11° Baumé. In 2014 the average alcohol reading for Madeira's principal grapes was as follows:

- Malvasias 10.6% abv.
- Boal 9.75% abv
- Verdelho 10.31% abv
- Sercial 9.30% abv
- Tinta Negra 9.65% abv
- Terrantez 9.89% abv.

Towards the end of the harvest Tinta Negra may occasionally reach a potential of 12% abv and the best Verdelho and Bual grapes from the south side of the island may register as much as 13 or 14% abv. The grapes are characterised by their naturally high levels of acidity, with total acidity (measured as tartaric) reaching 8 or 9 grams per litre. At these levels they would make unpalatably acidic table wines but the acidity is crucial to the ageing and overall balance of a fine madeira wine. Ricardo Diogo of Barbeito says that he takes as much notice of levels of acidity as Baumé in the best white grapes.

Since 2008, IVBAM has tightened up the *fiscalização* (control) of the island's growers. Following a system similar to that used for port on the mainland, each and every grower selling grapes to one of the shippers is issued with a card (*Cartão de Viticultor*). IVBAM send their representatives to audit the vintage and this card has to be produced for every transaction. Information such as vineyard plots, planting dates, grape varieties, volume of production and the sugar content of the grapes are now held by IVBAM on a computer system. As a result production statistics have become a great deal more trustworthy than they were in the past.

Until 1992, the price of grapes was fixed by the then IVM in conjunction with the shippers and growers. Now there is a free market and IVBAM only intervenes to buy up grapes that are considered unsaleable (below the minimum of 9° Baumé). The growers are paid for their grapes according to weight and sugar reading, with a premium paid for white grapes. In 2014 the average price for a kilo of Tinta Negra Mole and other authorised red varieties was €1.1 a kilo, with Sercial, Verdelho, Bual and Malvasia commanding an average of €1.5 a kilo. Under the most recent POSEI programme, growers with Sercial, Verdelho and Malvasia (three varieties in short supply) are awarded an extra €1 a kilo. But given that Tinta Negra is a much more productive variety than the traditional white varieties, this financial incentive does not seem to have brought about the desired increase in production for the latter. There is now also a shortage of Boal, a variety that was left out of the POSEI programme.

RECENT VINTAGES

'There is almost no such thing as a bad vintage in Madeira' were the words of one producer. 'Some years are better than others but we produce at least some good wine every year.' It is therefore hard to generalise about Madeiran harvests. A common problem on the south side of the island in those vineyards at lower altitudes is lack of winter dormancy, which ultimately weakens the vines for the growing season ahead. Could this possibly be being exacerbated by global warming?

With so many different grape varieties, meso-climates and micro-climates on the island something, somewhere nearly always comes good in the end. Evolution in wood is important. It is only after about seven years that the shippers really know whether a wine will be a great or not. The following appraisal of vintages over the past fifteen years (2014 to 1999) is based on the reports from a number of shippers, which are more detailed in some years than others. They give an indication of some of the good wines to come.

2014: a warm and very wet early September with 112.6 mm of rain falling, mostly in the first two weeks of the month. The picking of Malvasia de São Jorge began on 23 August well before the rain, but there was a shortage of Boal which was generally mediocre in quality. The best performing grape was Verdelho, especially in Raposeira. The harvest concluded with the picking of Sercial at Jardim da Serra on 6 October and Verdelho in Porto Moniz on the following day.

2013: a cold, dry winter helped the vines to rest, followed by a warm and wet early spring and a dry summer. A very good crop of Tinta Negra and excellent Sercial and Verdelho of potential 'vintage' quality. Verdelho picked as late as 11 October at Porto Moniz. A poor year for Bual, reasonable for Malvasia.

2012: a large harvest following a good, largely dry growing season. An early start (16 August at Quinta de Santa Luzia in Funchal), concluding on 4 October with Sercial from Jardim de Serra just after the first heavy rain. Excellent, potential 'vintage' quality from Tinta Negra, Sercial and Verdelho with sugar levels above average. Good Bual and Malvasia.

2011: a cold winter ensured a good dormancy period, leading to an increase in production on the previous year for all varieties except Malvasia de São Jorge, which suffered a collapse in production due to mildew and oidium. Excellent Verdelho, though still in short supply due to demand for unfortified wines at the Adega de São Vicente. Very good Sercial, with good Bual and Tinta Negra.

2010: this was the year of the February mudslides and floods (see page 28) which damaged some vineyards and reduced production. However, warm dry weather in the run up to vintage meant the crop was ripe and healthy, though rather smaller than average. Excellent Tinta Negra and Verdelho, the latter with small bunches and good concentration. Very good Sercial. Low production and only medium quality Malvasia.

2009: the wettest growing season since the mid-1970s, with a late harvest hampered by lack of ripening and rot. One of the worst years in living memory for Bual, both in quality and quantity. A problematic year for all grape varieties, which struggled to ripen to the 9° Baumé minimum.

2008: a long harvest, stretching from 25 August until 12 October when the last Sercial grapes were picked at Jardim de Serra (800 metres altitude) at 10.3% abv. Good sugar levels were registered both in the north and south of the island. An excellent year for Tinta Negra but much less so for the white grapes with only Verdelho showing real promise with an average Baumé of 12.7°. Sercial and Verdelho both in short supply.

2007: a late harvest, especially on the north side where July and August were overcast and wet. Excellent year for red grapes on the south side and white grapes from the south and west, especially Verdelho and Bual. Much less good for Malvasia de São Jorge in the north. Sercial and Verdelho again in short supply.

2006: good weather with only two days of rain in mid-September. Two weeks of 'leste' (hot, dry wind from the east) resulted in good maturation, especially Tinta Negra which registered the best sugar levels for a decade. Very small and rather poor production of Sercial. Half of the island's Verdelho went to the Adega de São Vicente for the production of unfortified wine. Bual of medium quality. Excellent production of Malvasia with good sugar levels.

2005: early harvest with Justino Henriques receiving grapes on 18 August. Warm, dry weather throughout with some stress in the vineyards slowing the maturation in the final weeks of the harvest. Excellent Sercial from Seixal, although rain on 7 October reduced Baumés at Jardim da Serra. Exceptional Verdelho from Raposeira but this variety was again in very short supply. Bual and Malvasia suffered mixed fortunes. Very good Tinta Negra.

2004: a relatively late harvest and a year of two halves: excellent grapes coming from the southwest of the island, much less good in the north. 'The best vintage for sixteen years' in the words of Ricardo Diogo of Barbeito, with excellent sugar levels in Verdelho and Bual from Prazeres and Raposeira (up to 14° Baumé for the latter). Verdelho in very short supply due to the demand for unfortified wines. Sercial very poor from the north but excellent from Jardim da Serra. Malvasia the least good of the traditional white varieties. The harvest was dominated by politics, with elections falling on 17 October. The last grapes were picked on 13 October (Sercial from Jardim da Serra and Bual from Campanário).

2003: very dry year in general, many vines suffering from severe stress. This was the year when the minimum Baumé of 9° for grapes destined for madeira wine was properly enforced for the first time. Good year for Sercial although grapes from Seixal failed to reach 8.5° Baumé. Exceptional Verdelho from Raposeira and good Bual. Much less good for Malvasia.

2002: excellent Bual from Calheta picked as early as 26 August though much less good in Campanário due to poor ripening. Good Sercial from Porto Moniz and Arco de São Jorge. There was a severe shortage of Verdelho due to the increasing amount of unfortified wine being made at the Adega do São Vicente although the quality was generally very good. A mediocre year for Malvasia due to oidium.

2001: a year classified as 'good' in terms of quality and 'very good' for quantity. However, Malvasia de São Jorge, Sercial and Verdelho from the north side of the island suffered from low production and poor quality. Boal seems to have been the most successful of the traditional white varieties.

2000: a very productive year, especially in Câmara de Lobos where the picking of Tinta Negra began on 23 August. Quality could have been better, the best grapes coming from the north side of the island where production was lower. Large crop of Bual from Câmara de Lobos and Calheta. Barbeito produced some fabulous Malvasia. The harvest concluded on 6 October with Sercial at Corticeiras and Jardim da Serra.

1999: a large harvest followed a good growing season. Picking began with Tinta Negra in Camara de Lobos on 17 August and continued until 1 October (Sercial). Very promising Sercial and Bual, both of which were described by the Madeira Wine Company as being of potential 'vintage quality'.

PRESSING THE GRAPES

Vintage today is a more efficient but much less colourful event than it was a generation or two ago. Before the network of sweeping new roads was built to connect the countryside to Funchal, grapes were foot-trodden *in situ* and transported to the winery as *mosto* (grape must). The traditional *lagares* that were once used to extract the must are no longer in use other than for wine for local consumption. Those that remain are museum pieces, and there is one on display at the entrance to the Henriques & Henriques wine lodge and another in the Blandy Wine Lodge.

The Madeiran *lagar* is quite different from the impressive banks of stone *lagares* still in use in the Douro, being much closer in concept to those once used in Jerez. In his book *Madeira,* published in 1961, Rupert Croft-Cooke describes a recent visit during the harvest: 'The

lagar or wine press is a square wooden trough raised above the level of the ground, high enough for butts to stand before it into which the wine can be run when the grapes are trodden. It is not more than ten foot and sometimes less across and barely three feet deep … there is room in the trough for four men to work.' He goes on to say that 'many of the *lagares* in Madeira stand alone in a small dark building and this gives the rather macabre scene … the atmosphere of a witches' midden'.

Henry Vizetelly describes a Madeiran *lagar* in Santa Cruz, a scene that can have barely changed from the sixteenth century until as recently as the early 1980s:

TREADING GRAPES IN THE LAGAR OF MESSRS. KROHN BROTHERS AT SANTA CRUZ, MADEIRA.
(*p.* 157.)

'The casa do lagar, *or pressing house, was in the centre of the vineyard, the* lagar *itself being a huge wooden trough similar to that used in the sherry district. Instead, however, of a huge iron screw, a huge wooden beam, like those in use in the neighbourhood of Lisbon and the Upper Douro, hangs across it, and aids the extraction of juice from the piled up grape skins after these have been well trodden by several pairs of brawny feet. Before, however, the treaders mount into the* lagar *the grapes' own weight produces a steady flow of juice into the adjoining vat – a rivulet which becomes a torrent when treading commences. The men dispersed over the* lagar *commence with a slow, steady movement, then spread out their arms and grasp the huge intervening beam, rapidly advancing one from another, occasionally turning rapidly half-way round, now to the right and now to the left, their frantic movements presently subsiding into a slow monotonous kind of jig.'*

The treading was done in shifts, sometimes lasting through the night. Traditionally, only men trod the grapes with the women joining in the singing that accompanied the process. The Madeiran guitar or *machete* (which was eventually taken to Honolulu where it became the ukulele) would be used to beat out a slow, laborious rhythm during the first treading. The songs were often improvised, telling stories about the workers or the owner of the grapes, and sometimes sung as if in a dialogue with verses being made up as they went along.

A second treading would follow the first, known as the *repisa* (re-tread). The music and the mood became more upbeat during the *repisa* as the treading became easier. The men moved faster and, fuelled by alcohol, the songs became increasingly bawdy until no more juice could be extracted from treading alone. At this stage the skins, stalks and remaining pulp would be raked into the centre of the *lagar,* piled up and bound by thick rope made from local sisal or plant roots. A board was then placed on top and the weight of the crossbeam was brought to bear on the rope. The men turned this and tightened it until every last drop of juice was squeezed from the grapes. The pressure was then released, the cord unwound and the mass of grapes would be re-bound and subjected to yet more pressure. The *mosto* or juice so released was known as *vinho da corda.* Finally, once all the juice had been extracted from the grapes, water would be added to the dry mass of grape skins, stalks and pips to ferment overnight into *agua pé* – 'foot water' – to be drunk by the vineyard workers.

Vizetelly makes the contemporary observation that 'Madeira vineyards being, as a rule small in area, and planted with several varieties, it is not worth the cultivator's while to separate the different species before pressing them in the *lagar*. Consequently the whole get crushed together…'. Only in the larger vineyards are 'the various types of grapes crushed separately, and the *mosto* from each is kept apart, especially that of the sercial, bual and malvasia varieties'. No mention of the then underdog, Verdelho.

Once the pressing was complete the musts would be sulphured and transported to the *armazens* (wine stores). Where the roads were good, the must would be transported in cask by bullock cart. However most of the musts from the outlying vineyards on the south coast around Funchal were carried in goatskins by processions of men known as *borracheiros*. Each goatskin would contain a *baril*, equivalent to between 9 and 10 gallons, with twelve *barils* making up a pipe (92 imperial gallons or 418 litres). On arrival at the *armazém* a clerk would randomly test the goatskins for volume and sugar content to make sure that the grape must had not been watered down en route. This was a necessary but laborious process given the poor state of the roads in Madeira, many of which were not fit for vehicular transport until well into the twentieth century. The last of the *borracheiros* worked into the 1980s. During the course of a day a *borracheiro* might make two or three return journeys to Funchal carrying the equivalent of 45 kilos on his back.

Wines from the north side of the island, already fermented, were transported by sea. There being no pier at Funchal until 1890, the casks would be thrown overboard and swum to the beach. Croft-Cooke remarks that this was still the situation at Porto Santo in the late 1950s: 'The casks are rolled to the sea-shore and into the water where a strong swimmer impels each to the ship that will take it to Madeira. It is hauled aboard by ropes.' I sometimes wonder if this means of transport accounts for the distinct saline character present in some older wines, or could it be my imagination working overtime?

In the past growers collected their grapes in baskets (*cestos da vindima*) with a capacity of 60 kilos. Around twenty baskets would fill a *lagar*, sufficient to produce 900 litres of *mosto*. Nowadays grapes are collected either in large stainless steel *dornas* or small plastic crates with a 20-kilo

capacity. Smaller crates are often lent by the shipper to prevent better quality grapes from being crushed under their own weight and from fermenting before they reach the press. The colourful but labour-intensive process described above is now carried out in a matter of minutes by a series of machines. Rupert Croft-Cooke visited Madeira at the start of a time of profound change. Ever the romantic, he laments this as follows: 'the treading of grapes by foot, like all other old and excellent processes is facing competition from machine presses… Such presses are certainly faster than the *lagar*, if that is any advantage. But in efficiency they are like so many of the mechanical innovations of this century, a millennium behind the methods of the ancient world. They break the pips, and the precious jelly under the skin is not so cleanly extracted. It is disturbing to find they have gained the most popularity in the region of the finest grapes, Cama de Lobos (sic) where they press nearly half the harvest.'

LANDING CASKS OF WINE FROM THE NORTH SIDE OF THE ISLAND.

In the twenty-first century 'efficiency' is the byword in the wine trade, alongside hygiene, and most of Madeira's growers now deliver their own grapes to central wineries belonging to the shippers themselves. Having been weighed and sugar readings taken, the grapes are off-loaded into a reception area where an Archimedes screw (known in Portuguese as a *semfim* or 'without end') conveys the grapes to a crusher/de-stemmer. The stalks themselves are always under-ripe and are often detrimental to the quality of madeira wine, bringing a 'green' character from the pyrazines. However a number of shippers retain a proportion of the stalks from the white grapes to increase levels of acidity and tannin in the wine.

The larger wineries have two reception areas, a large one for red grapes and another smaller area for white. Juice from red grapes (which make up the vast majority of production) is generally fermented on the grape skins, particularly if the wine is destined for a sweeter style, deemed to require a deeper colour. This will either reduce or negate the use of caramel for the colouring. White grapes are generally pressed in pneumatic presses prior to fermentation in a process known in Portuguese as *bica aberta*. This term survives from the days of the *lagar* when the *bica* (outlet) was left *aberta* (open) to separate the juice from the skins. Some shippers are now conducting short periods of maceration on the grape skins in order to obtain more varietal character in their wines. In 2007 Barbeito introduced an automated stainless steel *lagar* to achieve a more vigorous skin maceration from Tinta Negra (as a substitute for caramel). They have followed this up with Malvasia and Boal in order to obtain more aromatic character from the skins.

FERMENTATION

In the past nearly all Madeira was fermented dry at the outset and sweetened at a later stage, after *estufagem* and fortification. Vizetelly describes the process thus: 'the mosto continues fermenting, with the bunghole of each cask covered over with a fig leaf, generally until the middle of November. Either before or after the fermentation a small quantity of brandy is added, varying in quantity according to the quality of the mosto, but seldom exceeding three percent.' The best wines were adjusted with *vinho surdo* or *abafado*, unfermented or partially fermented grape juice that had been previously fortified to retain its natural sweetness. Many wines were artificially sweetened with either *arrobo* (a mixture of grape juice, sugar and tartaric acid) or *calda* (boiled up sugar, effectively caramel). Although caramel is still used to colour some wines, the use of *arrobo* and *calda* for sweetening are, thankfully, prohibited. If adjustment is needed post-fermentation, wines are now sweetened either with *surdo* or rectified concentrated grape must (RCGM). The latter maybe added either before or after fermentation (up to a maximum of 2° Baumé).

Most madeira wine is now made (like port wine) by arresting the fermentation with grape spirit. The spirit kills the active yeasts and, depending on the point of fortification, leaves the wine with natural residual sugar. Richer wines (including those made from Malvasia and Bual) will ferment for as little as forty-eight hours leaving them with 3.5–6.5° Baumé of residual sugar. The drier styles of wine will ferment for longer, perhaps four or five days, until most or all of the sugar has been fermented into alcohol. The white grapes will ferment for longer still, up to eight days for a bone-dry Sercial.

The fermentation itself usually takes place in stainless steel vats at controlled temperatures. White grapes are fermented at much lower temperatures than red, ranging from 16°C for the whites to as high as 32°C for reds. For the larger shippers, fermentation temperatures are pre-programmable according to the grape variety, and are computer controlled. Unless there is a specific problem with the fermentation, wild yeasts are used for madeira wine. Some shippers use autovinification, a process adapted from the port shippers on the Portuguese mainland which aids the extraction of colour from red grapes. A few shippers continue to ferment their wine in wooden or cement vats and H. M. Borges still ferment a small proportion of their white wine in the time-honoured way, using old wooden casks known as *pipas* (lodge pipes).

DOES ANYONE KNOW HOW TO MAKE MADEIRA?

In the spring of 1991 I wrote an article for *Decanter* magazine entitled 'Does Anyone Know How to Make Madeira?'. In retrospect the title was perhaps rather facetious but it was meant as a genuine reflection on the state of the madeira wine business as I had found it on a recent visit to the island. Having been fed the standard story (propagated by the Madeira Wine Company) as a recent WSET Diploma and MW student in London, I subsequently found that there were as many ways to produce madeira wine as their were shippers on the island (eight at that time). The article went on to say 'the difficulty is that Madeira's shippers set about making wine in so many ways. There are accepted textbook methods, but most producers choose to make wine their own way, occasionally cutting some tight corners in order to reduce production costs for the most basic wines.'

My visit was shortly after Portugal had joined the then EEC and, with the benefit of hindsight, the madeira wine industry was probably close to its nadir at the time, starved of investment both in the vineyards and in the winery, and lacking in direction. There was a serious shortage of good grapes (direct producers and hybrids were outlawed for wines for export but the 85 per cent varietal rule was yet to be introduced) and no one had quite worked out the best way to make wine now that pressing in *lagares* and fermentation in cask were no longer practicable. *Estufagem* was crude with most wine entering the *estufa* unfortified to save on the cost of valuable alcohol, some of which would otherwise be evaporated away at significant cost. The disadvantage of this was that the resulting wine would often taste burnt and insipid, and if fortification was delayed for too long the wine would easily be attacked by acetic bacteria. Sacks of sugar were stacked by the bottling lines and the use of *calda* (boiled-up sugar) for sweeting was clearly commonplace. A story that I learnt at the time – but never published – was that in order to avoid the vats of caramel boiling over, one shipper was using surplus butter (effectively pouring oil on troubled waters). This goes some way to explain the rancid, synthetic cheese character which was the way of identifying inexpensive (as well as some not so inexpensive) madeiras in blind tastings in the 1980s and early 1990s. 'Pukey' was the rather less polite tasting term that was also in use at the time. In conclusion I wrote 'you only need to look at Madeira's export figures to find out how the majority of the island's wines are made. In 1989 well over half the island's production of 3.8 million litres was exported in bulk ... and used for cooking. Not surprisingly, careful wine-making does not feature very highly on most shipper's list of priorities in this price sensitive market and so some fairly crude practices have evolved.' Twenty-three years later and so much has improved, largely due to intervention by the EU but also thanks to investment by the Symington family who were shocked by the standard of the industry at the time (see page 118). Without this, I doubt that the madeira wine industry would have survived.

FORTIFICATION

The spirit used to fortify madeira is 96% abv in strength. This is a much purer spirit than that used for fortifying port wine, which is 77% abv. Throughout the nineteenth century and much of the twentieth, most of the spirit used to fortify Madeira was distilled from sugar cane grown on the island (*aguardente de cana* at around 70% abv) but its use has been prohibited since 1967 (and it has to be said that this was greatly to the detriment of the local economy). The IVM continued to exercise a monopoly over the spirit until 1992, just as the Port Wine Institute did in the Douro. Nowadays all the spirit used to fortify madeira is of grape origin and comes mostly from either France or Spain. Shippers seek to buy the most neutral spirit available with the minimum of dry extract and high levels of ethanol. The initial fortification generally takes the wine to between 17 % and 18% abv. Under the 2015 legislation madeira wine must be fortified to between 17 and 22% abv but in exceptional circumstances, and with authorisation from IVBAM, madeira may be sold at a minimum of 15.5% abv.

Following fermentation and fortification, the wine is known as *vinho claro*. The wines are left to rest in vat until November when they are classified, according to style and quality, into different *lotes* or batches. Most firms then fine and filter their wine. After 15 November the shippers are required to make two declarations to IVBAM: the *Declaração de Compras* (Buyer's Declaration) and *Declaração de Produção*. (Production Declaration). In theory these should match up with the *fiscalização* undertaken by IVBAM during vintage. When details have been found to be correct and the wines have been analysed, the wines are registered by IVBAM on a *conta corrente* or current account. This system closely imitates that used by the *Instituto dos Vinho Douro e do Porto* (IVDP) to monitor the port industry. The *conta corrente* remains open until the last drop of wine a company has has been sold, whether it be after a few months as a modified wine into the food industry or after many years as a venerable *frasqueira* or vintage.

ESTUFAGEM

Most madeira wine, especially that made from the main red grape varieties Tinta Negra and Complexa, is then subject to a unique heating process known as *estufagem*. This process was developed in the late eighteenth century (see page 11) and named after the *estufas* (hot houses) in which the wines were originally aged. *Estufagem* has been used, and sometimes abused, by wine shippers ever since. The *estufagem* process at Cossart Gordon in the mid-nineteenth century is described in detail by Vizetelly in that 'the common wines are subjected to a temperature of 140 degrees Fahrenheit – derived from flues, heated with anthracite coal – for the space of three months. In the next compartment wines of intermediate quality are heated up to 130 deg. for a period of four and a-half months; while the third set apart for superior wines, heated variously from 110-20 deg. for a period of six months. The fourth compartment, known as the "Calor" possess no flues but derives its heat varying from 90–100 deg., exclusively from the compartments adjacent; and here only high-class wines are placed'. A similar sort of hierarchy still applies to the *estufagem* process today.

MESSRS. COSSART, GORDON, & CO.'S ESTUFAS.

Estufagem was once a fairly brutal process but it is essential to the character and development of most young madeira wine. Modern *estufas* are vats of between 20,000 and 50,000 litres capacity (although Justino's have an *estufa* with a 100,000 litre capacity), made from stainless steel, in which the wine is heated by passing water heated to 72°C through an external jacket. Every shipper has a slightly different *estufagem* regime but they are all obliged to abide by the law. The temperature of the wine maybe raised to a maximum of 55°C (there is no minimum) for a period of at least ninety days based on the principle that the longer and slower the heating process, the better the quality of the wine. Most producers heat the wine to a maximum of 45–50°C. IVBAM regulates the *estufagem* process, during which time the vats are sealed.

In spite of the controls, the *estufagem* regimen varies between shippers. In the past small shippers relied on the sun to heat their wines, either leaving casks outside or in specially constructed greenhouses (*estufas do sol*). The disadvantage of this approach is the diurnal heating and cooling which is detrimental to the wine. Some shippers still use wooden or epoxy-lined concrete vats with an internal serpentine but this tends to burn the wine excessively, which can be ameliorated by regular pumping over. In the past shippers would frequently use charcoal (carbon fining) to 'deodorise' wines following *estufagem* which would strip them of much of their character.

The standard of *estufagem* has improved greatly in recent years, such that in some three-year-old wines it is almost impossible to detect other than via a slightly toasted character, whereas in the past almost all young wines tasted stewed and baked. In the past many wines were not fortified until after *estufagem*, to save on the alcohol that was lost in the process (see above). This generally produced unpleasantly burnt and, often, volatile (acetic) wines. Even now, the cooling period can be particularly risky and the temperature must return to near ambient levels over a period of four weeks before the wine is removed from the *estufa*, otherwise excessive oxidation can occur.

Most wines would be completely destroyed by *estufagem* and, if handled badly, some are still wrecked by the process. But through the oxidation of primary (fruit) aromas and the caramelising of the natural grape sugars, the *estufa* transforms a naturally acidic but otherwise distinctly bland *vinho claro* into a completely different wine. As a rule of thumb it is reckoned that three months in an *estufa* roughly equates to the wine spending two years in wood. Research undertaken by the Universidade Católica in Porto, Portugal and the Universidade da Madeira shows that *estufagem* produces a powerful aroma compound and sugar lactone called soloton which contributes greatly to the typicity of madeira wine. First isolated in 1975 from the herb fenugreek, soloton is a lactone also found in high concentrations in lovage, and is a major flavour component in artificial maple syrup. In high concentrations soloton may smell like curry, but at lower concentrations it is more like nuts and brown sugar. Sweeter madeiras, subject to *estufagem*, have higher concentrations of soloton than drier styles. Soloton can also be found in *vin jaune*, some sherries and wines made from botrytised grapes.

AGEING

It is a common misconception, even in the wine trade, that all madeira wine is subject to *estufagem*. Although it is entirely up to the shipper to decide on which wines to *estufa*, those destined to be bottled young (after three or five years) gain the most. But whereas the Madeira Wine Company only subject their three-year-old range to bulk *estufagem*, Justino Henriques *estufa* all their three-, five- and ten-year-old wines. One small producer, Barros e Sousa, flatly refused to subject any of their wines to *estufagem* and I have seen back labels offering a financial reward to anyone who could prove otherwise, just to reinforce their point!

Wines produced from the traditional white grapes (Sercial, Verdelho, Bual and Malvasia) are not usually subject to any *estufagem* at all. Instead these wines are generally aged in 'lodge pipes', wooden casks which can vary from 400 to 650 litres in size. Some wooden vats (*balseiros*) used for ageing large volumes of wine have a capacity of up to 2,500 litres. The origin of the wood itself is largely immaterial as its prime function is not to impart flavour but to develop and nurture the wine over a decade or more. Most casks are of indeterminate age, having undergone successive repairs by skilled coopers who replace warped wood and often rebuild entire casks weaving banana leaves between the staves to ensure a tight fit. Most of the casks on the island are made from American or Portuguese oak but a small number of newer casks are made from French oak. Since 2001, Justino's have been using casks that were previously used to age cognac. Henriques & Henriques have set up a lucrative business ageing madeira for two years in old bourbon barrels which are then sent on to Scotland for ageing whisky. Most of the madeira aged in this way goes into wine destined for the food industry (see below).

Larger vats or *balseiros* are generally built from Baltic oak or Brazilian satinwood. A number of shippers have been experimenting with new French oak for ageing their *colheitas,* with a significant effect on the style of the wine. However, with the contraction of the wine industry over the past sixty years, there is no shortage of old wood on the island.

The ageing process causes the wine to maderise. This is a pejorative term when applied to a normal table wine, suggesting it is brown, badly oxidised and usually well on the way to being undrinkable. However, with madeira wine the high level of natural acidity and alcohol, together with the small quantity of oxygen in the cask, serve to inhibit the formation of volatile acidity whilst promoting the formation of fragrant esters and aldehydes. In 2005 research conducted in Madeira, mainland Portugal and Spain identified sixty-eight odorants in madeira wine, with soloton (see above), phenylacetaldehyde and wood extractable aromas being more important than varietal aromas. Oxygen is crucial to the ageing process and casks are never completely filled but left with a small headspace for air. As it ages the wine is slowly stabilised by oxygen until, in time, there comes a stage where it cannot be damaged by further exposure to the air. This goes a long way to explaining why madeira is the longest living of all wines and why, once a bottle of old madeira wine has been opened, it can remain on ullage for months, even years.

One of the enemies of madeira is the flor yeast that transforms a relatively bland palomino wine into a distinctive fino or amontillado sherry. Henry Vizetelly rather charmingly mentions the 'so-called flowers of wine' on his visit to Madeira. There is a risk of the growth of flor on the surface of a madeira wine if it is fortified too late and aged in unhygienic conditions. This leads to the formation of excess acetaldehyde, which is a defect in madeira.

The maturation of Madeira wine depends to a large extent on how and where it is kept. Wine kept in smaller volumes (lodge pipes) will develop more rapidly and quite differently than that left to age in larger *balseiros*. Some wine stores or 'lodges'[3] are inevitably warmer than others and accelerate the maturation process. Wines are generally only stored in the warmest lodges (or on the upper floors) for the first few years of their life where the average temperature can be as high as 28°C (for example, the Sotão de Amêndoa in the Blandy Wine Lodge). During this time, the annual evaporation rate can be as high as 6 or 7 per cent. However, humidity is crucial. If the relative humidity in the lodge remains below 85 per cent there is little or no loss of alcohol. The alcohol level may dip slightly in the first and second year of ageing, but as the water content evaporates there is a concentration of alcohol from 17% abv to between 19–20% abv. The natural sugars, acidity and dry extract in the wine also concentrate with age, and intensity of flavour starts to increase. Madeira normally starts with a high level of natural acidity, registering 7–10 g/l at the outset. This will fall by a gram or so with fortification but rise to 12 g/l with thirty or forty years of cask age. Volatile acidity after twenty years will rise to about 1 g/l, to reach over 2 g/l in some very old wines. The maximum permitted levels of volatile acidity permitted by IVBAM under the 2015 legislation are as follows: wines of 10 years old and less, 20 mEq/l; wines between 10 and 20 years old, 25mEq/1; wines of 20 years and older, 30 mEq/l. Whether the acidity and volatile acidity are noticeable will depend on the concentration of sugars and the overall balance of the wine. A good

3 The term 'lodge' is not a Madeiran expression but has been imported from the port trade in Vila Nova de Gaia. It is, however, increasingly used in English to denote an *armazém* or wine store.

madeira should never be acetic or vinegary but it may be described as 'lifted' or 'high toned' if the volatile component in the wine is relatively high. With increased concentration the level of dry extract rises, starting out at around 22g/l for a three-year-old wine and increasing to as much as 40 g/l for a old Malmsey. These terms are explained more fully in the glossary on page 237. A typical analysis of a madeira wine is appended to the category descriptions below.

After four or five years in relatively warm conditions, a wine destined for long ageing will be transferred to cooler lodges, either on the lower floors or to a different building at higher altitude. Before moving to new purpose-built lodges outside Funchal, Barbeito used to have three different sites to age their wine, varying in altitude, with evaporation rates ranging from 2 to 6 per cent a year.

Over time there is, nevertheless, a substantial loss of wine to evaporation. For example a single 620-litre cask of a Barbeito 1996 Bual had diminished to 404 litres by the time it was bottled in 2011. In general a shipper can expect to lose over half the initial volume of wine to evaporation by the time a *frasqueira* or vintage madeira has been bottled at a minimum of twenty years old.

Unlike other wines, madeira is very rarely racked. Most shippers leave the wine in cask or vat, undisturbed, for years at a time and will only rack from one cask to another when it is transferred from one wine store to another. However a madeira from a single outstanding year may spend fifty or more years in wood. With the quantity steadily diminishing through evaporation, the wine will require topping up and, occasionally, refreshing with a small quantity of younger wine. A wine left in cask untouched becomes undrinkably viscous and concentrated. This is something that I experienced on tasting a Sercial from a cask that had been abandoned for over fifty years. When the cask was discovered, just 30 litres out of the original 250 remained and the wine was as viscous as black treacle. To avoid this excessive concentration, older wines will be transferred from wood to glass demi-johns, where the rate of evaporation is greatly reduced and maturation slows to a near standstill.

A wine that has been aged in wood for a minimum of two years without being subject to *estufagem* may legally be called a *Vinho do Canteiro*. The name comes from the scantling racks (*canteiros*) on which the casks are placed on the floor of the lodge. Since 1992 an EU-funded campaign known as *POSEIMA (Programma de Opções Específicas para o Afastamento e Insularidade da Madeira e dos Açores* – now known as POSEI) has greatly increased the amount of *canteiro*-aged Madeira. Under this EU-funded scheme the shippers are currently paid 5 cents per hectolitre per day over a period of five years to promote the ageing of wine in cask.

BLENDING AND BOTTLING

The nerve centre for every madeira wine shipper is the tasting room, often a small atmospheric space near the laboratory stacked high with half-filled bottles of wine. These are reference samples representing some of the many different wines ageing in the lodge. Every shipper has an experienced taster who knows the company's wines like his or her own family. More often than not, the wine maker is also responsible for blending. The tasting year begins shortly after the vintage, assessing and blending young wines to meet the company's future requirements.

The first task is to identify the different *lotes*: parcels or batches of wine ranging in size from thousands of litres for three-year-old blends or everyday wine in vat, to small quantities (sometimes as little as a

Vinho do canteiro *ageing in Barbieto's warmest wine store, the Armazém de Afonso*

single cask) for colheita and vintage wines. With the help of heavy leather-bound stock ledgers or, nowadays, computer records, blends will be made up to fit the market. All shippers are required by IVBAM to hold stocks equivalent to eighteen months' worth of sales based on their average sales over the past three years.

When it comes to making up a blend for a relatively large, internationally known brand (e.g. Blandy's Duke of Clarence) the shipper will be looking to secure consistency from one bottling to the next, planning ahead to ensure that there are sufficient stocks to meet seasonal demand. Conversely when it comes to identifying wines of potential *frasqueira* (vintage) quality, the shipper will be looking to set aside small quantities of a distinctive wine that will age for a minimum of twenty years. The *transfega* or racking process is an opportunity for these *lotes* to be continually reassessed and, if they fail to meet expectations, they may be demoted and blended into a larger stock *lote*.

TASTING AND BLENDING

Francisco Albuquerque, chief wine maker at the Madeira Wine Company, describes his responsibility in the tasting room immediately after the vintage: 'In November I spend time tasting all the wines in cask. I spend eight days tasting maybe eighty-five different wines. I start at 10 a.m. I take a break for fifteen minutes. I taste up to twelve wines each time and I do it alone. When I taste I need to be alone, without interruptions, the mobile phone switched off. The most important thing in tasting is to be honest with yourself. If there is any commercial pressure I know from experience that it will produce problems in future.

'What do I look for? The first thing is the wine must not have defects and as this is a blind tasting I try to judge the age of the wine and its potential. If I discover something very good I make a note that it has the either the potential to be a vintage or a *colheita* and when it should be bottled. I rate wines from nought to five. To me the tasting is the key. Beside me, I also have an analytical report from the lab and if both are excellent I recommend a bottling date. Otherwise, if both are very good, I identify them as wines for blending. Memory is all-important as I need to ensure that our blended wines maintain their characteristics.'

Harvest in a traditional *latada* vineyard at Jardim da Serra.

Above: Clouds and vines – looking towards Porto Santo from the north coast of Madeira.

Below: Quinta do Bispo, São Jorge, with the *capacete* or 'helmet' of cloud covering the summit of Madeira.

Above: Terraced *latada* vineyards at São Vicente in spring time.

Below: A heavy crop of Tinta Negra hanging from a young *latada* vineyard in São Vicente.

Left: Inspecting the grapes at a modern *espaldeira* vineyard at Campanário.

Below: Picking Malvasia Cândida at the famous Fajã dos Padres vineyard on the south coast of Madeira.

When a *lote* is finally assembled for bottling it is given up to six months further ageing for the components to marry and settle. Nearly all large *lotes* are subject to further fining, cold stabilisation and filtration before bottling. Carbon fining may also be used again at this stage to remove colour from dry wines at the three- and five-year-old level which are expected to be paler than sweeter wines. Refrigerating the wines to -7°C removes natural tartrates, which would otherwise precipitate as crystals in bottle if the wine became subject to low temperatures. Scandinavia and Canada, both cold climates, are significant markets for madeira wine.

Wine shipped in bulk used to make up the lion's share of Madeira's exports (see page 73) but, following in the footsteps of the port and sherry producers, bulk shipments have been officially prohibited since 1 January 2002. The only wine that may now leave the island without first being bottled is that which is previously 'modified' or *desnaturado* (denatured) by the addition of additives (basically salt, pepper or malt extract) for use in the *indústria agro-alimentar* (the food industry): flavouring sauces, deserts, chocolates, etc. There is also a category known as 'disqualified' wine which is unmodified but may be exported in bulk for a specific purpose and may not be bottled. There is a significant market for this category of madeira in Scandinavia where it is used for flavouring schnapps. There are controls on the sale of modified and wine that has effectively been disqualified from bottling (*madeira sem aditivos*): neither category may be sold until 31 October in the year after the wine was made. Depending on the year, these hidden categories still account for up to a third of Madeira's total sales (see Appendix IV).

CATEGORIES OF MADEIRA WINE

Throughout its long history, madeira wine has been classified in a number of different ways. In the eighteenth and nineteenth centuries it was not uncommon to find madeira named after its locality of origin (for example, São Martinho or Cama [Câmara] de Lobos), the ship that transported the wine (for example, Hurricane or Southern Cross madeira), the country to which the wine had been transported (for example, East India Madeira), or even occasionally the name of the customer. However, none of these names gave any indication of the style of the wine. Although the name of the grape variety on the label might give an indication of style, it was by no means obligatory and it was not unheard of to find a Malvasia that had been fermented dry. In the period between the First and Second World Wars it became common to name all madeira wine after one of the four traditional grape varieties. Accordingly dry wines would be labelled as 'Sercial', medium dry as 'Verdelho', medium sweet as 'Boal' or 'Bual' and sweet wines as Malmsey or Malvasia, whether or not they were made from the stated grape. This misleading practice was only brought to an end following Portugal's entry into the then EEC (EU) in 1986. Subsequently any wine stating one of the permissible grape varieties on the label (Sercial, Verdelho, Boal/Bual, Malvasia/Malmesy, Terrantez, Bastardo, Moscatel and, recently Tinta Negra Mole) must be made from at least 85 per cent of that variety. All other wines are bottled with an indication of style as follows:

Extra seco / extra dry: 0–15 g/l residual sugar (0–1° Baumé)

Seco / dry: 20–50 g/l residual sugar (1–1.5° Baumé)

Meio seco / medium dry: 50–75 g/l residual sugar (1.5–2.5° Baumé)

Meio dôce / medium sweet / medium rich: 75–100 g/l residual sugar (2.5–3.5° Baumé)

Dôce / sweet / rich: > 100 g/l residual sugar (> 3.5° Baumé)

Varietal wines are officially defined by IVBAM as falling into one of the following categories, although exceptions may be granted by the official tasting panel:

Sercial: dry or extra dry

Verdelho: medium dry

Boal: medium sweet

Malvasia: sweet

Terrantez: medium sweet or medium dry

Age is important to madeira (see above) and a hierarchy has emerged with most (though not all) categories legally defined by the IVM in 1982, revised in 1998 and again in 2015. The accepted categories, in ascending order of age, are as follows:

Corrente or 'Three Year Old'

Although 'three year old' is not an official designation, IVBAM stipulates that all wine subject to *estufagem* may not be bottled for at least three months after it has left the *estufa* and never before 31 October of the second year after the harvest. In effect this puts the minimum age of a madeira wine at between two and three years old, and these are officially designated as *corrente* ('current') by IVBAM. Invariably these wines are made from red grapes (basically Tinta Negra) and can be sold under one of the designations above. In the past many of these wines were sold as 'Finest', 'Selected' or 'Choice': misleading adjectives for the most basic of wines. Most wines in this category are now sold under the shipper's brand name e.g., Blandy's Duke of Clarence, Barbeito's Delvino or Leacock's St John. By definition, madeira of this age is never the most complex of wines but it should taste clean, if still perhaps slightly spirity, with the drier wines displaying a soft, appetizing savoury character and the sweeter wines showing easy-going raisiny richness of flavour. A typical analysis of a wine at this level will show a wine with 5.5 g/l total acidity, volatile acidity of around 0.3 g/l and dry extract of around 22 g/l. See the glossary for an explanation of these terms.

Rainwater

This is taken to mean a pale-coloured wine ('pale to gold') from dry to medium-dry (1–2.5° Baumé) that is lighter in style, around 18% abv, bottled with a maximum of ten years of age. There is some speculation over the origin of the name but it is thought that some casks awaiting shipment were left unstoppered on the beach overnight and rain diluted the wine. The name started to appear on wine lists at the end of the eighteenth century but was never patented and became a generic term, particularly in the US.

Wine with an indication of age

Eight age designations are officially permitted for use on the label of madeira. It should be emphasised that these do not amount to an exact age, a minimum age or average age, but are merely an indication of the age of the wine. They are, in fact, style categories. In the past there was plenty of scope for the shippers to make up their own blends from stock but recent legislation has become much more specific in its requirements. Each category must be accompanied by a *conta corrente* or current account detailing the wines used in the final blend. The ultimate arbiter is IVBAM whose *câmara de provadores* (tasting panel) have to pass all the wines before they are granted a seal of origin and released. The designations in inverted commas are those permitted by the current legislation, some of which are still rather misleading. Under the 2015 legislation any wine that is considered to 'stand out' in its age category is entitled to use the term 'Seleccionado', 'Selected', 'Choice' or 'Finest' on the label. The words 'Fino' or 'Fine' may be used on any wine that has 'the perfect balance of freshness and acidity in conjunction with aromas associated with ageing in wood'.

Five Year Old ('Reserva', 'Velho', 'Reserve', 'Old' or 'Vieux') blends are generally based on the Tinta Negra Mole grape although both the Madeira Wine Company and Barbeito also bottle varietal wines made from Sercial, Verdelho, Bual and Malvasia. Most, though by no means all, of the wines at this level have been subject to *estufagem*. These wines have considerably more lift and presence than the basic 'three year old' category and begin to hint at the complexity of older wines. Dry wines should show attractive nutty-toasty complexity and sweeter wines should be rich, with some concentration and fresh acidity as a counterbalance. The sweetness should never be cloying. A typical analysis would show a wine with total acidity of around 6 g/l, volatile acidity of around 0.4 g/l and dry extract around 24 g/l.

Ten Year Old ('Reserva Especial', 'Special Reserve', 'Reserva Velha', 'Old Reserve', 'Very Old') are generally made from one of the four white grapes (Sercial, Verdelho, Bual or Malvasia), with wines which have not previously been subject to *estufagem*. There are two notable exceptions as both Justino's and Pereira D'Oliveira bottle ten-year-old wines based on Tinta Negra. At this level, the wines should be starting to show some of the concentration and ethereal beauty that comes with age. A good ten year old will have fine, lifted aromas that sometimes sing from the glass and an incisive tang with great persistence of flavour. It should express some positive varietal character where one of the traditional white varieties has been used. Typical analysis: total acidity of 6–8 g/l, depending on the variety, volatile acidity around 0.5 g/l and dry extract of around 25g/l.

Fifteen Year Old ('Reserva Extra', 'Extra Reserve'), a category used by some shippers generally for wines made from either Sercial, Verdelho, Bual or Malvasia (and occasionally Terrantez) although Pereira D'Oliveira base their fifteen year old on Tinta Negra. These wines should display great complexity with fragrance, pungency, concentration and poise. Typical analysis: total acidity of 7–9 g/l (as much as 12 g/l for Sercial), volatile acidity around 0.6 g/l and dry extract up to 30g/l.

Twenty Year Old, Thirty Year Old, Forty Year Old, Fifty Year Old and Over Fifty Years Old: although officially permitted, these designations were rarely used with twenty years being the minimum age for a wine to qualify for *frasqueira* or vintage. However, recently both Barbeito and Borges have released some outstanding blended wines at these age designations. It is to be expected that more will follow in future, especially given the restrictive definition of *solera* (see below). Typical analysis: total acidity of 8–12 g/l, volatile acidity 0.7–1.5 g/l, dry extract up to 40 g/l.

Colheita

Meaning 'harvest' in English, *colheita* signifies a wine from a single year or harvest that has been bottled after spending at least five years in wood. This relatively new category has only emerged from the legislation in 2000 and was initially only applied to wines made entirely from Sercial, Verdelho, Bual or Malvasia. Now wines from Tinta Negra may also be sold as *colheitas*, as well as wine made up from blends of different varieties. Commercially, this has already proved to be a very significant category as it permits a wine to be sold with the year of vintage on the label long before it qualifies as vintage or *frasqueira* (see below). Not to be confused with a *colheita* port, which is essentially a dated tawny, a *colheita* madeira is in effect an early bottled vintage. If the effect of *colheita* on sales of madeira amounts to even a fraction of the effect of Late Bottled Vintage on port sales in the 1980s and 1990s, then it will be the saviour of the island's industry. *Colheita* certainly adds an important point of interest to madeira wine and, not surprisingly, all the shippers have now embraced this category. *Colheitas* vary considerably according to house style. Without the concentration and complexity of a good *frasqueira*, *colheitas* should be fine, individual wines expressing both the harvest and the grape variety from which the wine is made. Barbeito have taken the *colheita* category one step further by bottling wines from a specific numbered cask. A back label informs you where the grapes came from, how the wine was aged and how many bottles make up the *lote*. The English word 'harvest' is interchangeable with *colheita* on the label but most shippers prefer to use the Portuguese expression. Sales of *colheita* are still small (less than 1 per cent of the total by volume).

Solera

Though *solera* is a term more closely associated with sherry rather than madeira, the *solera* system has nonetheless been used widely on the island since the late eighteenth century. The *solera* in Madeira has always been different from that used in Jerez and was based on the *lote* system explained in the section on blending above. The date on the label supposedly referred to the oldest wine in the blend. Ill-defined and open to fraud, Madeira's *soleras* were effectively abolished following Portugal's accession to the EU (there is a rumour that they simply forgot to include it in negotiations). Only wines that had already been bottled could continue to be sold as *soleras*. There are still a number of fabulous late nineteenth-century *solera* madeiras available from the shippers on the island, and older wines which crop up at auction in London and New York. A number of old *solera* wines are described in Chapter 6, along with the story behind Blandy's 1811 Solera Bual which explains how this famous wine came about. Since 1998 the *solera* category has been officially reintroduced and defined much more tightly by IVBAM. Under the new legislation, the basis for the *solera* must be wine from a single year or harvest, of which not more than 10 per cent can be withdrawn in any one year. This must be replaced (or refreshed) by another younger wine of similar quality. The maximum number of additions permitted is ten, after which all the wine in the *solera* must be bottled at the same time. As yet, none of the newly defined *solera* madeiras have reached the market and most shippers have turned their backs on the new definition.

Frasqueira (vintage)

At the top of the madeira hierarchy, wine from a single year or vintage has officially been designated *frasqueira* and is sometimes referred to as *garrafeira*. Both terms literally mean a 'wine-vault': a place to keep your very finest wines under lock and key. The term came about when the *Instituto do Vinho do Porto* (IVDP) objected to the use of the term 'vintage' being applied to madeira in the same way as it is attached to port (although as the shippers will tell you there is 'vintage champagne' and there are 'vintage cars'). The term '*frasqueira*' is still some way from entering the international wine lexicon and most people still prefer to use the word 'vintage' to identify wines in this category. To qualify, the wine must be made from a single 'noble' grape variety (although Tinta Negra will shortly be permitted) and aged in wood for at least twenty years before bottling. Wines destined to be bottled as *frasqueira* are generally selected around a decade after the harvest. In general the wines with higher levels of dry extract are those that show the greatest potential. Shippers are obliged to maintain a 'current account' for each of their *frasqueira* wines recording the amount of wine and when it was bottled. It is only since 2015 that shippers have been obliged to put the date of bottling on the label, although most shippers have been including it in recent years. With older bottles it is therefore quite possible for the same wine to be bottled at a number of different stages, say at twenty years then forty years, by which time (with an extra twenty years of age in wood) the wine will be very different in style. Vintage madeiras are generally bottled in tiny quantities, representing the very best wines from the year's crop. Although all the shippers bottle and sell vintage wines, there is no discernable pattern to the years on sale. Unlike port, where a particular vintage is 'declared' by a number of houses, in madeira the shippers quietly squirrel away tiny *lotes* of wine only for them to re-emerge in bottle decades later. At the Madeira Wine Company the oldest wine, still unbottled, is a Bual dating from 1920. D'Oliveira, who pride themselves on their huge stock of old wines, have only recently bottled their 1901 Malvazia.

'Vintage' madeira is without doubt one of the world's most thrilling and haunting of wines. The pungency, power and concentration of a great wine is as mind-numbing as the fragrance and delicacy is enchanting. No other wine deserves quite the same respect as a madeira from, say, the early nineteenth century which appears to combine the freshness of the day it was made with intensity, concentration and the ethereal complexity of age. These wines are, inevitably, expensive. But, because of the way they have been aged, they are also virtually indestructible. This means that you can revisit a bottle of vintage madeira again and again for months, even years, after the wine has been uncorked. No other wine can give the same amount of pleasure for so long! (See pages 215–17 on cellaring, decanting and serving madeira wine.) Bottled in small quantities, often by hand, vintage madeiras are identified nowadays by the name of the shipper, the year and the grape variety, hand-stencilled on the bottle. There is no such thing as a typical 'vintage' madeira but an analysis might give a total acidity of up to 12 g/l for a Sercial, volatile acidity of up to 2.5 g/l and dry extract between 30 and 40 g/l.

Chapter 6 contains more specific information on historic madeira wines. A review of recent vintages can be found at the end of Chapter 3.

DO MADEIRENSE AND IG TERRAS MADEIRENSES

Since 1999, the unfortified wines made on the island have become entitled to their own denomination: initially VQPRD and now DO Madeirense. Unfortified wines (*vinho seco*) have always been made on Madeira, generally from poorer quality grapes, and sold in *tascas* and bars around the island. Since the mid-1990s, however, a number of producers have been making unfortified wines from Tinta Negra, Verdelho or a number of international grape varieties. The fashion began in 1992 with Atlantis, a medium dry rosé made from the Tinta Negra by the Madeira Wine Company. Sales of this wine now amount to over 50,000 bottles a year.

The construction of a new *adega* in 1999 beside the old cooperative at São Vicente gave the impetus for a new wave of unfortified wines. This small but impressively well-equipped winery belongs to the IVBAM and is used by a handful of growers, mostly on the north side of the island, who pay for the space and services. A large number of grapes are permitted including all the traditional Madeiran varieties as well as international grapes like Sauvignon Blanc, Chardonnay, Merlot and Cabernet Sauvignon. There is also an obscure grape variety named Arnsburger, developed in Germany which, with the help of a German consultant, has found its way to the north side of the island. The wines made at the Adega de São Vicente are still very variable in quality and are, as yet, unlikely to be found outside the local market. Unfortunately Tinta Negra is not capable of producing very interesting unfortified wine. There is, however, an interesting project at Caniçal on the south side of the island where Touriga Nacional, Syrah and Merlot have been planted to produce red wine. Their results are quite encouraging but the wines are not really competitively priced to sell outside the local market.

Since 2001, there has also been a Vinho Regional (now an IG or Indicação Geographica) covering Madeira and named Terras Madeirenses. Equivalent in status to a French *Vin de Pays*, the Vinho Regional permits more flexibility in terms of the grape varieties that may be used.

5

MADEIRA WINE PRODUCERS

At the end of the nineteenth century there were over 150 wine producers on the island of Madeira, including shippers and numerous *partidistas* or intermediaries who either made or bought in wine and carried the stock until it was required by the shippers themselves. Crises, closures, takeovers and mergers have taken their toll and the number of Madeira wine producers has fallen to just six registered shippers or exporters. There is just one *partidista* remaining.

Nearly all the survivors result from mergers and amalgamations: for example, the Madeira Wine Company (which began as the Madeira Wine Association) has as many as twenty-six names under its umbrella. Like the port trade on the Portuguese mainland, madeira is now essentially about brands. Every shipper trades under one principal brand name, retaining a number of associated brands targeted at specific customers or markets. Short profiles of some of the more important shippers that have ceased to exist may be found in Chapter 6.

In the nineteenth century many of the shippers had small vineyard holdings of their own, mostly on the outskirts of Funchal. These were sold off for urban development leaving just one shipper, Henriques & Henriques, owning a substantial vineyard. Consequently the shippers rely on an army of independent growers for their grapes, employing agents in the field to work with the farmers and to coordinate the harvest. Following in the steps of the port shippers who have been securing an ever-greater share of their own production since the 1970s, the Madeira Wine Company leased two vineyards on the north side of the island in 2012. They also have access to a small family-owned vineyard at Quinta de Santa Luzia in Funchal. The individual shippers exercise much greater control over quality than they did just a generation ago, when trained oenologists or wine makers were unheard of on the island. All the shippers now employ at least one trained oenologist.

Until as recently as the 1980s, the madeira wine shippers were largely concentrated in the centre of Funchal around the Rua dos Ferreiros, Rua dos Netos and the Rua do Carmo. They occupied cramped but atmospheric buildings known as *armazens* ('wine stores' in English) where the wines were aged. A number of traditional *armazens* still exist (see Barros e Sousa, Borges, the Madeira Wine Company and D'Oliveira below) and these attract large numbers of visitors. Taking advantage of funding from the European Union, two major shippers decided to relocate lock, stock and barrel to more modern purpose-built premises outside the city. In the 1990s the Madeira Wine Company also had plans to relocate their main lodges and *adega* to Cabo Girão, but chose one of the few locations on the island that was not on solid rock. The cost of stabilising the site was inordinately expensive and the project was abandoned. In 2014 they moved the bulk of their production from the centre of Funchal to the *Zona Franca* (Freeport) at Caniçal to the west of Machico.

The following madeira producers are listed in alphabetical order with the full company name, address, telephone and website. Where passing visitors are welcome to visit and taste, I have included current opening hours – but be aware that these may change.

As well as a commentary on the history and background of each shipper, I have also included tasting notes from the current range in order to convey something of the unique character of the wines. I am not a fan of rating wines by points and have awarded the wines a star rating as follows (see page 133 for a fuller explanation):

***** an outstandingly beautiful wine, that leaves you with a sense of awe and wonder

**** an excellent wine in its class, highly recommended for its beauty, depth and articulacy

*** a good wine with some complexity and much to recommend it

** an enjoyable but simple and straightforward wine

* a very ordinary wine without faults, but with no great merit

No star: faulty

Frasqueira or 'vintage' wines, some dating back to the early eighteenth century, can be found rated on the same basis in Chapter 6. For further information on tasting, buying and serving madeira wine, see Chapter 7.

Barbeito

Vinhos Barbeito (Madeira) Lda, Estrada de Ribeira Garcia, Parque Empresarial de Câmara de Lobos, Lote 8, 9300-324 Câmara de Lobos
Tel. (351) 291 761829 / 291 762434
Email: info@vinhosbarbeito.com.pt
Website: www.vinhosbarbeito.com
Opening hours: Monday to Friday, 9.00–13:00 and 14.00–18.00

Established by Mario Barbeito Vasconcelos in 1946 (see page 21), this company is a relative youngster among the madeira shippers but has a stock of some historic wine. Mario Barbeito started working for the now defunct Companhia Vitícola da Madeira (CVM) but, with access to substantial stocks of wine of his own, he set up as a shipper in his own right. Like the other major shippers in the post-war period, Barbeito made money mostly from selling bulk wines for export, building up lucrative markets in Scandinavia and Japan. From its inception the company occupied an old cane sugar factory situated on the edge of a cliff, fortuitously but incongruously, in between Reid's and the Cliff Bay hotels.

Mario Barbeito died in 1985, leaving the business with his daughter Manuela de Freitas, almost certainly the first woman ever to take charge of a madeira wine shipper. Mario Barbeito's grandson, Ricardo Diogo Freitas, took over the helm from his mother in 1991 and changed the firm's orientation, bravely ending bulk shipments over a decade before they were officially suspended. The company's turnover immediately fell by half, but Diogo was helped in his single-minded drive for quality by the Kinoshita family of Japan who became joint partners in Barbeito in 1991. Kinoshita had been Barbeito's Japanese distributors since 1967 and Japan had become the most important market for their three-year-old wine, Delvino. Barbeito now have a market share in Japan of over 60 per cent. The cooperation between the two families brought about investment in new wine-making facilities. In 2008 the company left the cliff-top sugar factory for new purpose-built premises above Cabo Girão Câmara de Lobos. The old site is now being incorporated into the adjacent Cliff Bay Hotel.

Although Barbeito always prided themselves on some impressive old wines, it is the younger wines that are now attracting the most interest. A historian by training, Ricardo Diogo has a refreshingly open view of the world, including the world of wine. His penchant for late-harvest wines, especially Riesling, goes some way to explaining the character of his company's wines today. Since the early 1990s the company has been making a much more restrained, delicate style of madeira with less power and pungency which initially marked them out from other houses on the island. They also have a purity and honesty about them. Diogo states openly that he has mostly given up using caramel as a colouring agent, something that the other shippers still use but rarely, if ever, mention. Since 1995 Barbeito invested heavily in improving their *estufagem*, the first madeira shipper to do so. The old concrete *estufas* were decommissioned and replaced by modern stainless steel tanks with external jackets where temperatures are computer controlled. These produce much cleaner wines without the burnt, caramelised flavours that resulted from the heavy-handed *estufagem* in the past. About three quarters of the company's wines are subject to *estufagem*.

Barbeito operates from three sites, each with very different characteristics when it comes to ageing wine in cask. Their new *adega* and main wine lodge with a capacity for 220,000 litres in ageing cask is located on a business park above Cabo Girão. At 610 metres above sea level it is much the highest and coolest wine lodge on Madeira and with annual evaporation rates of around 3 per cent it produces the gentlest wines. Another *armazém,* called the Adega do Afonso at Estreito de Câmara de Lobos, at an altitude of 400 metres has a slightly higher evaporation rate. The old Barbeito *adega* at Ponte dos Frades in Câmara de Lobos has been retained for ageing around 120,000 litres of wine and, being at 80 metres above sea level, this has a higher annual evaporation rate of around 4 to 5 per cent. Ricardo Diogo is continually experimenting and for a time he was ageing wines, some in new oak, at the family quinta at Barreiros just above Funchal. Here, in buildings that were not much more than garden sheds, evaporation rates reached 5 per cent. He has reached the conclusion that new oak has nothing to contribute to madeira other than for the company's three-year-old wines which spend between three and six months in 225-litre *barricas*. These three sites, along with cask sizes ranging between 225 and 2,000 litres, give the company a wide range of different *canteiro* wines for blending.

The company's most recent innovation is a mechanical stainless steel *lagar*, similar to those being used for port wine in the Douro. This is used for Tinta Negra, the extra maceration giving a much deeper and darker wine than would be obtained by pumping over in tank. Diogo is a fan of Tinta Negra as a varietal and the *lagar*-fermented wine is more full bodied, making it suitable for ageing in *canteiro*. The deeper-coloured Tinta Negra is also used as a substitute for caramel in Barbeito's three-year-old blend.

Barbeito produce a complete range of Madeira wines, starting with a competent and characterful three-year-old blend, continuing through five and ten, and culminating in wines dated twenty, thirty and 'Over 40 Years Old'. The latter wines fall into what the company terms its 'Signature Series'. These are supremely good wines blended with great sensitivity and extend to the Historic Series commissioned by Emmanuel Berk of the Rare Wine Company in Sonoma, California. Bottled with evocative names like Charleston Sercial, Savannah Verdelho and Boston Bual, these wines have done much to revive the market for madeira in the US. Mr Madison's Madeira and Baltimore Rainwater (see below) are attempts at imitating the style of madeira shipped to North America in the eighteenth century, with short ageing in wood and limited oxidation.

In 2001 Barbeito launched a series of numbered single-cask *colheitas*, often from a single vineyard with detailed information on the back label. Many of the family's *frasqueira* or vintage wines pre-date the company, including a rare but remarkable 1795 Terrantez (one of the oldest wines I have ever tasted), which originally belonged to the Hinton family and came to Mario Barbeito through Oscar Acciaioli (see pages 139–46 for more information on these historic wines). Recent wines set aside to become *frasqueiras* promise just as much excitement for the future.

The Barbeito family have no vineyards of their own (other than a small experimental vineyard alongside the *adega*), although they used to own a property named Jardim do Sol in Caniço, east of Funchal. Barbeito's 1957 Boal originates from there (see page 141). Since 2015 the company has employed a viticulturalist, Rita Alves, who used to work for IVBAM and has an intimate knowledge of the island's vineyards. Barbeito buy in grapes from between 120 and 140 growers, mostly in Estreito de Câmara de Lobos and São Vicente, with Malvasia coming from São Jorge and Fajã dos Padres.

Ricardo Diogo's experiments do not end in the wine lodges. He has been proactive in matching madeira wine and food, taking a road show to both the US and the UK. A tasting with Ricardo Diogo is the experience of a lifetime and can range from a pairing of a ten-year-old Sercial with *escabeche*, octopus in aspic flavoured with cherry vinegar, or a medium dry *colheita* with Yorkshire pudding and onion gravy. (For more on matching madeira wine with food, see pages 222–4.) Ricardo Diogo is the most open and inventive of all madeira producers and thoroughly deserves to succeed.

Barbeito's range changes regularly with new and numbered *lotes*, innovative blends and single-cask bottlings. The wines are very clean and pure from the start, as was immediately evident on tasting some very expressive aromatic 2014 wines made from Sercial, Boal, and Bastardo in early 2015. With cask age, many of Barbeito's wines seem to take on delicate aromas of wood smoke whilst retaining their varietal purity. From extensive recent tastings I have identified the following wines as worthy of note.

Barbeito Dry

A three-year-old wine from Tinta Negra given short ageing in relatively new wood: pale amber; simple, straightforward and a touch spirity with a hint of peach and watermelon, off dry and quite delicate with a touch of curried spice on the finish. ***

Barbeito Rainwater 5 Anos

A blend of Tinta Negra and Verdelho, without any *estufagem*: pale orange/amber, gentle toasted aromas and a savoury character with a touch of citrus. ***

Barbeito, 'Mr Madison's Madeira'

A 'one off' wine bottled in 2014 for the American market, this is a Malvasia aged for five years with very limited oxidation: deep, golden straw colour; not very expressive but unusual primary grape and pineapple aromas with fresh, sweet fruit on the palate and a slightly savoury dusty finish. A curiosity. ***

Baltimore Rainwater

A blend of Sercial and Verdelho aged for five to seven years in wood, keeping oxidation to a minimum: deep golden colour with lovely smoky aromas and savoury-toasted flavours offset by a touch of dried apricot sweetness. Not complex but very pure and appetising. ****

Barbeito 10 Year Old Boal Reserva Velha

A very worthy silver medal winner at the *Decanter* World Wine Awards in 2014: mid-orange/amber; gently singed on the nose with a lovely candied peel character underneath; pure candied citrus and marmalade sweetness, gentle and linear with a fine streak of acidity lingering onto the finish. ****/*****

Savannah Verdelho, Special Reserve

A wine bottled specially for the Rare Wine Company in the US which includes some very old wines in the blend: mid-pale mahogany, green tinge; lovely aromatic quality, floral, leafy hedgerow character on the nose; very fine and expressive with lovely concentration and depth, touch of butterscotch offset by leafy acidity. Peacock's tail of a finish. ****/*****

Barbeito, Riberio Real Verdelho, Lote 1, 20 Years Old

One of a pair of recently launched blended wines with 15 per cent Tinta Negra and 85 per cent of the stated variety, named after the Ribeiro Real estate owned by the Favila family (see page 175), 200 metres above sea level at Câmara de Lobos. Wines from Ribeiro Real form an important component of the blend: pale-mid amber; wonderful, pungent, focused, smoky nose (gunsmoke) matched by delicate, toasted, savoury flavours backed by a hint of grapefruit and lemon and lime marmalade. Long, elegant and fine. ****

Barbeito, Ribeiro Real Boal, Lote 1, 20 Years Old

See the wine above for background information: mid-amber/orange; perfumed orange blossom and jasmine aromas with a touch of savoury bonfire smoke underlying; wonderful texture and concentration, *marmelada* (quince marmalade) with caramelised oranges and a lovely long, pure finish. Very fine. ****/*****

Malvasia 20 Anos Lote 12089

A trophy winner at the *Decanter* World Wine Awards in 2013: mid-deep-green-tinged amber; lovely smoky perfume, touch of autumn bonfire and decaying flowers; lovely depth (extract) and mouthfeel, very refined, vanilla and quince marmalade, very complex but with a lightness of touch and so fresh for a twenty year old. The follow up *lote* is numbered 14050, bottled in 2014, and is just as refined and elegant. ****/*****

Barbeito 40 Year Old Mãe Manuela Malvasia

A wonderful tribute to Manuela de Freitas who ran Barbeito from 1972 to 1991. A very worthy silver medal winner at the 2014 *Decanter World Wine Awards*: mid-deep amber/mahogany; rich, complex slightly autumnal aromas; butterscotch and dried fig, wonderful weight and texture with real depth and concentration, offset by a fine streak of acidity. Long and very fine. ****/*****

Artur Barros e Sousa Lda.

c/o Pereira D'Oliveira (Vinhos) Lda., Rua dos Ferreiros, 107, 9000-082 Funchal
Tel. (351) 291 220784
Email: perolivinhos@hotmail.com

Stepping off the pavement of the Rua dos Ferreiros into the lodges of Barros e Sousa was like taking a walk back in time. The pebble-cobbled floors, simple whitewashed walls and dark wooden casks reek of old Madeira, both the island and the wine. But this small, family company is a relative newcomer to madeira. It was established in the early 1920s when Dr. Pedro José Lomelino recruited his nephew, Artur Barros e Sousa, to sort out his collection of old madeira wines. The company was first registered under the name Lomelino but this name was already in use (see Madeira Wine Company) and it was re-registered under the name of Artur de Barros e Sousa. The business was owned and run by his three grandsons: Artur, Edmundo and Rui. Artur was the wine maker, Edmundo received visitors and made the sales and Rui was a sleeping partner. In 2013 the company was bought by their larger next door neighbour, Pereira D'Oliveira. At the time of writing they plan to keep Barros e Sousa as a separate entity, maintaining the traditions that kept the company unique for so long. However, the doors that used to welcome visitors off the street are currently closed.

Producing less than 300 cases of wine a year, everything at Barros e Sousa was done on an artisan scale. The company had no vineyards but kept longstanding contacts with growers. They didn't even own a press and borrowed one belonging to Pereira d'Oliveira. The must was then brought down to Funchal where it was fermented in old casks, outdoors on a *canteiro*, in an atmospheric little courtyard in the middle of the lodge. Barros e Sousa were totally traditional: there was no stainless steel, no temperature control, no filtration and certainly no *estufagem*. Some bottles even had a back label offering a substantial financial award to anyone who could prove the wine had been through an *estufa*. All the wine was aged in pipe in a three-storey lodge behind the courtyard. With its creaking wooden floors propped up with rough-hewn tree trunks, the lodge feels like the hold of a ship and Barros e Sousa's wines are probably the closest in style to those that used to complete the round voyage across the tropics. The wines spent the first ten years or so on the top floor where the annual rate of evaporation is around 3 per cent and are then transferred to lower floors where the evaporation rate is reduced to around 1 per cent. The pipes themselves are between forty and a hundred years old.

It almost goes without saying that the wines were hand bottled. Many of the bottles are hand painted and stencilled 'ABSL' for Artur Barros e Sousa Limitada. The youngest wines available were classified 'Reserva' which are blends of around ten years' average age. Reserva Velha used to denote blends of ten years plus with some up to thirty years old. There are also unblended *colheita* and *frasqueira* (vintage) wines although these expressions were never used on the label. When a single variety is stated on the bottle, Barros e Sousa used to point out that the wine was made from 100 per cent of the variety, not the 85 per cent permitted under the law.

The company was also unique in bottling a tiny quantity of Listrão from the neighbouring island of Porto Santo. Faded family photographs on the wall of the tasting area illustrated the harvest in Porto Santo in the 1970s. They also maintained small quantities of aged wines from Terrantez, Moscatel and Bastardo, grapes that are in very limited supply. The Moscatel was allowed to macerate on the skins for several months following the harvest, in the manner of a Moscatel de Setúbal from the mainland.

Barros e Sousa were never officially registered as an exporter: until they were taken over they were technically a *partidista* (intermediary) only able to sell wines on the island although a few bottles were occasionally sent to private customers overseas. Some of the wines have a rusticity about them, perhaps not surprising given the circumstances in which they were made. The family preferred to follow their own rules; something that shows in notes on the eclectic range of wines that follows. Although D'Oliveira intend to maintain the brand it remains to be seen if they will follow these time-honoured artisan traditions.

ABSL, Boal 1998 (bottled 2004)

Pale golden amber; pure, fresh blossom scent to the nose, very expressive for such a young wine (still technically a *colheita* when I tasted this in 2005); lemon and lime marmalade, quite dry in style for Boal but racy and very fine indeed. ****

ABSL, Terrantez Reserva

Golden amber colour with a distinct olive-green tinge to the rim; perfumed aromas with a hint of something savoury; fine and delicate on the palate, bone dry, savoury toasty flavours with the merest hint of candied peel. Wonderful finish. ****

ABSL, Moscatel Reserva Velha (bottled 2002)

Mid-deep amber with an apple-green rim; fragrant, floral nose, more expressive of the type of ageing than the grape variety; very sweet and rich but stops short of cloying. Tawny marmalade tang with vibrant acidity. Lovely concentration from about twenty years in wood. ****

H. M. Borges

Rua 31 de Janeiro, 83, PO Box 92, 9000 – Funchal, Madeira, Portugal
Tel. (351) 291 223247
website: www.hmborges.com
email: info@hmborges.com
Opening hours: Monday to Friday, 9.00–12.30 and 14.00–17.30

This small independent family company can date itself back to 1877 when Henrique Menezes Borges, a food wholesaler, began using his profits to buy up old wines. He became a *partidista* (intermediary) who supplied many firms especially Krohn Brothers, who were significant shippers to Russia before their business came to an end after the October Revolution of 1917 (see page 190). Henrique Borges himself died a year earlier leaving the company to his two sons and a daughter. It was only in the 1920s that the firm began to export wines in its own right, at which time they moved to the present site, an old flour mill on the Rua 31 de Janeiro. During the difficult decades of the 1920s and 1930s a number of takeovers and mergers brought the firms of Adega de Exportadora de Vinhos de Madeira, J. H. Gonçalves, Araújo Henriques & Co. and Borges Madeira under the same roof. Alongside H. M. Borges, these names are still used occasionally as brands by the company. H. M. Borges is now run by two cousins, Helena and Isabel Borges, who are great-granddaughters of the founder. The wine maker is Ivo Couto who used to be at the Madeira Wine Company in the 1980s.

The company has no vineyards of its own but they buy in grapes from the Araújo family, who are shareholders in Borges and own vineyards at Estreito de Câmara de Lobos. In total the company buys in 200,000 kilos of grapes a year of which 80 per cent is Tinta Negra Mole and the remaining 20 per cent is mostly Malvasia. Vinification takes place in a small *adega* next to the *armazens*, the traditional white grape varieties being fermented in cask. Only wine destined for three-year blends is sent for *estufagem*. The remainder is aged in oak and satinwood vats and pipes in cramped but atmospheric *armazens* on four floors in the centre of Funchal. There are paintings by Max Romer in the highly polished tasting room and a letter from Winston Churchill hangs on the wall thanking the Borges family for a gift of wine. The company can count on around a million litres of stock. Borges produce a full range of wines bottled at three, five, ten and fifteen years as well as *colheitas* and the occasional twenty year old, thirty year old and *frasqueira* or vintage wine. There is not room to carry much stock and many of the wines are bottled to order. Many older vintages from the Borges family reserves are outstanding (see pages 160–4) but with stocks of these largely exhausted, Borges main strength lies in their blended ten-year-old wines designated 'Reserva Velha' or 'Old Reserve' wines, some of which are very good indeed. Scandinavia is the main export market. The following notes give a flavour of some of their best wines but it is worth making your own way to the Borges tasting room in the centre of Funchal.

H. M. Borges Meio Seco 3 Year Old

Mid-amber colour; straightforward, clean, caramelised fruit character, some raisiny sweetness offset by fresh acidity and a satisfying savoury-sweet finish. **

H. M. Borges Meio Dôce 5 Years Old

Pale to mid-amber; quite rich but a touch stewed on the nose, lovely figgy flavours with good depth and cut leading to an attractive spicy finish. **

H. M. Borges 'Old Reserve' Ten Year Old Sercial

Made from grapes grown in Jardim da Serra: pale to mid-amber, olive-green tinge to rim; lovely lifted, leafy aromas; dry yet full savoury-nutty flavour followed up by bracing acidity and a slightly green finish. Not too punishing: well balanced Sercial. ***/****

H. M. Borges 'Old Reserve' 10 Year Old Malvasia

Mid-amber/mahogany; rich and lifted on the nose, slightly autumnal with a touch of savoury beef stock; rich and mellifluous with lovely texture, slightly blunt but soft figgy fruit balanced by fresh acidity. Very good. ****

H. M. Borges 15 Year Old Boal

Mid-amber/mahogany, distinct olive-green-tinged rim; quite rich with a touch of toffee on the nose; rich and well developed, fresh, clean tawny marmalade flavours offset by vibrant acidity. Good length of flavour. ****

H. M. Borges Colheita 1995 Verdelho

A wine bottled in 2006: pale orange/amber; fine, delicate and distinctly smoked on the nose, toast and salted nuts underneath; similarly savoury, toasted flavours, dried apricots and a touch of dried fig, rich yet off dry with good complexity all the way through to the finish. ****

H. M. Borges 20 Year Old Verdelho

Pale-to-mid amber/orange; lovely smoked, slightly singed aromas, flinty too, very expressive; fine savoury, toasted flavour with more concentration mid-palate than *colheita* (above), long and quite complex in character. A good representation of this variety. ****/*****

H. M. Borges 30 Year Old Malvasia

Mid-mahogany; deep and pungent on the nose; a lovely butterscotch character with a touch of treacle and molasses underlying; rich, tangy and satisfying all the way to the finish. Quite profound. ****

J. Faria

J. Faria & Filhos Lda. Travessa do Tanque, 85/87, 9020-258 Funchal
Tel. (351) 291 742 935

Founded in 1949, the name J. Faria is best known on the island for its range of liqueurs, *poncha* (fruit punch) and *aguardente de cana* (sugar cane spirit). The company only became associated with wine in the late 1990s when it began buying in wines from a family-owned Câmara de Lobos based *partidista* called P. E. Gonçalves. J. Faria moved to purpose-built premises near Madeira Shopping on the outskirts of Funchal in 2006. The company produces a limited range of wines, so far confined to the three-, five- and ten-year-old levels. All are non-varietal. Most wines are sold on the island although J. Faria also produce madeira for the Portuguese supermarket chain Pingo Dôce.

Henriques & Henriques

Avenida da Autonomia, 10, Sítio de Belém, 9300 – 138 Câmara de Lobos, Madeira, Portugal
Tel. (351) 291 941 551/2
Email: HeH@henriquesehenriques.pt
Website: madeirawine@henriquesehenriques.com
Opening hours: Monday to Friday, 9.00-13.00 and 14.30-17.30

Henriques & Henriques is unique among Madeira wine shippers in that the company has almost always owned its own vineyards. The firm was established in 1850 but the Henriques family were already large landowners in Câmara de Lobos, having planted vineyards at Pico de Torre in the middle of the fifteenth century, only a few years after Madeira was first discovered and colonised. When João Joaquim Henriques founded the wine-producing company they were already in possession of some old wines. The firm acted initially as a *partidista,* only selling wines to other shippers. When João Joaquim's two sons took over in 1912, the company was reconstituted as Henriques & Henriques, and by the mid-1920s the company was selling most wines under its own label. Sales grew rapidly and the company built up strong markets in the USA and Scandinavia.

The younger of the two brothers, known as João de Bélem, invited two friends to join the business: Alberto ('Bertie') Nascimento Jardim and Carlos Nunes Pereira. In 1938 he also took in Peter Cossart, the younger brother of Noel Cossart, who had been advised by his mother not to join the family firm, Cossart Gordon. When João de Bélem died in 1968 without an heir he left the business equally to the three partners. When Peter Cossart died in 1991, after fifty-three vintages with the company, his son John took over in conjunction with Carlos Perreira's nephew, Luís, as winemaker and production director alongside Humberto Jardim. John Cossart quickly grasped the complexities of the madeira wine trade. He was an ambassador for the island's wines, travelling the world looking for new ways to promote both madeira and his firm's wines; in order to illustrate the effect of heat on madeira wine he once held a tasting in a London hammam! When John Cossart died suddenly in February 2008 he was the last of a long line of Englishmen involved day-to-day in the madeira wine trade. His death precipitated the sale of the company to La Martiniquaise who also own Justino's (see below). Humberto Jardim, the last representative of the three partners, still retains a shareholding and now manages both companies and acts as the chief wine maker, having learned the ropes from Luís Pereira. Despite being jointly managed, both companies have kept their separate identities and only share a bottling line.

The fact that Henriques & Henriques have long sourced a significant proportion of their grapes from their own vineyards and are therefore in control from the vineyard to the bottle perhaps goes some way to explain the consistently high quality of the company's wines. There was a brief hiatus when, after the 25 April Revolution of 1974, the company was forced to sell its vineyards to the tenants (see page 23), other than 1.4 hectares on precipitous *poios* at Ribeira de Caixa below Estreito de Câmara de Lobos. In 1993, H&H bought land at Quinta Grande, 600 to 800 metres above Câmara de Lobos, and planted 10 hectares of vines, now planted entirely with Verdelho. With help from technicians from the port wine region on the mainland, it was the first vineyard on Madeira to be mechanised. It remains by far the largest single vineyard on the island. The vineyards at Ribeira de Caixa have been replanted with Malvasia Candida and Terrantez.

Until 1994, H&H occupied cramped lodges in the centre of Funchal but, with help of European funds, they were able to invest in purpose-built premises at Câmara de Lobos. A new winery was established below the vineyards at Ribeira de Escrivão, Quinta Grande, and a new *armazém* and visitor centre were built by the sea at Sítio de Belém where the Henriques family owned land. Sadly the founder's house in front of the *armazém* has been demolished by the local council and replaced by an ultra-modern library. Apart from the wines and casks (many of which date back before 1850) the only piece of equipment to make the journey from Funchal to Câmara de Lobos was the company's trusty steam boiler. Built in Liverpool in the 1850s, it still produces steam for the new stainless steel *estufas*.

Henriques & Henriques produce a full range of wines, totally independent of Justino's. H&H's three- and five-year-old blends, made predominantly from Tinta Negra, are subject to *estufagem* in tank, whereas the ten-, fifteen- and twenty-year-old wines, made from the traditional white grapes, are all *canteiro* wines. The company's lodges at Sítio de Belém are on four levels, and have large south-facing plate glass windows enabling the wine to be heated naturally by the sun (almost a modern day *estufa do sol* – see page 11). With much of the concentration of flavour found in even older madeiras, the ten- and fifteen-year- old ranges are quite outstanding and regularly win gold medals in international wine competitions. H&H are one of the few companies to maintain sizable stocks of old wine in cask and in bottle. *Frasqueira* wines are bottled under the name '*garrafeira*' as well as 'vintage'. At the time of writing, wines dating back to the nineteenth century are still on sale at the lodge in Câmara de Lobos. Although these wines are sold without a vintage year, some of them were considered to be old when H&H was founded in 1850. Notes on some of these wines can be found on pages 180–6.

Like most Madeira shippers, Henriques & Henriques produces wines under a number of different labels. Carmo Vinhos, Belém's Madeira Wine, Casa dos Vinhos da Madeira and António Eduardo Henriques are the names owned by the company, as well as the recently defunct Veiga França and Silva Vinhos. H&H also bottle madeira wine for Sandeman. But, as the slogan goes, 'there are only two names in Madeira'…

Henriques & Henriques Monte Seco

First made as a prank by Peter Cossart in 1937 as a substitute for his favourite La Ina fino sherry which was unobtainable on the island; during the Second World War it came to be used as a substitute for vermouth in dry Martinis! Originally made from the Listrão grape, Monte Seco is now produced from Tinta Negra: pale amber; simple appley fruit, toasted and a touch salty on the finish. Made in 'extra dry' style with 25 g/l residual sugar. **

Henriques & Henriques Full Rich

A three-year-old wine, made entirely from Tinta Negra: deep amber; straightforward, clean raisiny aromas and raisin and sultana flavours with some depth already evident on the finish. Rich and satisfying. ***

Henriques & Henriques 2001 Sercial 'Single Harvest'

Iridescent, pale orange/amber; lifted, leafy aromas, very characteristic of Sercial; lovely dried-apricot dimension and concentration offset by seemingly saline acidity, a lovely aperitif wine with a long, crystal clear, off dry finish. A fine representation of Sercial. ****

Henriques & Henriques 1997 Colheita

Made entirely from Tinta Negra in a rich style with a proportion of the wine aged in new Iberian oak: mid-deep amber/mahogany; vanilla evident on the nose with a toasted character underlying; lovely rich and mellifluous dried-fruit compote offset by racy acidity and a touch of soft vanilla sweetness underlying all the way to the finish. ***

Henriques & Henriques 15 Year Old Sercial

Regular medal winners in the *Decanter* World Wine Awards, the H&H fifteen-year-old range is truly exemplary and the best in its class. There is really no better introduction to fine madeira: mid-amber; powerful, incisive high-toned savoury aromas; quite rich in style for a Sercial with a hint of dried apricot; some gentle sweetness evident at first, a tang of tawny marmalade followed by a fine dry, savoury finish. ****

Henriques & Henriques 15 Year Old Verdelho

Mid-deep amber/mahogany with an olive green rim; restrained and slightly singed on the nose, a touch of beef stock; lovely fresh, clean savoury character (consommé) sweet fruit underlying, dried figs and dried apricots, offset by rapier-like acidity on the finish. Great poise. ****

Henriques & Henriques 15 Year Old Bual

Mid-deep mahogany, olive-green rim; very fine, fragrant aroma, leaves, green tea and flowers; rich toast and marmalade character yet at the same time gentle, beautifully concentrated with an incisive finish. Very finely poised. ****/*****

Henriques & Henriques 15 Year Old Malmsey

Deep mahogany; olive-green rim; enchanting nose, dusty and floral, slightly lifted; wonderfully rich, concentrated flavours, toffee apple, with fine incisive acidity (5.2 g/l) on the finish offsetting 120 g/l residual sugar. An outstanding wine in its class. ****/*****

Henriques & Henriques 20 Year Old Verdelho

A gold medal winner at the *Decanter* World Wine Awards in 2014: mid-amber; smoky, autumnal aromas, obvious concentration with a touch of dusky forest floor; clean and toasty with hazelnut and salted almonds on a long, incisive off-dry finish. Very fine. *****

Henriques & Henriques 20 Year Old Terrantez

Pale to mid-green-tinged amber; lovely crème brûlée character on the nose, just a touch autumnal; rich texture with characteristic bitter-sweet lemon and lime freshness with pruney richness offset the natural astringency on the finish. Lovely balance and poise. ****

Henriques & Henriques 20 Year Old Malmsey

A silver medal winner at the *Decanter* World Wine Awards in 2014: very deep red/mahogany; powerfully concentrated fig, truffle and raisin on the nose, beautifully lifted and quite expressive; rich and mellifluous, *bolo-de-mel*/parkin character, very clean with lovely texture and weight, a lovely clear, delineated finish. ****

Justino's

Justino's Madeira Wines SA, Parque Industrial da Cancela, 9125-042 Caniço, Madeira
Tel. (351) 291 934 257
Email: justinos@justinosmadeira.com
Website: www.justinosmadeira.com
Not open to visitors

Vinhos Justino Henriques (VJH) was a small family-owned shipper on its last legs when Siegfredo da Costa Campos bought the company in 1981. A former army colonel in the colonial wars of independence and with no previous wine trade experience, Costa Campos turned the company round with considerable vision and passion. In 1993 it became part of the French wine and spirits distribution group La Martiniquaise, owners of the Porto Cruz brand. Now rebranded Justino's, the company is the single largest shipper of madeira wine, producing around 1.6 million litres a year. Known locally and rather cynically as the 'good colonel', Siegfredo da Costa Campos died in 2008. Since 2009 the company has been totally owned by La Martiniquaise. In 2010 La Martiniquaise bought a majority stake in Henriques & Henriques and put both companies under joint management (see page 103).

Justino Henriques was founded in 1870 as a small family shipper. By the 1930s it was mostly trading with Brazil and when this market collapsed they developed a market in Canada. It remained in the family until the 1960s when it became associated by the now defunct Companhia Vinícola da Madeira (CVM). The company continued to operate from cramped lodges on the Rua do Carmo in the centre of Funchal until it moved to an industrial estate at Cançela east of the city in 1994. Partly financed by the European Union, the new premises have served Justino's well even though they have none of the charm of the old *armazens* in Funchal. The Cancela site has two parallel wine-making facilities, one of red grapes and a much smaller one (almost a 'boutique' winery) for small *lotes* of white grapes. With stainless steel vats ranging in size from 1,000 to 350,000 litres, the company now has a storage capacity of 8 million litres of wine, 2 million of which is in wood. At the time of writing Justino's have a project to increase their ageing capacity in wood by another 2 million litres. Heavy investment in wine making, bottling and especially in the *estufagem* process has improved the overall quality at all levels whereas, in the past, many of Justino's wines were rather heavy, stewed and soupy in style. Porto Cruz is the largest single brand of port wine and the lion's share of Justino's wines are sold under the Madère Cruz label in 20 cl flasks, more than a million of which are sold in France each year. To put this into perspective, Cruz accounts for 90 per cent of the bottled madeira sold in France, which itself is the largest single market for madeira wine. Justino's also produce smaller quantities of wine for the Broadbent label, established in the US by Bartholomew Broadbent in 1996. He is the son of Michael Broadbent who was the Head of Christie's wine department in London from 1966 to 1992 and published Noel Cossart's book on Madeira. Broadbent's wines are made by Justino's and selected by Broadbent father and son.

Justino's is primarily geared to export and the wines are not widely available on the home market. The company is very efficiently run with a small permanent staff of twenty. Wine making is the responsibility of Juan Teixeira, his Spanish Christian name explained by his Venezuelan birthplace. The company produces a wide range of wines under their own label including three-, five- and ten-year-old blends, *colheitas* and *frasqueiras*. Since 1995 the company has been building up a stock of good *colheitas* (a category which they claim to have invented). These are made either with Tinta Negra (at least ten years old) or, where stated, traditional white varieties (at least fifteen years old). Most are aged in French oak casks from Seguin Moreau that were previously used for cognac or armagnac for at least eight years previously. Some of the older *frasqueiras* came from the old CVM.

Having never owned any vineyards of their own, Justino's buy in grapes from a variable number of growers according to the year, usually around 800 but up to 1,130. The three-year-old and five-year-old ranges are all subject to *estufagem* in stainless steel. An ever increasing quantity of wine from Tinta Negra as well as the white grape varieties (used only for ten-year-old blends, *colheita* and *frasqueiras*/vintages) is aged at ambient temperatures in wood. At 300 metres above sea level, Justino's have one of the cooler lodges on the island and use solar panels to heat the interior of the *armazens*. Annual evaporation rates can be regulated to between 2 per cent and 5 per cent.

Justino's also produce an increasingly good range of unfortified red, white and rosé wines for the local market under the 'Colombo's' label from grapes like Merlot, Cabernet Sauvignon, Tinta Roriz, Touriga Nacional and Syrah grown at Caniçal.

Justino's Fine Dry

A three-year-old madeira from Tinta Negra: pale amber with fresh appley fruit and a touch of amontillado character, off-dry (40g/l residual sugar), very clean and straightforward. **

Justino's Fine Rich

Mid-deep amber; soft caramelised fruit, raisiny, slightly toasted with a hint of butterscotch. **/***

Justino's 10 Year Old Sercial

Pale to mid-amber; very elegant, lifted aromas with a touch of vanilla and a hint of amontillado; soft in style for a Sercial with vanilla sweetness (45g/l residual sugar), not in any way aggressive. ***/****

Justino's 10 Year Old Bual

Winner of a silver medal at the *Decanter* World Wine Awards in 2013: mid-deep amber/mahogany; attractive high-toned aromas, rich raisin and dried fig fruit; very rich and sweet on the palate, butterscotch, just short of unctuous initially, but offset by zesty, seemingly salty acidity on the finish. ****

Justino's 10 Year Old Malvasia

A silver medal winner at the *Decanter* World Wine Awards in 2014: mid-deep red-tinged mahogany; not very expressive on the nose, touch of mocha and malt, but with good toffee richness underlying; fine, dried fig flavours with lovely richness offset by a streak of acidity on the finish. ***/****

Justino's 1996 Colheita

From Tinta Negra: mid-deep amber/mahogany; not very expressive on the nose, clean toffee-apple character; gently rich with good expression on the palate and a lovely appley finish with a touch of *salgadinho*. Toffee apple all the way through. Another silver medal winner at the *Decanter* World Wine Awards in 2014. ****

Terrantez 'Old Reserve'

A wine that came up from the Carmo in Funchal in 1994, now at least sixty years old: bright orange/amber colour; very clean, floral aromas with a touch of vanilla caramel; soft, savoury character with fresh acidity and a lovely gentle finish. Not particularly complex but very elegant in style. ****

Madeira Wine Company

Rua dos Ferreiros 82, 9000 Funchal, Portugal
Tel. (351) 291 740100
Website: www.madeirawinecompany.com
Opening hours: Monday to Friday, 09.30–18.30; Saturday, 10.00–13.00

Despite being the best-known wine name from Madeira, the Madeira Wine Company (or MWC for short) is a relatively recent creation, although with a long and cumulative history. The company began as the Madeira Wine Association (MWA), formed when three shippers, Hinton, Welsh & Cunha and Henriques & Câmara, joined forces in 1913. Hinton was forced to leave four years later but so many other firms joined in the lean years that followed that for a time the MWA became known as 'the shipper's cemetery'. In 1925 the Blandy and Leacock families amalgamated their wine interests with a Portuguese–Jewish firm called Viuva Abudarham followed by Miles, Lomelino and, eventually, Cossart Gordon in 1953. The Association became an unwieldy body with a huge number of different companies and brand names including Viuva Abudarham Lda., Aguiar Freitas & Ca. Sucrs Lda, Barros Almeida, Bianchi's Madeira Lda., V. Donaldson & Co Lda., F. Martins Caldeira & Co. Lda., F. F. Ferraz & Co Lda., Funchal Wine Co Lda., Luiz Gomes (Vinhos) Lda. Krohn Bros. & Co Lda., Tarquino T. da C. Lomelino, Madeira Victoria & Co Lda., A. Nobrega (Vinhos da Madeira) Lda., A. Pires Scholtz & Co., J. B. Spinola Lda., Power Drury (Wine) Lda., Shortridge Lawton & Co. Lda., C. V. Vasconcelos Lda. and Welsh Bros. (Vinhos) Lda. Ferdinando Bianchi, general manager in the 1960s and early 1970s, recalled that in Germany alone, the Association had seventy agents, each representing a different madeira brand in a different part of the country. In the UK each of the brands was represented by a different distributor, even though many

NOBREGA

Fine MADEIRA wine

SHIPPED BY
A. NOBREGA (Vinhos da Madeira) LDA.
FUNCHAL-MADEIRA
Produce of Portugal

of the wines were coming straight out of the same vat.

The MWA was forced to change direction in the wake of the 25 April Revolution of 1974. During the so-called *verão quente* ('hot summer') of 1975 the newly nationalised banks cut off lines of credit to the company and, for a time, it looked as though it might not be able to pay its workforce. A new executive committee was set up chaired by Anthony Miles, with Richard Blandy and William Leacock each representing their family's interests and the principal shareholders within the Association. Once the political troubles of 1974–5 had been quelled, long-overdue rationalisation began to take place. Reflecting the shareholding and the fact that term 'Association' had no legal meaning in Portugal, the Madeira Wine Association was renamed the Madeira Wine Company in 1981. Depending on the market, by the 1980s the MWC traded in the names of nine companies: Blandy, Cossart Gordon, Ferraz, Freitas Martins, Gomes, Leacock, Lomelino, Miles and Power Drury. This was still too many and proved to be difficult logistically.

After a search for strategic partners, the Blandy family entered into a joint venture with the Symington family of Oporto in 1988. The Symingtons, owners at the time of the Dow, Graham and Warre port houses, eventually took a majority share in the business. Invited into the partnership to secure greater international distribution for the Madeira Wine Company, the Symingtons were profoundly shocked by the poor standard of viticulture and winemaking that they found on the island. With a talented trained oenologist in Francisco Albuquerque, MWC's wines were gradually transformed. By 1997 James Symington was sufficiently confident in the revamped three-, five- and ten-year-old ranges to be able to present them with pride to wine writers and opinion formers in London. The Symingtons came in for a huge amount of criticism, especially on Madeira where they were accused of bringing in outside practices and turning madeira into port wine, but without their technical know-how and long overdue investment, it is doubtful that the MWC would have survived.

The Blandy–Symington partnership worked very successfully for over twenty years. It was a meeting of like minds from two proud family companies. However in 2010, shortly before Blandy's celebrated their bicentenary in Madeira, the Symingtons announced that they wanted to withdraw. Having purchased the assets of Cockburn's in 2006, their madeira interests were becoming a distraction. Consequently the Symingtons sold most of their holding to the Blandys, retaining a small stake in the MWC which helped to guarantee access to the Symington's distribution network (the very reason they became involved in the first place). Having previously worked alongside the Symingtons in Oporto, Christopher Blandy now manages the MWC, bringing in a new era of family involvement.

At the time of writing, the Madeira Wine Company operates from three sites: two in the centre of Funchal and one out east in the Freeport of Caniçal. The company's showpiece *armazens* on the Avenida de Arriaga, the *Adegas de São Fransisco*, date back to the sixteenth century. Originally a monastery, the site was acquired by the Blandy family in 1834 following the dissolution of the religious orders and has now been rebranded as the Blandy Wine Lodge. These atmospheric buildings are the oldest working *armazens* in Madeira and attract over 100,000 visitors a year. Like other traditional *armazens*, the wines are stored on three floors, with the younger wines stored in the attics where the temperature and evaporation rates are highest. The Blandy Wine Lodge has a capacity of 700,000 litres split between demi-johns, lodge pipes and Brazilian satinwood vats containing up to 10,000 litres each.

The second site at Mercês used to belong partly to Miles and partly to Lomelino until these separate family firms joined forces with the then Madeira Wine Association. Built in the 1960s but thoroughly revamped under the Blandy–Symington partnership from the mid-1990s onwards, this is still the company's vinification centre. A recently equipped stainless steel winery has the capacity to produce a million litres of wine a year, mostly by auto-vinification. The MWC relies on grapes from around 500 growers including a new vineyard at Quinta de Santa Luzia in Funchal belonging to Andrew Blandy. The main lodge at Mercês housed concrete *estufas* and storage vats as well as an *armazém de calor*, where wooden lodge pipes were warmed either by heating pipes or by proximity to the *estufas* themselves. Much of the storage at Mercês was in large *balseiros* or vats made from Brazilian satinwood and American oak, which are used to homogenise *lotes* in the final six months before bottling.

In August 2014, the *Via Rapida* (expressway) east of Funchal was closed overnight for a move – lock, stock and barrel – to newly constructed *armazens* at the *Zona Franca* in Caniçal. There is nothing at all romantic about the long single-storey warehouse which is designed as a super-efficient and hygienic 'line in/line out' operation for the majority of madeira wine produced from red grapes. The new stainless steel *estufas* are the most energy efficient on the island, saving an estimated 50 per cent of the energy expended in the past (the water in the jacket is now heated to 72°C rather than 90°C in the old internal 'serpentines', and the tanks and the *armazém* are well insulated – see page 75 for an explanation of *estufagem*). Heated to a temperature of 45°C, the wine in the new *estufas* will lose just 3°C of heat over a period of fifteen days. With a capacity of 700,000 litres, all the wine from the previous year's harvest will have been subject to *estufagem* by February the following year. There are now plans to build a new vinification plant alongside the *armazém* at Caniçal as well as a specialist, small-scale *adega* for white grapes at a location in the vineyards to the west of Funchal.

Although no longer the largest shipper on the island in volume terms (that accolade belongs to Justino's), the Madeira Wine Company is the most famous wine shipper on the island. The much-rationalised company produces a full range of wines under four brand names: Blandy, Cossart Gordon, Leacock and Miles. Of these, Blandy and Cossart Gordon are given the most prominence. All the MWC's three-year-old blends are made from Tinta Negra Mole and are subject to *estufagem*. All other wines are made from the traditional white varieties and are aged in wood. A radical departure from tradition is Blandy's 5 Year Old Alvada, a suave blend of Bual and Malvasia with the influence of new oak (see below). In general terms the MWC's three- and five-year-old blends have improved greatly over the past decade from the time when the wines used to have a distinct *rancio* character. This could still be picked up in some of the ten- and fifteen-year-old blends until the early 2000s, as well as in the occasional dated wine from the 1970s and 1980s. Since the early 2000s, the Madeira Wine Company has been a strong proponent of *colheita* wines and these wines give fine expression to the white, 'classic' grape varieties at a relatively young age. The company's great strength lies in its huge stocks of older *frasqueira* (vintage) wines. On the ground floor of the Blandy Wine Lodge there are small quantities of Bual from the 1920 vintage still waiting to be bottled. At the time of writing the company has sixteen different *frasqueira*/vintage wines on sale dating from 1984 back to the famous 1920.

Although the different brands within the Madeira Wine Company have much in common, some stylistic differences between the wines are maintained. I have therefore separated the four main brands and included a history of each of the firms and the families behind them. Some of the other companies that make up the Madeira Wine Company can be found in Chapter 6 on Historic Wines.

Blandy

Rua dos Ferreiros 82, 9000 Funchal, Portugal
Tel. (351) 291 740100
Website: www.madeirawinecompany.com
Opening hours: Monday to Friday, 09.30–18.30; Saturday, 10.00–13.00

I should open this short profile of Blandy's by repeating the family interest: my wife Katrina is the daughter of the late Richard Blandy who managed the family firm with great dexterity until shortly before his untimely death in 2002 (he is profiled on page 26). The island's Blandy lineage began in 1808 when a young man named John Blandy from Dorset in England set sail for Madeira. For many years it was believed that he came to Madeira as a soldier (it was the time of the Napoleonic Wars), but in 2006 madeira wine specialist Emmanuel Berk uncovered a letter of introduction addressed to Messrs. Newton, Gordon, Murdock & Scott (subsequently Cossart Gordon). It read 'We beg to introduce Mr John Blandy who visits your island on account of ill heath'. Having been briefly employed on the island Blandy sailed back to England in 1810, returning to Madeira (with his brothers Thomas and George) as a married man a year later. He quickly established a successful shipping firm that is so well known on the island today that one could simply write 'the rest is history'! By the time of his death in 1855 John Blandy had a business that was trading from Russia to the Americas.

The company grew rapidly under his son Charles Ridpath Blandy (see page 15) and by the 1870s the company had the largest stock of

wine on the island, amounting to 5,000 pipes. Charles Ridpath Blandy prospered from others' misfortunes, buying up stocks of wine during the oidium epidemic of the early 1850s which finished off many other shippers. By this time Blandy's had diversified into a ship's agency business, coal bunkering as well as general merchants, importing and exporting. The company also began a banking business (at one stage even issuing their own coinage) which survived in family hands until it was sold to the Espirito Santo family in the 1960s. A decade later all Portuguese banks were nationalised.

When phylloxera came to the island in the 1870s Blandy's were sufficiently well stocked with wine to weather the storm. Henry Vizetelly describes the company's *armazens* at the time: 'no fewer than forty stores connected by passages, staircases, platform landings and doorways pierced through massive stone walls.' A flavour of this can still be found by visiting the *Adegas de São Francisco* (now rechristened the Blandy Wine Lodge) on the Avenida de Arriaga in the centre of Funchal.

Under successive generations of the family, Blandy's became one of the most important family firms on the island, expanding further into flour milling and into the local media under John Burden Blandy who also set up a business on Las Palmas in 1886. They even owned their own fleet of small ships by the end of the century. In 1885, John Burden Blandy acquired Quinta do Palheiro, one of Madeira's most stately properties. Bought from the Conde de Carvalhal, it remains in the family and, besides the private house and magnificent formal gardens, there is a hotel (Casa Velha do Palheiro), a golf course and a housing development.

Red Jacket

One of the Blandy family's ships was a former clipper known as *Red Jacket*. It had been launched in 1853 and set a speed record the following year, crossing the Atlantic from New York to Liverpool in thirteen days, one hour and twenty-five minutes. This is a record for a sailing ship that has never been broken. After thirty years' service, *Red Jacket* was sold to Blandy Bros., stripped of her masts and rigging and used as a coal hulk. In a storm on 15 December 1885 the ship was torn from her moorings and was wrecked in heavy seas. Mahogany salvaged from the ship was used to construct the main staircase in the old Blandy offices at no. 20, Rua da Alfandega in Funchal and the staircase at Quinta de Santa Luzia.

The diversity of the Blandy family business left them much less exposed to the vicissitudes of the wine business than other shippers dealing purely in madeira wine. They survived the First World War, increasing their wine sales at a time when other shippers – with previously lucrative exports to Russia, Germany and France – were shut out of the market. One of the Blandy family's most respected and able employees was Tom Mullins who joined the wine shipping firm in 1914. He became the first Managing Director of the Madeira Wine Association in 1925 and, with the Blandy family occupied with their other interests, Mullins effectively ran the wine business until his retirement in 1946.

In 1937 the Blandy family took control of Reid's Hotel, which they received in lieu of a bad debt. The hotel was forced to close three years later but re-opened in 1949 just in time for the visit of Sir Winston and Lady Churchill in January 1950. Local residents lent their furniture to the hotel to make the Churchills more comfortable. At a dinner in the hotel Sir Winston ordered a bottle of Blandy's 1792 Solera, the very wine that had been taken on board HMS *Northumberland* with Napoleon when he was exiled to St Helena in 1815 (see page 197).

The 1974–5 revolution brought radical change to Madeira (see page 23) and challenged the hegemony of all the Anglo-Madeiran families on the island. Although the Blandys had never owned any vineyards they were large property owners in and around Funchal and avoided expropriations by initiating development projects and launching into strategic joint ventures. At a time when many other well-known families fell by the wayside, the Blandys prospered by reinventing themselves. Ultimately this included selling off trophy assets. In 1989 they established a partnership with the Symingtons to run the Madeira Wine Company (see above) and in 1996 sold Reid's Palace Hotel to the Orient Express Group. With tourism growing exponentially the family subsequently became partners in the Porto Bay group of hotels which includes the much newer Cliff Bay Hotel adjacent to Reid's. Since 2001 the company has been chaired by Michael Blandy, representing the sixth generation of the family. In 2011, the year of the company's bicentenary, the family bought back the majority stake in the Madeira Wine Company and since 2012 the MWC has been managed by Christopher Blandy, the seventh generation of the family to be involved in madeira wine.

From extensive tastings I have selected the following wines from the current range as being worthy of note. Vintage wines back to 1811 can be found in Chapter 6.

Blandy's Duke of Clarence, Rich

A bestseller among madeiras and a worthy silver medal winner at the *Decanter* World Wine Awards in 2013: deep mahogany in colour; rich and pruney on the nose with a slightly roasted edge; intensely raisiny on the palate with some depth and weight. Straightforward, long and satisfying, retaining freshness on the finish. ***

Blandy's Alvada 5 Year Old Rich

A radical departure for Madeira, launched in the early 2000s, Alvada is a 50:50 blend of Bual and Malvasia with a touch of new oak, intended as a desert wine. The uncompromising pink and black label is part of its appeal. Mid-deep nut-brown with a tinge of green; lovely lifted aroma with a touch of balsamic and a hint of mocha; fine figgy fruit offset by pronounced acidity. Very smooth, rich and quite seductive in style with a touch of coconut and spice towards the finish. ****

Blandy's 10 Year Old Sercial

Deep gold to pale amber; fine and gentle on the nose with toasted walnuts and brazil nuts, quite complex with a hint of acacia; soft and gentle in style for Sercial, savoury nutty flavours, dry, slightly biscuity with racy acidity on the finish. ***/****

Blandy's 10 Year Old Malmsey

Mid-deep mahogany, green tinge on the rim; rich raisiny aromas with a touch of crème brûlée. Very rich, verging on unctuous initially with dried fig and prune flavours, offset by a fresh counterpoint of acidity on the finish. Very satisfying. ***/****

Blandy Colheita Bual 2002

Bottled in 2014: mid-amber; lovely heady, rich aromas, already quite pungent smoky-sweet; dried fig richness with the tang of thick cut orange marmalade mid-palate and rich tangy finish. ****

Blandy's Colheita Sercial 1998

Representing the first of the new generation of *colheitas* and a silver medal winner at the *Decanter* World Wine Awards in 2014: pale amber/orange; quite restrained on the nose with aromas of orange peel and blossom; a touch of honeyed sweetness initially giving way to a savoury, seductive almost saline off-dry finish. ****

Blandy's 1993 Bual Colheita (Lodge 2, Cask no 14011)

This is Blandy's response to the single cask wines initiated by Barbeito, from numbered casks, the bottles carrying the signature of Michael Blandy: pale green-tinged amber; fine, lifted, incisive aromas, gentle yet quite expressive; fine, bitter-sweet lime marmalade character, pronounced citrus streak but gentle too with a lovely clean finish. Delicious. ****

Cossart Gordon

Rua dos Ferreiros 82, 9000 Funchal, Portugal
Tel. (351) 291 740100
Website: www.madeirawinecompany.com
Opening hours: Monday to Friday, 09.30–18.30; Saturday, 10.00–13.00

Founded in 1747 by Scotsman Francis Newton who was joined by his fellow Scot Thomas Gordon in 1758, Cossart Gordon is the oldest shipper of Madeira wine still in existence (albeit as part of the Madeira Wine

Company). In 1791 another Scotsman named Thomas Murdoch joined the partnership and the firm became Newton, Gordon & Murdoch, as was the custom. The Scottish line was broken by the arrival of William Cossart, an Irishman from a family of Huguenot origin who had been acting for the firm in Ireland and London. He set sail for Madeira in 1802, was captured by the French and finally arrived on the island in 1808. In 1861, with the last Newton and Murdoch having departed, the company took on its present name. The last Gordon, Russell Manners Gordon, left the firm in 1857 when he became the Count of Torre Bella (see page 205) and adopted Portuguese nationality (the statutes of the firm maintained that the partners should be British).

The firm then became the property of Peter Cossart and his five sons. By all accounts the family lived in great style at Quinta do Monte (then known as 'Quinta Cossart'), described as a 'fine house with deer in the park, pheasants in the woods and trout in the stream'. The Cossarts could afford this lifestyle as, by the mid-nineteenth century, Cossart Gordon had established a huge market in North America and was described as shipping 'half the growth of the island'. But the firm continued to be attached to its British roots and retained a branch of the business in London until the 1950s. At the end of the nineteenth century Cossart Gordon expanded into shipping their own brand of port, sherry, Tarragona, Marsala and Malaga as well as representing a number of French producers in the UK. Cossart Gordon suffered greatly from the imposition of prohibition in the US in 1920, and when Noel Cossart (see page 24) took control of the company in 1936 sales were in serious decline. When Blandy and Leacock joined forces within the Madeira Wine Association in 1925 this created a serious competitor for Cossart Gordon and the company struggled to survive. The Second World War inflicted further damage, including to the company's London office at 75 Mark Lane which was destroyed in the 1941 blitz. After the war Cossart Gordon had some success in the North American market, shipping wine in barrel rather than bottle due to the shortage of glass. But when Rutherford & Miles joined the MWA in 1949, Cossart Gordon was left on its own. In 1953 Noel Cossart bowed to the inevitable and took his firm into the Association. He was left with a 7 per cent share of the new company, putting him in a weak position when the Blandy and Leacock families each owned a third. From then on the Cossart Gordon brand lived in the shadow of Blandy's, although it has recently been revived for a series of excellent *colheitas*. Noel's son David continued to represent the company in the UK until the mid-1980s but eventually left the wine trade, and in 1990 the family's shares were sold to the Symingtons.

A full range of wines is still bottled under the Cossart Gordon label, from the three-year-old Good Company to some outstandingly good *colheitas* and *frasqueira* (vintage) wines (see Chapter 6). An *armazém* within the Blandy Wine Lodge is dedicated to Cossart Gordon. The wines, originally destined for the US, were always slightly drier in style than Blandy's, whose main market was the UK. This distinction has been maintained since the two houses were brought under one roof.

Cossart Gordon, Good Company, Rich

Mid-deep amber: soft, smoked fig aromas, rich and raisiny on the palate and spicy with spirit still evident towards the finish. Very similar in style to Blandy's Duke of Clarence, only slightly and almost imperceptibly drier. **/***

Cossart Gordon 1988 Sercial Colheita

An early *colheita* bottled in 2005: pale amber/orange; baked, savoury, toasty nutty aromas; fresh, zesty yet soft savoury flavours. Lovely balance and a fine linear finish, quite expressive of Sercial ***

Cossart Gordon 1995 Colheita Verdelho

Pale amber/orange; pure aromas, tea leaf, dried flowers and tobacco; fine, well defined cognac-like flavours, off-dry, slightly smoky with racy acidity on the finish. Very good indeed. ****

Leacock

Rua Dos Ferreiros 82, 9000 Funchal, Portugal
Tel. (351) 291 740100
Website: www.madeirawinecompany.com
Opening hours: Monday to Friday, 09.30–18.30; Saturday, 10.00–13.00

John Leacock arrived in Madeira in 1741 and, after being apprenticed to a Scottish merchant named John Catanach, established a wine shipping firm with two partners, George Spence and Michael Newlan. The partnership came to an end in 1799 with the death of Michael Newlan. The most famous member of the family was Thomas Slapp Leacock, born in 1817, who had a 13-acre vineyard at Alto de Pico de São João, then on the outskirts of Funchal. Leacock's vineyard was attacked by phylloxera but he went to great lengths to combat the plague (see page 41), and reputedly saved many of the island's traditional grape varieties. However, the family firm suffered from the phylloxera outbreak and Thomas Slapp Leacock's son, John Milburne Leacock, left the island for the Canaries to try and develop the production of wine there. He soon discovered that there was no future for wine but built up a substantial business shipping bananas instead.

Edmond Erskine Leacock, born in 1891, took over the management of the family business in 1908 and continued to control the firm until 1968 when he handed over to his son William. In 1929 the Leacock interests were divided into two: Leacock & Co (Wine) Ltd. and a series of companies, which embraced the manufacture of embroidery, fertilisers and tobacco as well as car distribution. Leacock's built an important market in Scandinavia with a brand named St John after the family's famous vineyard. In 1925 Leacock's pooled their wine resources with the Blandys and joined the then Madeira Wine Association (MWA). Thereafter there was considerable rivalry between the two families which was clearly not conducive to the smooth running of the MWA during its early years. At nearby Cossart Gordon (not yet part of the MWA) there were two dogs that fought each other. One was called 'O Bland' and the other 'Leacock'!

For a time the Leacock family owned a third of the MWA and William Leacock joined Richard Blandy and Anthony Miles in rescuing the company after the 1974–5 revolution. The Blandy family eventually acquired the Leacock's stake in the company. Members of the Leacock family continue to live on the island and their family property, Quinta da Casa Branca, is now a luxury hotel; they no longer have any connection with the wine firm bearing their name. The Leacock brand is still strong in Sweden, a country where Madeira used to be one of the bestselling wines. An *armazém* within the Blandy Wine Lodge is dedicated to Leacock wines.

Leacock St John, Rich

Three year old: mid-deep amber, rich and pruney on the nose and palate, fresh acidity with spirit still quite noticeable on the finish. Straightforward, warming and satisfying. **

Leacock Rainwater

Bright orange/amber in colour; lightly toasted on the nose with a touch of Demerara sugar, not nearly as burnt as in the past; soft light, with appetising toasty flavours and a spicy-peppery finish. **

Miles

Rua dos Ferreiros 82, 9000 Funchal, Portugal
Tel. (351) 291 740100
Website: www.madeirawinecompany.com
Opening hours: Monday to Friday, 09.30–18.30; Saturday, 10.00–13.00

Established in 1814 and, like other shippers, the company was originally known by the names of its partners: Rutherford & Grant followed by Rutherford & Drury. The Rutherfords left the island in the 1870s when the phylloxera epidemic was at its height, leaving the company in the hands of

Henry Price Miles. Miles took over the firm's stocks of wine and agreed, under the name of Rutherford & Miles, to supply Rutherford & Co. in London. The firm would ship all their wine through the Rutherfords in London provided they placed all their international madeira wine business with Miles. Although nothing was ever written down, this gentlemen's agreement survived through generations of both families until Martini Rossi bought Rutherford, Osborne & Perkins in the 1960s. Two of the Rutherford's main UK brands were Old Trinity House and Old Custom House. In 1872 Henry Price Miles established the first brewery on the island which subsequently became known as the 'Atlantic Brewery' and, as the Empresa de Cerveja da Madeira, is still the producer of the main brand of beer on the island, known as Coral. The Miles family continued to run the brewing business until they sold their share in 2004. Their family property was Quinta do Til.

Miles continued to prosper as a madeira shipper until the late 1940s when, under Major Charles Henry Creed Miles, it lost its share of the lucrative Brazilian market and joined the Madeira Wine Association in 1949. At the time this left Cossart Gordon as the only independent British-owned shipper. The company's substantial stocks, then located in the Largo da Saúde adjacent to Lomelino's lodges, became part of the Association. Until 2014, the Madeira Wine Company's bottling hall occupied the site. Anthony Miles remained a director of the MWA until 1989 and helped to steer the company through the challenging times that followed the 1974 Revolution. Miles is the smallest of the four main brands within the Madeira Wine Company. The range is now limited to three- and five- year-old wines, sold on the island. There are no longer any vintage wines bottled under the Miles name, but old bottles under the name Rutherford & Miles sometimes crop up at auction (see page 204).

Miles 5 Year Old, Seco

Deep straw to pale amber; light, gentle savoury nutty-biscuity aromas and flavours with a touch of grapey sweetness. Soft and toasty if a little bland. **

Miles Five Year Old, Doce

Mid-deep amber; slightly singed dried fig aromas; some lovely fig and fruit cake flavours with depth and spice towards the finish. ***

Pereira D'Oliveira

Pereira D'Oliveira (Vinhos) Lda., Rua dos Ferreiros, 107, 9000-082 Funchal
Tel. (351) 291 220784
Email: perolivinhos@hotmail.com
Opening hours: Monday to Friday, 09.00–18.00; Saturday, 9.30–13.00

Founded in 1850 by João Pereira D'Oliveira, D'Oliveira is the second oldest shipper still trading on the island. Like most other Madeira shippers, the company now incorporates a number of other old firms, including Júlio Augusto Cunha Succrs. (dating from 1820), João Joaquim Camacho Succrs., Vasco Luís Pereira Succrs. and Adegas do Torreão (Vinhos) Lda., the later being an old *partidista* bought by the D'Oliveiras in 2001. In 2013 D'Oliveira also bought up Barros e Sousa located next door on the Rua dos Ferreiros (see page 99).

Pereira D'Oliveira is a small company with sales averaging just 150,000 litres a year. It has a wonderful stock of wine in cask, the oldest dating back to the mid-nineteenth century. The wines are bottled under a single brand, D'Oliveira, although it is the company's intention to retain Barros e Sousa. Three brothers, Aníbal, Miguel and Luís Pereira D'Oliveira, represent the fifth generation of the family to run the firm. Aníbal and his son Filipe are responsible for the wine making whilst Luís runs the wine stores and looks after sales and marketing. Since 1911 the company has operated from an old school building dating back to 1619, situated at the bottom of the Rua dos Ferreiros. The family have a number of other *armazens* scattered around the centre of Funchal. There are plans to convert the old Vasco Luís Pereira *armazém* on the Rua Visconde de Anadia in the heart of the city into a new visitor centre.

The D'Oliveira family were well known for their vineyards, owning fourteen small parcels above São Martinho until the 1990s. Like most in the vicinity, these have now been sold for property development and the money was reinvested in *armazens* in the centre of Funchal. The company buys in grapes from 90 to120 growers around the island (mostly Estreito de Câmara de Lobos, São Vicente and Calheta with Sercial from Seixal), and has an *adega* near Camacha where *estufagem* is also carried out. Production varies from year to year: 'Our aim,' according to Luís D'Oliveira, 'is to keep all our casks full,' which stops the wood from drying out. The company carries 1.5 million litres of wine in stock: 'We have never been in a hurry to sell'. Between 70 and 80 per cent of production are Tinta Negra-based wines, all of which are subject to *estufagem*. This includes the three-, five-, ten- and fifteen-year-old ranges. D'Oliveira's main strength is their remarkable stock of old dated wines. Many were absorbed from other companies and between the 1930s and 1970s the wines were only sold on the island. There are wines up to eighty years old still in wood and even older wines in glass demi-johns awaiting bottling. The oldest wine in stock dates back to the company's foundation in 1850. The company has had a somewhat quirky policy as regards *frasqueira* or vintage madeiras, some of which are stencilled '*colheita*' (even though they qualify for vintage status) and, until 2010, others were stencilled '*reserva*'. The D'Oliveiras could never give me a satisfactory explanation for this policy. However Luís D'Oliveira does not believe in using the term '*reserva*' for their five- and ten-year-old wines as the legislation now permits. D'Oliveira's dated wines are often extremely good, characterised by the power and concentration that comes from long cask ageing (see Chapter 6). Many of the older wines share a charming rusticity. Usefully, they generally had the year of bottling on the back label long before others followed suit. These old wines are available to taste by the glass at the company's *armazens* which are popular with Madeira tourists. At the time of writing there are over sixty *colheita/frasqueira* wines for sale from 2002 to 1850, including eight from the nineteenth century. Wines made from Tinta Negra are designated merely as 'Old Wine'.

D'Oliveira's Meio Seco/Medium Dry

A three-year-old wine: mid-golden-amber; spicy but somewhat spirity 'cognac' aromas with a vestige of simple, clean (nothing baked or stewed) grapey fruit; soft, smooth and easy to drink. **

D'Oliveira's Dôce/Sweet

Deep, red-tinged amber; very clean but rather empty on the nose; soft, raisins and sultanas, offset by fresh lemony acidity. **

D'Oliveira's 5 Year Old Seco/Dry

Mid-amber; savoury, slightly casky aromas with much less spirit evident than the three year old; clean, soft, off-dry, simple dusty-biscuity flavours. **

D'Oliveira's 5 Year Old Doce/Sweet

D'Oliveira's bestseller: mid-deep mahogany red; clementine and fruit cake aromas; dried fruit compote and a savoury-sweet, Christmas cake finish with some lingering depth. ***

D'Oliveira's 10 Year Old Doce/Sweet

Mid-deep amber; rich heady, figgy aromas with a touch of *rancio*; fine Christmas cake aromas; rich and concentrated with a lovely fat texture balanced by fresh slightly saline acidity and fine finish. Good. ****

D'Oliveira's 1994 Colheita

A wine bottled in 2014: mid-deep amber; a lovely, expressive smoky-savoury bouquet, complex and appetising with savoury flavours (pretzels) backed by racy acidity and a touch of orange peel with a slightly peaty finish. ****

D'Oliveira's 1988 Colheita Terrantez

A wine bottled in 2003: pale mahogany, green tinge; fragrant, floral and complex, candied fruit and rose petals; not particularly rich but very fine and delicate with ravishing acidity and length. Beautiful wine. ****

6

GREAT (AND SOME NOT SO GREAT) VINTAGE MADEIRAS AND HISTORIC WINES

Nearly every madeira wine worshipper has come to it after having had a Damascene moment. I recall my own quite vividly. I had only been in the wine trade for two years when I attended a pre-sale tasting in October 1986 at Christie's in London for an auction held to commemorate the six-hundredth anniversary of the Treaty of Windsor. Having been told how to spot madeira in a blind tasting by my elders in the trade (the buzz word in those days was the rather unattractive 'synthetic cheese ball' character described on page 73), I suddenly found that there was a great deal more excitement to be found in older vintage madeiras. I was an immediate convert, but the experience left me mystified and struggling for the correct vocabulary to describe the wines. Some of the spellbindingly complex madeira wines that I taste today still leave me lost for words.

A large part of the appreciation of any great wine lies is its depth and mystery, and there are few wines as magical or mysterious as old madeira. The purpose of this chapter is to share information on some of the background to the great wines (dating back to the early eighteenth century) that I have had the opportunity to taste during my career; madeiras that are increasingly sought after by collectors. This section of the book is very far from encyclopedic and there is much here that will always remain a mystery to me and to others. Over the years I have tried to build up a pedigree for some of these wines, including background information on the shippers that made them.

Madeira vintages are not nearly as well documented as port vintages. Until recently, few records of climatic conditions were kept and even fewer of the insightful socio-economic observations that pepper the vintage reports and visitors' books of the port shippers. There are a number of reasons for this. Firstly, unlike port, there is little or no consensus among shippers as to what constitutes, in port terminology, a 'declared' vintage. In any one year there is a wide variation of aspect and altitude to consider as well as the performance of individual grape varieties grown on tiny plots. One shipper may hit on a great Verdelho; another may not. Although terse and succinct, the notes left by the late Noel Cossart and published in his book *Madeira, The Island Wine* reflect this. His notes on individual vintages go back to 1774 but they are no more than one line entries with remarks like 'Sercial fine' or the occasional 'Cama de Lobos and São Martinho good'.

It has to be said that modern records are much more detailed (and the main shippers now file quite detailed vintage reports – see Chapter 3), but when it comes to older vintages much of the information has been lost in the mists of time. At the Madeira Wine Company, for example, there is a whole room full of archives dating back over 200 years. The Blandys have recently employed an archivist to work through them but it will be many years before they are able to piece together the history and pedigree of many of their historic wines. Without the sequential pattern and weight of the unanimous or majority declaration of vintage port, great vintage madeira is much more sporadic and random in nature. In short, it is much more difficult to generalise about vintage madeira than it is, say, for port or bordeaux. This, in my opinion, adds greatly to the magic and occasional sense of awe about individual wines.

This chapter has a historical slant but, with madeira's inbuilt longevity, it is still very much about some of the remarkable wines that are still available in limited quantities today. Small stocks are still held by Madeira families and are drip-fed onto the market. Others appear from country house cellars elsewhere in the world and come to auction, usually in good condition given madeira's near indestructibility. Some shippers on the island also hold substantial stocks of older wine which they release from time to time, often to coincide with significant anniversaries.

NAME AND IDENTITY

The current classification and nomenclature of madeira is covered in Chapter 4 but the means of naming and identifying a bottle of madeira has evolved throughout its history. Consequently the titles affixed to some of the famous old wines defy convention and the rules laid down today. As previously noted, where the shipper and/or grape variety is unknown, the wine may be designated by its geographic origin (e.g. São Martinho, or very occasionally the *quinta*), the name of a ship on which it was transported (e.g. Hurricane, Southern Cross), the country to which the wine was sent (e.g. East India Madeira) or sometimes the name of the customer or collector. Some customers amassed significant collections that have become famous in their own right and which are profiled throughout this chapter.

Madeira is a small island and the same surnames often crop up in different contexts with bewildering frequency. Alongside the historic family brand names that have made Madeira (the islands and the wines) internationally famous, families like Acciaioli, Abudraham, Araújo, Borges, Ferraz, Freitas, Henriques and Lomelino continually crop up in the history of madeira wine. Many of these families were traders and stockholders in their own right, and their wines were absorbed by larger shippers through mergers and acquisitions and then frequently rebranded. Many of the wines listed below undoubtedly came through these families but the records of where they originated have long been lost.

One of the frustrations about tasting older madeira is that there is rarely an accurate record of the bottling date. It is quite possible, indeed probable, for the same wine to have been bottled on a number of different occasions throughout its history. Most shippers now display the date of bottling but this has only been mandatory since 2015. This still leaves generations of older wines without any indication of the date of bottling whatsoever. This gives the prospect of two bottles of ostensibly the same wine being very different, one having been bottled, say, twenty years later than the other. It is for this reason that in the compendium below I have added the date I tasted the wine (although this is not much of a guide). Again I look on this absence of information as part of the mystery and academic fascination of madeira!

Soleras are another challenge. Until 1998 there was no enforcable definition of what constituted a *solera* madeira (see page 88). In his book, *Madeira, the Island Vineyard*, Noel Cossart devotes an entire chapter to historic *soleras* and explains at the outset that these are based on the *lote* system rather than the system of fractional blending that is used to such great effect in Jerez. Cossart dates Madeira's *soleras* to the mid-nineteenth century when shippers, facing acute shortages due to oidium and phylloxera, were forced into blending wines from different years (rather in the same way that the port shippers were forced to blend wines from different quintas to make a house vintage port). There are, however, a number of *soleras* which pre-date this (see notes on Blandy and Cossart Gordon wines below). Noel Cossart goes on to offer a logical definition of how a dated *solera* in Madeira used to work: 'The date indicates the year in which the original wine was actually vintaged. This is called the *vinho madre* or *matriz* (mother wine). When the decision is made to turn a vintage into a *solera*, as it becomes ullaged, the *matriz* is topped up from a back-up *lote* of old wine of the same style, and in turn the back-up is replenished with a blend to suit the style. Usually the *solera* is topped up either when ten per cent down or annually, which ever occurs first, but the figure varies from ten per cent to twenty five per cent.' No doubt this is how a *solera* should work, but there have been many disreputable *soleras* and Cossart singles out those sold pre-war to unsuspecting passengers on liners from *bambotes*, the so-called 'bum-boats' that used to be rowed out to ships in Funchal bay. I suspect these were not the only ones and a number of shippers also pushed the boundaries of credibility. But the fact remains that a good *solera*, no matter how it is put together, is often a wonderful wine with balance and poise like no other (see the story of Blandy's 1811 Solera on page 159). But, for a cautionary tale, see my note on Justino Henriques 1748 Solera on page 189.

CORKS AND RECORKING

It is a fact of life that most madeiras were bottled with short corks, often of poor quality. Due to the shortage of cork on the island (cork trees do not grow on Madeira), many of these were recycled. Francisco Albuquerque, wine maker at the Madeira Wine Company, remembers boiling up previously used corks to sterilise them as a child. Given the prolonged ageing for madeira in cask and demi-john, the cork was thought to be of little significance serving merely as a barrier to foreign objects in the outside world. As madeira is stored with the bottles standing upright, the corks dry out quickly and usually crumble as soon as they are penetrated by a corkscrew. Any bottle of venerable madeira being cellared for any length of time should therefore be recorked roughly every twenty to thirty years. In the case of a few well-cellared wines, the date of recorking is recorded on the bottle (e.g. 1870 São Martinho, bottled 1893, recorked 1953, recorked 1960, rebottled and recorked July 1996). This, however, is the exception rather than the rule. When a wine is recorked I always wonder if there is a temptation to taste a little of the original wine and replace or refresh it with something younger. It may be my suspicious mind at work but, again, perhaps this is just part of the mystery of uncorking an old bottle of madeira. Since 1990, vintage wines from the Madeira Wine Company tend to have longer, top quality corks.

SERVING AND TASTING OLD MADEIRA: A PERSONAL PERSPECTIVE

There are sections on serving and tasting madeira in Chapter 7, but it is worth emphasising a few points specific to older wines here. Nearly all older madeiras benefit from decanting well in advance of serving. As a stoppered glass bottle is a reductive environment for wine to age in, bottle stink can develop which can be hard to shake off. Noel Cossart recommends decanting four to eight hours before serving, but from experience I take the view that to enjoy it to the full, an old madeira should be decanted at least a day beforehand. Cossart does add the sensible caveat that 'the period for allowing an old wine to breathe cannot be overdone in the case of Madeira'. It is likely that there will be a certain amount of sediment at the bottom of the bottle, so pour the wine slowly and carefully into a decanter, separate the sediment back, rinse out the bottle and pour the clean wine back in again. Don't dispose of the sediment – hold it back for cooking!

Even once a wine has been decanted, it is striking how it can change in the glass. At the Blandy's bicentennial tasting held in London in 2011, the wines were decanted off their natural deposit three months previously and rebottled. Served immediately prior to the start of the tasting, they changed and improved noticeably over a period of two to three hours. One wine (Blandy's 1954 Malmsey) which had been showing quite badly at an earlier tasting in San Francisco was much better in London and scored my highest mark. The extended decanting process had helped to rid the wine of the bottle stink that marred the nose in San Francisco three months earlier.

The question of length of time that you can leave a bottle of old madeira opened and on ullage for is one that I have never satisfactorily answered for myself. I regularly uncork old bottles, serve perhaps half at a dinner then put them back in the cellar to help myself to a glass when I feel like it. The bottles sometimes sit there for years, seemingly to no ill effect. Cossart offers no advice on this but Francisco Albuquerque, wine maker for the Madeira Wine Company, believes that 'you can keep a bottle of madeira open for five years if you store it in the dark'. This will give heart to madeira wine drinkers the world over, myself included: you can uncork one of these rare (and expensive) bottles and come back to experience its unique qualities again and again and again. That is something you just can't do with fine (and equally expensive) claret, burgundy or vintage port!

The language of madeira

All tasting notes are to a certain extent synthetic. They serve to convey the character of a wine, either as a useful *aide memoire* to the taster or to an interested observer. The language of tasting has become increasingly florid of late and this, I think renders it increasingly meaningless especially when tasting expressions become too remote from our everyday experience. Madeira requires a completely different tasting vocabulary from other wines. The volatile and oxidiative characteristics which would count as faults elsewhere are positive facets in madeira, provided that the wine is stable and that they are in proportion and under control. In madeira, as in any other wine, balance is everything.

Tasting old madeiras with other *aficionados* and collectors has also made me realise just how much the appreciation of a great wine is a matter of personal taste. One person's 'lifted' or 'high toned' can be another's excessive volatility. 'Ethereal richness' can be interpreted as 'soupy' by someone else (usually me). I look for definition and focus in a wine. The notes that follow are my interpretation, built up from tasting madeiras over a period of nearly thirty years in the wine trade. I have avoided the purple prose increasingly favoured by wine writers but certain expressions recur and these may require some explanation. (A guide to tasting can be found on page 218.) I hope these notes convey the character of the wine as well as a sense of awe and wonder in those wines that truly merit it.

I am not a fan of rating wines by points and eschew the 100-point scale where a wine that scores less than 80 is immediately cast into outer oblivion (whereas 80 is thought of as a rather good pass mark in most exams). There are no absolutes in tasting, and my feeling is that there is no such thing as perfection so I would never award 100 points! In my own tasting notes I use an arcane code of ticks and crosses that I picked up from my years in the tasting room at The Wine Society in England. I have converted these into broad star ratings based on the following criteria, as in the previous chapter, I have written the equivalent marks out of twenty in brackets.

***** an outstandingly beautiful wine, one that leaves you with a sense of awe and wonder (19-20)

**** an excellent wine in its class, highly recommended for its beauty, depth and articulacy (17-18)

*** a good wine with much to recommend it (15-16)

** an enjoyable but simple and straightforward wine (13-14)

* a very ordinary wine without faults but no great merit (10-12)

No star: disagreeable (8-10) or faulty (below 8)

NB: a +? signifies that a doubt exists in my own mind - where, for instance, a wine might have scored better if it had been adequately decanted and would improve on ullage.

Where I have tasted the wines on more than one occasion I have included all my notes. Given that the bottling date of one bottle may be different from another, it is quite possible to have two different notes on what is ostensibly the same wine (see above). Where the bottling date is known, I have included the information as well as any background material which helps to establish the pedigree of the wine. Many of the wines below have been shown at tastings in London and New York. I am especially grateful to Patrick Grubb MW for sharing so many great and often unique wines at his annual tastings in London between 1998 and 2013. I also acknowledge the work of Emmanuel Berk and Roy Hersh in setting up a series of tastings in New York ('Velhissmo Verdelho' in 2013 and 'The Beauty of Bual' in 2014) as well as their research into some of the wines. Other notes come from pre-sale tastings at Christie's, wines shown by individual shippers and bottles shared with friends, some from my own cellar.

The wines below are listed under the headings of producer (or the collector where the wine is known by this name) rather than by date. Some of the shippers have gone out of business long ago but I have included relevant background information on them where possible. There are also sub-sections on significant collectors and historic collections, many of which have now been dispersed.

THE COLLECTIONS

Viuva Abudarham

José Abudarham arrived in Madeira in the second quarter of the nineteenth century. He had dual nationality: English and French. He established himself as a general trader and became a shipping agent and money lender. In 1860 he set up as a wine trader with stores near the old Funchal Post Office, close to Cossart Gordon. His trade was in bottled wines, principally with Germany and France. Following his death in 1869 the company was inherited by his widow (*viuva*), hence the name Viuva Abudarham & Sons. The company then moved into the former Post Office. The Abudarhams' considerable interests on the island were built up by Jacob Abudarham who founded the *Companhia de Seguros Aliança Madeirense.* But following his early death in 1903 his only daughter sold Viuva Abudarham to her husband António Bettencourt de Câmara and business partner António Justino de Freitas. The wine company joined the Madeira Wine Association alongside Blandy and Leacock in 1925.

Acciaioli ('Acciaioly')

The Acciaiolis were a noble family originating from Florence, with Guigliarello, a descendant of the Dukes of Burgundy, recorded as having lived there in 1181. Two centuries later, Remeiro Acciaioli had many titles conferred on him including that of Duke of Athens; Laudomia Acciaioli married Pier Francisco de Medici in 1462 and their great-great-granddaughter married King Charles I of England. Simon Acciaioli arrived in Madeira from Florence in 1505 and it is said by the family that he brought Malvasia Babosa vines from the Greek islands. The Madeira branch of the family entered the wine business and made their market in Scandinavia, receiving a royal warrant from HM King Gustav Adolf VI of Sweden (1950–1973).

The Acciaioli business failed in the 1950s. When Oscar Gil Borges Acciaioli died in 1979 his cellar in Funchal was split between his second wife (who sold them to Mario Barbeito) and his two sons Michael and David, one living in England, the other in North America. A large amount of bottled 'Acciaioly' wine was bought by Manuela de Freitas of Barbeito in the late 1980s. The bottles were decanted into demi-johns for aeration and given a light filtration before being rebottled, the original bottles having been rinsed with sand to remove the crust. The wines were shipped to London in the autumn of 1988 and sold in a remarkable sale at Christie's in June 1989. I have notes from the pre-sale tasting and a subsequent tasting in 2013. Given the large quantities that were sold in 1989 (flooding the market and reducing the price), bottles labelled 'Oscar Acciaioly' are still around and return from time to time at auction.

Oscar's Verdelho Special Reserve 1839 / Dry

A 'generally very good' vintage, records Noel Cossart: mid-amber, wonderful high-toned, slightly singed aromas, rich spicy-raisiny flavour initially leading to long and rather drier finish (but certainly not 'dry' as stated on the label), ****. Second note from the Velhissimo Verdelho Tasting in New York (spring 2013): tasting mid-deep mahogany, thin green rim; lovely, lifted leafy aromas, green leaves with a touch of toffee apple; sweet initially, greengage fruit, rich and intense with wonderful texture and length, fresh citrus finish with a touch of butterscotch. Verdelho in a rich and rather atypical style: 'slutty' according to one of my fellow tasters at the time! ****

Oscar's Boal Special Reserve 1837

From a 'very good' vintage, 'especially Malmsey' notes Noel Cossart; 210 bottles of this wine came to auction in 1989. Two notes: mid-amber colour with glorious, lifted, warm aromas; crisp and beautifully balanced with a lovely tang lingering on to the finish. Among the best of the range of Acciaioli wines to come to auction, *****. From Patrick Grubb's 1998 tasting: quite pale-to-mid amber; compost heap meets honeysuckle on the nose, tastes similar with remarkable green, leafy complexity, an extraordinary wine that somehow works! ****/*****

Oscar's Malmsey 1836

One rather sketchy note on this from the pre-sale tasting when 227 bottles of this wine came to auction at Christie's, London in 1989: mid-deep amber colour; rather overpowering earthy and peaty on the nose (possibly bottle stink due to inadequate decanting); very rich, round, sweet and spicy, with a long, warm, slightly earthy-malty finish. ***/****

Oscar's Special Reserve Terrantez 1832

There were as many as 243 bottles of this wine divided into twenty-six lots at the 1989 sale. I was less impressed by this wine at the time: mid-mahogany, green-tinged rim; perfumed, distinctly high toned, just stopping short of volatile and looking much less fresh than the 1802 (below); quite gentle, medium-rich yet quite austere and a little unbalanced but still very fresh and distinctively Terrantez, ***. Second note, rather more positive, from 2002: mid-mahogany; perfumed, gentle floral aromas, not especially pungent, typically Terrantez, very dry, but elegant and fresh with supreme elegance. ****

Oscar's Terrantez Special Reserve 1802

Ninety-nine bottles of this wine were sold at Christie's at one sale in 1989: mid-amber with olive green rim; ethereal, fragrant and high-toned bouquet, rich, crystalised fruits offset by beautiful, rapier-like acidity and a long searing finish. Great poise and precision. Given its age, the rarity of Terrantez and its undisputed quality, this is now one of the world's most sought-after madeiras. *****

'Especial' Old Malmsey

A wine that was never marketed by Oscar Acciaioli but kept for entertaining at home. The age of this wine was unknown when eighteen bottles came to auction in 1989, a rather sketchy note as follows: mid-deep amber, olive-green rim; very rich and concentrated, almost chocolatey in its intensity, full yet refined with a lasting citrusy tang that offset the richness. ****

João Carlos Aguiar

Diogo Afonso de Aguiar was sent to Madeira by King Afonso V to marry one of the daughters of João Gonçalves Zarco. The family became prominent in Câmara de Lobos where João Carlos Aguiar was a producer in the eighteenth century. J. C. Aguiar & Co. was also a *partidista* who supplied the major shippers into the early years of the twentieth century.

J. C. A. & Co. 1795 Velhissimo

Believed to be Terrantez from Ferraz, bottled in 1931, this wine tasted at Patrick Grubb's tasting in 2005: mid-amber; subdued and rather stewed on the nose with the smell of an old archive; quite rich with fine acidity, burnt toast leading to a rather musty finish. **/***

J. C. A. & Cia. 1795 Velhissima Moscatel

From a burgundy-shaped bottle, circa 1840: deep, reddish mahogany; powerful, rich with an unusual hint of chocolate on the nose; big rich, sweet chocolate and toffee flavours, so powerful and concentrated as to make this the essence of Muscat with a lovely pruney depth and a savoury leathery finish that goes on and on. A fantastic oddity. ****/*****

Araújo

The Araújo family came to Madeira from mainland Portugal at the end of the fifteenth century (there are also Araújos involved with wine in northern Portugal), and their descendants are living and working on the island today. They own vineyards at Jardim da Serra and Estreito de Câmara de Lobos, and produce very fine Sercial and Verdelho. The family continue to farm at Quinta do Jardim da Serra, having once owned Consul Veitch's old country residence. The family has a shareholding in H. M. Borges and are related to Manuela de Freitas at Barbeito. The Araújos also hold stocks of old wine.

Araújo de Barros 1895 Verdelho

From Prazeres on the south side of the island, bottled in 1949 and rebottled in 1973 and 1998: mid-deep amber, sings from the glass with a lovely, lifted leafy character, classically Verdelho; very fine, pure and crisp, clean and steely with racy acidity and a relatively dry, long finish. Delicious and remarkable for its age. *****

Quinta Araújo de Barros 1891 Sercial

Recorded as being from the Prazeres district above Jardim do Mar on the south west side of the island. Two quite similar notes, the first on a wine that was in cask for 58 years before bottling: mid-amber; rich and not very expressive on the nose, singed around the edges; fine, mature with rapier-like acidity, austerely dry on the finish with a distinctly rustic / peaty finish, **. The second from a tasting in 2008, wine labelled 'Sercial 1891, Reverta, Prazeyres. José Gomes Henriques Araújo': mid-deep amber; fine, floral, expressive high-toned aromas; caramelised, casky flavours, bone dry, rustic but quite powerful in style. The acidity is searing rather than steely and the finish rather coarse and woody. ***

Sercial 1790 (Araújo Family)

From the private reserves of the Araújo family, tasted at Patrick Grubb's annual tasting in 2009: mid-nut brown/mahogany, olive tinge; fragrant and delicate, very fresh, floral (jasmine) aromas, very fine; dry, savoury, nutty character (brazil nuts and almonds), very delicate, the wine plays on the tongue, crystalised fruits (Elvas plums) on the finish. A remarkable wine for its age. *****

Avery

In the 1950s and 1960s, the British wine merchant Avery's of Bristol was a rich source of old madeira from a stock built up by Ronald Avery. Most of the wines are believed to have come from the then Madeira Wine Association and the estate of Sir Stephen Gaselee (see page 177).

Avery's Verdelho Reserva Velhissima, Visconde Val Pariso circa 1846

Tasted in New York in 2013; mid-amber, thin green-tinged rim; gentle, lifted although not especially expressive on the nose, just a touch beefy;

firm and spicy, peppery even, very clean and quite powerful with a fine focused linear finish and the merest touch of cask, a very beautiful wine, just a touch savoury though perhaps drying out. (See note on Val Pariso on page 208.) ****

Avery's Verdelho 1838

This wine probably originated from the collector Sir Stephen Gaselee. André Simon wrote that 'some of the Madeira notables sold to Gaselee some priceless wines which they would not have let any wine-merchant buy for sacks of gold'. This wine, tasted along with other old Verdelhos in March 2013, lives up to its billing: mid-deep mahogany, reddish glint, thin green-tinged rim; not as pungent as some of the wines here, savoury bouillon nose, fine and well defined, savoury – toasty character, caramelised nuts, leading to a deliciously savoury finish. Very, very fine, finishes beautifully. *****

Avery's Verdelho 1822

Possibly a *solera*: most of Avery's 1822 Verdelho was labelled '*solera*' but some were not. This bottle is one of the few where the label does not say '*solera*' although the bottle is newish, suggesting it was bottled in Bristol in the 1950s: mid-deep amber with a green-tinged rim; fine savoury aromas, beef consommé (this wine demands it!); soft and savoury, yes this is beefy yet gentle and delicious, not much depth but a lovely, gentle old wine. ****

Barbeito

The madeira shipper Barbeito is profiled in detail on page 93. Although the company was only founded in 1948, Mario Barbeito Vaconcelos bought in old wines (including those of the late Oscar Acciaioli) and bottled them under the company name. Some of the founding wines are listed here. In the 1950s the family used to own a vineyard called Jardim do Sol, at Caniço, east of Funchal.

Barbeito 1992 Sercial

From Ricardo Diogo's first vintage in charge, a thousand bottles filled in 2011 with no more to follow: pale amber; lovely appetising, saline character, salted nuts and pretzels, very fine and delicate in style, characteristically Sercial but not too austere with some richness and sweetness (58g/l residual sugar) towards a savoury finish. ****

Barbeito 1992 Boal

Bottled June 2013, tasted in 2015: mid-amber; rich but lifted butterscotch and caramelised citrus aromas; full and mellifluous, dense with *marmelada* (quince jelly) richness and a long tangy finish. ****

Barbeito 1992 Verdelho

A wine bottled in 2013, tasted most recently in 2015: mid-amber/orange; lovely, gentle savoury-smoky aromas, a touch of bonfire; again very gentle on the palate, toasty-savoury character with very pure dried apricot fruit lingering on the finish. Still a relative youngster, there is still more ageing in pipe still to bottle. ****

Barbeito 1988 Sercial

Bottled in 2003, tasted in April the same year: mid-amber/orange; high toned, slightly rubbery initially (though this disappears after an hour in the glass), porridge and honey on the nose; dry but not over austere (1.4° Baumé), caramelised oranges offset by clean, steely Sercial finish. ****

Barbeito 1982 Boal

Bottled May 2007, tasted October the same year: pale amber; fine and focused if slightly singed on the nose; clean, quite delicate with savoury-spicy length, ***. Second bottling in February 2012, the wine having returned to oak from demi-john in June 2007 and kept at warm temperatures in Câmara de Lobos with evaporation at 8 per cent per year: mid-deep amber, slightly turbid; roasted, high-toned aromas, almost *vinagrinho* (1.62 g/l volatile acidity); very rich and concentrated, quite sweet for Boal, rather lacking in focus and verging on soupy, just about redeemed by powerful acidity towards a rather burnt finish. **/***

Barbeito 1981 Verdelho

Tasted in 2005: pale amber; fine high-toned aromas, sings from the glass; bitter-sweet fruit, greengage freshness with the concentration of dried apricots, great poise. A really lovely wine. ****

Barbeito 1978 Sercial

Bottled January 2011 and tasted in April 2011: pale-mid amber, slight green tinge; very expressive on the nose, aromatic, fine, meadow flowers and grass, lifted and slightly smoky; deliciously pure and delicate, not austere at all (1.2° Baumé), a touch savoury-smoky with great poise and expression on the finish. ****

Barbeito 1978 Verdelho

Aged in oak from February 1979 until October 2001 when it was transferred to glass demi-johns before bottling in March 2001; 1,493 bottles in total. Tasted in 2002 and again in 2014: very genuine mid-amber hue with green-tinged rim; quite subdued with slightly caramelised aromas and a bonfire of autumn leaves underneath; soft and slightly smoked initially, dried apricot richness offset by fresh acidity rising in the mouth leading to a smoky-flinty finish. ***/****

Barbeito Boal 1978

Bottled June 2007, tasted October 2007: mid-orange/amber; lovely, caramelised oranges, very pure and clean, spicy marmalade flavours, seemingly quite dry and delicate for a Boal, ****. Second bottling from January 2011: pale mahogany; apple, toffee and bonfire, lovely concentration and depth, rich and quite powerful, savoury-sweetness offset acidity on an explosive finish which is just a touch casky. ****

Barbeito Boal 1957

A wine from Jardim do Sol in Caniço, tasted in 2005: pale-mid mahogany, rich but subdued on toffee-apple nose; singed fruit, bitter-sweet caramelised apples and allspice, good bitter-sweet length of flavour. ****

Barbeito 1954 Moscatel

From Patrick Grubb's 1998 tasting, a rare Moscatel: musty but scented on the nose, unusual charred-smoky flavours, not all that sweet, rich and well balanced. ***

Barbeito 1950 Malvazia

Tasted in 2008: amber/mahogany, lovely rich raisins and dried figs on the nose; fine and concentrated, peppery, spicy and rich, quite spirity but with fine figgy length. ***/****

Barbeito 1947 Verdelho

Note from Patrick Grubb's tasting in 2007: red-tinged amber; quite subdued and slightly caramelised on the nose; lovely pure, gentle, green-leaf flavours, long and fresh with a touch of lapsang suchong tea. ***/****

Barbeito 1946 Malvazia

A note from Patrick Grubb's 1998 tasting: dried fruit compote, figs, dates and raisins, lovely texture and depth with the richness offset by fresh, nervy acidity. Very fine. ****/*****

Barbeito 1920 Malvazia

From a magnificent vintage, 'especially for Malmsey' notes Noel Cossart; tasted with Ricardo Diogo in April 2011: very deep mahogany; stunning aroma, beautifully perfumed, lifted, leafy and expressive; rich, sweet, intensely so (6.3° Baumé), quite powerful and concentrated as a result but the richness is off-set by oh-so-fine steely acidity. This has everything going for it and is so beautiful on the finish that it made my eyes water! *****

Barbeito 1916 Malvazia

One of the first wines bought by Mario Barbeito, tasted at Patrick Grubb's annual tasting in 2009: mid-deep mahogany, olive-green rim; very pungent, rich, baked but slightly coarse in the context of a very fine line up of madeiras at the time: rich and caramelised on the palate, the richness offset by citrusy acidity, savoury-sweet length. Very satisfying. ***

Barbeito 1914 Malvazia

From Quinta de Piedade, a vineyard belonging to the Vasconcellos family in Jardim do Mar on the island's south coast. This wine tasted at Patrick Grubb's tasting in 2005: deep mahogany; rich but rather casky on the nose, singed fruit with a touch of molasses; rich and unusually unctuous on the palate, pruney fruit, quite impressive if a little rustic in style. ***

Barbeito 1895 Verdelho

At Patrick Grubb's tasting in 2008: mid-red-tinged mahogany; fine, savoury toasted character, toasted almonds and cashews; very fine, well poised, lime and lemon marmalade, great finesse, very clean with lovely nervy, fruity acidity. Remarkably fresh. Fantastic. ****/*****

Barbeito 1895 Boal

At Patrick Grubb's 2008 tasting: mid-amber; unusual dusty smell, redolent of dog biscuits, meaty but not terribly expressive (possibly bottle stink); much fresher on the palate, lovely medium rich quince marmalade flavours with nutty-savoury complexity, lovely length and purity despite the strange nose. Would it have been better with longer decanting time? ***

Barbeito 1875 Malvazia

One of the first wines bought by Mario Barbeito, at the same tasting in 2008: mid-deep amber; pungent, rich and quite expressive on the nose; prune and fig with a distinct tawny marmalade tang, sweetness offset by fine, fresh zesty acidity. Good balance, and poise. Overall very fine indeed. ****

Barbeito 1870 Boal RV

This is a wine from Teresa and Ricardo Vasconcellos, who were originally sugar-cane producers in Jardim do Mar where the family owned a small vineyard called Quinta de Piedade. It was acquired by Ricardo Freitas of Barbeito in demi-john in 2008. It was returned to cask for a few months before being bottled in the autumn of 2008. It was one of the last wines that Ricardo worked with in the old Barbeito wine lodge between Reid's and the Cliff Bay Hotels before it was demolished. Tasted in New York in 2014: rather cloudy and muddy in colour, thin green rim; stewed (singed), soupy aromas with a touch of Bovril, others said 'soy sauce'; quite rich, certainly better on the palate than on the nose but still rather soft and soupy in style (banana toffee) with some fresh grassy acidity on the finish. Balanced but just not my style of wine. **

Barbeito 1870 Sercial RV

From Quinta de Piedade (see note above), a small but successful vintage immediately prior to phylloxera, tasted in 2007: mid-reddish amber; smouldering leaves with roasted almonds both on the nose and the palate, some richness offset by brisk acidity. Beautifully balanced. ****

Barbeito 1863 Boal

There are many different bottlings of this wine, spanning half a century. It was part of Mario Barbeito's initial stock when he founded the eponymous company in the 1940s (along with 1795 Terrantez, 1834 Malvasia and 1863 Boal). This particular bottle, tasted in New York in 2014, was imported by the Rare Wine Company, Sonoma, in the late 1990s having been bottled in 1991 or 1992: mid-deep amber/mahogany; slightly sour nose initially, not unattractive and this began to disappear in the glass, delicate, quite complex with toasty-savoury undertones; lovely rich intensely powerful figgy flavours, almost syrup of figs but just stops short, aided by fresh acidity. Very long and fine, with great definition. ****

Barbeito 1856 Bual

A rarity, coming so soon after the outbreak of oidium. This bottle (tasted in New York in 2014) originated from Mario Barbeito who bottled some of the wine in the 1970s though this may come from a later date: deep, slightly cloudy mahogany, very strange dank aromas ('cockroaches' according to Ricardo Diogo Freitas!) and an equally strange saline taste (iodine?). Lead pencils. Burnt and concentrated. Badly flawed. No stars.

Barbeito 1837 Boal

Ricardo Diogo Freitas of Barbeito believes that this wine may be the same as the Acciaioly 1837 (see above) since his family did the decanting, airing and rebottling of these wines in the late 1980s. On tasting it in 2014 however I gave it a rather lower mark: mid-deep red-tinged amber/mahogany; not very expressive on the nose, a touch of toffee but surprisingly flat, even dull; not that rich, soft and rather simple initially, builds mid-palate, mellifluous, leading to a fine, gentle finish. Fresh and elegant, ***/****. Another, tasted in 2015 with Ricardo Diogo, decanted for approximately two weeks beforehand: much more expressive on the nose, torrefaction with a touch of mocha, toffee and thick-cut marmalade, followed up by crystalised fruit and a delightful bitter-sweet finish. Beautiful concentration. Very fine. (****/*****)

Barbeito 1826 Sercial

A 'generally fine vintage, Sercial especially', notes Noel Cossart. Tasted in 2005: pale-to-mid amber; lovely fresh green grassy fruit with just a touch of butterscotch; crisp and leafy on the palate with a lovely dry, delicate finish. ****

Barbeito 1802 Boal

From Ricardo Diogo Freitas' family collection, tasted in New York in 2014. I thought that this might be the same wine as the one below, but it isn't. Quite rare with very few bottles of 1802 Boal having appeared at auction: mid-deep amber honey and raisins on the nose with the merest touch of rubber, quite open and expressive; sweet, rich and mellifluous in style (herbal, touch of dill), harmonious, still very much alive and kicking. Sweet and delicate in the finish with great length and poise. ****/*****

MBV 1802 Boal

Tasted in 2011 at Patrick Grubb's annual tasting, bottled in 2011 from a demi-john in the private stock of the late Mario Barbeito Vasconcelos, whose monogram seal is impressed on the wax capsule. Deep amber, green-tinged rim; pungent *rancio* nose, powerful, aggressive, a touch of washing powder (!) perfume; rich but coarse burnt flavours, again powerful on the palate, fierce and austere, not that pleasurable but admirable. ***

Barbeito 1795 Terrantez

This wine came from the Hinton family to Mario Barbeito via Oscar Acciaioli (see above). I have tasted it on a number of occasions, most recently at a tasting hosted by Patrick Grubb in London in 2005. Barbeito still carry a small stock and occasionally release bottles for auction. This wine was bottled in the mid-1980s from demi-john by Mario Barbeito, the late father of Ricardo Diogo Freitas. In his book *Vintage Wine*, Michael Broadbent speculates as to whether it is a *solera* but Ricardo Diogo assures me that it is not. Amber/mahogany in colour; fine, gentle, slightly smoked-singed aromas, green tea, jasmine and a touch of lapsang suchong; fabulous concentration, crisp, almost searing acidity keeping the wine alive, clean, penetrating crystalised fruit flavours and a peacock's tail of a finish. An outstanding old wine. I tasted this wine again in 2015 from a bottle belonging to Manuela de Freitas Barbeito that had been open for twenty years and forgotten – still extraordinary in its depth and concentration. This wine is truly indestructible! *****

Barros e Sousa

Now in the ownership of Pereira D'Oliveira, Barros e Sousa (see pages 98 and 124) had sold off many of their old wines in the 1980s and 1990s and had very little stock as a result. However, some magnificent older bottles still turn up for sale, most recently in London through Patrick Grubb. Not technically a shipper, recent wines can be identified by the initials of the founder, Artur Barros e Sousa (ABSL) stencilled on the bottle.

ABSL, Terrantez 1980

Tasted in situ in the atmospheric Barros e Sousa *armazém* in 2004 and again from my cellar in 2014, a wine bottled in 1999: burnt umber to gold in colour; fine, perfumed, floral aroma, typical of Terrantez, with a touch of toffee; fine and sinewy, candied orange peel with a lovely streak of citrusy acidity to balance the texture and concentration. Very fine, seemingly bone dry and with great poise. ****

Barros e Sousa, Verdelho, Porto Santo n/v

There was no date on this wine (tasted with Patrick Grubb in 2013) but the design of the label places the bottling date sometime in the 1930s or 1940s. Before the airport was built on the island, Porto Santo had plenty of vineyards and the Barros family were large owners. This is the only Verdelho that I have ever seen from the island, the most commonly planted grape being Listrão (see page 51). This wine is notable for its comparable lack of acidity: mid-amber with a touch of mahogany; a rather coarse, meaty nose, a touch of Bovril; savoury, rich and full with good weight and texture but without much finesse. Beef stock flavours right the way through to the finish. Fascinating wine, difficult to mark as there is not much to compare it against but not a very pleasant drink.

Bygone Madeira: traditional pressing in a *lagar* (see pages 66–9 for a description).

Above (l): Stainless steel *estufas* at the Madeira Wine Company's new *armazens* at Caniçal.

Above (r): Wine ageing on *canteiro* at Barbeito's new *armazens* above Estreito de Câmara de Lobos.

Below: A *canteiro* in an artificially heated *armazém de calor*.

Above: Sotão de Amêndoa or 'Almond Attic': the warm upper floor of the Blandy Wine Lodge in the centre of Funchal.

Below: Bottles of 'vintage' madeira ageing upright in the *frasqueira* room at the Blandy Wine Lodge.

The old and the new: Blandy's 200-year-old Adega de São Francisco in Funchal (above). Barbeito's new *adega* and *armazém* located at the Parque Empresarial de Câmara de Lobos (below).

ABS Barros e Sousa 1880 Madeira Velho

From Patrick Grubb's tasting in 2013: slightly cloudy, pale-to-mid amber, subdued savoury aromas with pruney fruit underneath; rich and spicy initially, tawny marmalade character, slightly burnt and bitter sweet and astringent on the finish, not especially long, falls away on the finish. ***

PJL Barros e Sousa 1880 Boal

At the same tasting in 2013: mid-amber; lovely expressive aromas, pungent, dried figs and apricots, lifted and rich with a touch of marmalade; long, rich dried apricot fruit with a citrusy streak of acidity running all the way through, very sweet yet gentle with an almost mellifluous finish. ****

Barros e Sousa 1890 Boal

At the same tasting in 2013: mid-deep orange/amber; not quite so expressive, singed leaves, autumnal nose; medium-rich tawny marmalade character with a bitter sweet twist of orange peel towards the finish, long and pure. Very fine. **** / *****

Barros e Sousa 1860 Old Reserve

Tasted in 2013: mid-deep amber; rather a soggy, soupy nose, musty and not terribly attractive – a longer decanting time may have helped; tastes much better with a marmalade tang, pure and lean mid-palate, orange peel, extending on to the finish. Let down by the nose. *** +?

Blandy

The family shipping firm of Blandy is profiled at length on pages 115–119. Ever since Charles Ridpath Blandy's profligate buying spree in the 1850s, the Blandys have maintained substantial stocks of old wines, buying up more wine as other shippers fell on hard times. In an extensive and rather enviable tasting, Vizetelly describes some of the wines he found at the Blandy wine lodge during his visit in the autumn of 1877: a *solera* from 1792 (predating the founding of Blandy Bros. by nineteen years), 'a fine old concentrated wine from the Torre Bella vineyard'. Was this the same wine that had been shipped to St Helena with Napoleon in 1815 and was subsequently drunk by Sir Winston Churchill in 1950 (see page 197)? Vizetelly also tasted 'a remarkable

Sercial, vintaged half a century ago, and today emitting a wonderful aroma, and having a marked though pleasant pungent flavour'. During the first twenty years of its life this wine, we are told, 'was far too harsh to be at all palatable'. He also singles out certain 'growths' which had been kept separate, from Porto da Cruz and Ponta Delgado (sic) on the north side of the island and an 1870 from São Martinho ('an excellent wine of medium dryness' – see my note on the 1879 on page 179). Another São Martinho Verdelho 'already half a century old' is described as 'boasting a wonderful perfume … one of the most perfect old Madeiras we ever tasted'. It seems Blandy's was ever thus and, thanks to careful family custodianship through seven generations, the company can still claim to have some of the best and oldest stocks on the island today held in wood, in demi-john and in bottle. A large number of wines were brought out for the company's bicentennial in 2011 when commemorative tastings were held in both San Francisco and London. I was fortunate to taste all these wines in Funchal prior to these events. In 2014 Blandy's also bottled a number of old wines from demi-johns, specifically for auction at Christie's in London. Sealed with red wax, these became known as the 'Blandy's Demi-john Collection'.

Blandy 1988 Malmsey

Winner of the International Fortified Trophy at the *Decanter* World Wine Awards 2014. Just 1,589 bottles filled in 2013: mid-deep amber/mahogany; fine, expressive, gently high-toned aromas, a touch of *rancio* with obvious cask age and intensity; wonderfully figgy, raisiny richness perfectly offset by lime-citrus acidity. This has focus, power and concentration and finishes with great poise. ****

INTERIOR OF THE ARMAZENS OF MESSRS. BLANDY BROTHERS AT FUNCHAL, MADEIRA.

Blandy 1985 Malmsey

Bottled 2009, tasted in 2011: pale green-tinged mahogany; expressive but slightly stewed, pruney aromas with a touch of cheese-ball *rancio* (it belongs to *that* generation of madeira wine); lovely concentration of flavour, very forward and quite evolved for its age, figgy, pruney depth with lovely texture mid-palate and steely acidity working its way through on a clean finish. Very good but rather let down by the nose. ***

Blandy 1984 Verdelho

Tasted in 2005: pale amber/mahogany; attractive raisiny aromas, a touch of old-fashioned *rancio* and perhaps a bit simple for a wine of this age; lovely figgy fruit flavours with good weight and texture. Much cleaner on the palate with good length and depth. *** / ****

Blandy 1978 Malmsey

Tasted at the MWC in 2004, a wine bottled in 2000: mid-mahogany; lifted and perfumed, floral with a touch of tawny marmalade; rich, Elvas plums, lovely fat texture with the richness offset by zesty acidity. ****

Blandy 1977 Verdelho

Tasted in 2006, a wine bottled in 2004: mid-amber, attractive smoky aromas, singed autumnal leaves; fine, clean and savoury-sweet, figgy richness mid-offset by bracing acidity, clean green tea finish. *** / ****

Blandy 1976 Terrantez

Bottled in 1997, made from some of the last historic Terrantez before the variety became temporarily commercially extinct. Tasted in 2011: mid-mahogany, green rim; high-toned, savoury-smoky aromas, toast and wood-smoke and a touch of varnish; lovely, characteristically bitter-sweet fruit, very clean with apple and citrus acidity, something almost burgundian about this wine's gentleness and finesse, ****. A second note from the *Decanter* World Wine Awards in 2014: rich, caramelised and rather soupy on the nose, even a touch of molasses; very rich and powerfully concentrated, syrup of figs offset by fresh acidity. ***/****

Blandy 1976 Malmsey

Shown at Patrick Grubb's 1998 tasting: rather burnt, stewed, rancid aromas; soft, raisiny, sweet and figgy, a bit over-balanced and lacking acidity, **. Second note from a tasting at the MWC in 2005: mid-mahogany, rather cheesy, rancid nose, raisins and molasses too; much better on the palate with figgy fruit, dates and spice, raisiny length. **/***

Blandy 1975 Terrantez

Tasted twice, each time at the MWC in 2004 and 2007, a wine bottled in 2004: pale to mid-mahogany; not very expressive on the nose, touch caramelised; fine off-dry with spicy acidity, bitter sweet and rather austere, ***. Fine, high-toned and slightly singed on the nose; rich marmalade, bitter-sweet citrusy flavours, racy acidity with a rather coarse burnt character to the finish. **/***

Blandy 1974 Sercial

Tasted at the MWC in 2004: mid-amber colour, quite deep for Sercial; fine, fragrant and floral, singed leaves on the nose; quite rich in style for Sercial, lacking a little in definition mid-palate. ***

Blandy 1973 Verdelho

Two notes, the first from a tasting in 2003: pale amber in colour with gently caramelised aromas, slightly lifted with recognisably leafy Verdelho character; lovely toasted flavours with near perfect texture for a wine of this age, ****. The second note from 2015 at a dinner with

Michael Blandy, bottled in 2014: mid-amber; surprisingly demure on the nose, very clean with dried fruit character; lovely fresh dried apricot richness and a touch of toffee, quite rich for Verdelho, still seemingly quite young after forty-one years in wood. There is more of this still in wood and it will be even better in twenty years. ****+?

Blandy Bual 1971

Tasted at the Blandy Wine Lodge in 2007, bottled in 2004: mid-mahogany; quite subdued and slightly smoky on the nose; rich and sweet with lovely concentration, tawny marmalade flavours with the richness nicely offset by crisp acidity. ***/****

Blandy 1969 Bual

Blandy's new Managing Director, Christopher Blandy, sent me a sample of this wine in 2013 (bottled 2012) which he was very excited about, and with good reason. The year 1969 was singled out in early cask tastings by the late Noel Cossart as one of the best vintages for Bual: amber/orange in colour with clear, clean ethereal aromas, crystalised citrus peel with a hint of orange blossom; fine, almost delicate initially with beautiful poise maintained throughout, crisp lime marmalade with just a wisp of wood smoke towards the finish, long, linear and very beautiful to behold, ****/*****. Second tasting at the *Decanter* World Wine Awards in 2014 where it won a gold medal: toasted aromas, hazelnuts and dried fruit; fine tawny marmalade character, well defined with richness offset by a magnificent streak of acidity. It is deeply reassuring that wines as great as this are still being bottled in Madeira. *****

Blandy Terrantez 1969

One of the last vintages of Terrantez before the grape was driven to near extinction by commercial development west of Funchal, tasted at Patrick Grubb's tasting in 2009: mid-nut brown colour, olive rim; rather baked, savoury, slightly cheesy aromas, not really reflecting the grape variety but quite appetising nonetheless; rich bitter-sweet flavours (typical of Terrantez), gentle flavours, dried apricots, not especially long but with a fine savoury-sweet finish. **/***

Blandy 1968 Verdelho

Three not very positive notes, the first at Patrick Grubb's tasting in 1998: very gentle, delicate, slightly caramelised aromas, lacking pungency, fine off-dry but lacking complexity on the finish, ***. At a Masters of Wine seminar with Richard Blandy 1999, bottled 1994, 2000 bottles in total: mid-deep amber, lovely lifted aromas, high toned and ethereal, crisp, almost searing acidity, fine but slightly burnt on the finish, ***/****. In 2005 at the MWC: mid-amber; burnt, rubbery nose (possibly reduction) with a touch of Bovril and Cup-a-Soup; tastes better but still rather soupy in style with a beefy finish. **

Blandy 1968 Bual

Two quite consistent notes, first at Alex Liddell's book launch in 1998: mid-mahogany; high toned and floral, delicate and well balanced, sweet greengage fruit, ***. At the Madeira Wine Company in 2011: mid-mahogany, green tinge to the rim; lovely, lifted and expressive on the nose, figs and walnuts and wood smoke; very clean, piercing fruit, crystallised fruits, long and sinewy with good poise, length and concentration of flavour. ****

Blandy 1966 Sercial

Three very consistent notes, one from 2006 and two from 2011 on the same 2004 bottling: pale to amber, attractive savoury aromas, well-roasted almonds, clean and well-defined; similarly fine, toasted flavours, good texture with some richness offset by racy acidity. Gentle for Sercial, ****. Lifted aromas, a touch of varnish initially, almonds, slightly singed but gentle for Sercial; lovely lime marmalade flavours, seemingly just off-dry (though with 47g/l residual sugar), fresh tingling acidity (not searing as with many Sercials), clean and delicate rather than austere on the finish. Perhaps not very typical of Sercial but a beautiful wine nonetheless, ****. Pale amber colour, lovely gentle, floral, leafy high-toned aromas, not a hint of the rancid smell that often comes from wines of this era; very clean and pure, just short of bone dry with relatively delicate (rather than searing) acidity, apples and pears, quite austere on the finish but not shockingly so, long, pure and lovely. ****

Blandy 1964 Bual

Quite a lot of notes from 2004 (two) 2005 (two) and 2006. From the 1986 bottling: mid-deep mahogany; rich, high toned and quite varnishy on the nose, toffee, chocolate and torrefaction; wonderful concentration with a wonderful range of flavours, crystalised fruit offset by a wonderful streak of acidity, leading to a slightly singed finish, ****. All from the 2004 bottling: fragrant, gentle nose, green tea with a touch of jasmine; fine, sweet crystalised fruit offset by crisp acidity and length. Lovely purity, ****. Red-tinged mahogany, candied fruit, slight cigar box nose, fine acidity, ***. Open, high toned but with distinctly rancid undertones and slightly soupy in its lack of definition; soft and smooth initially with savoury-sweet richness and a fine streak of acidity. A lovely wine but just let down by the nose, probably inadequate decanting, ***. Analysis: 21% abv, residual sugar 90.6 g/l (3.5° Baumé), dry extract (excluding sugar) 37.10 g/l, V.A. 1.2g/l.

Blandy 1962 Sercial

Tasted at Patrick Grubb's tasting in 1998 and again in 2007: lacking scent but fine, delicate and high toned with a typically grassy/leafy finish, ***. Reddish amber in colour, rather wild and slightly stewed on the nose; much fresher on the palate with crystalised fruit and some residual sweetness cut by bracing acidity. ***

Blandy 1958 Bual

Two very similar notes made in 2003 and 2005: lovely ethereal aromas, figs, raisins and prunes, if a touch caramelised; rich, dense and pruney, beautifully offset by rapier-like acidity, fine and long. ****

Blandy 1957 Bual

From Blandy's Demi-john Selection, sold at Christie's, London in December 2013, this wine bottled in 2013 and sealed with a red wax capsule. A bottle from my own cellar tasted in 2014: mid-mahogany with a red glint; butterscotch with a touch of savoury malt on the nose; rich with lovely figgy intensity perfectly offset by fresh acidity leading to a clean honeyed finish. ****

Blandy 1954 Bastardo

Bottled in 1994 and tasted in 2011, the last wine in the company's collection made from this rare red grape that proved very difficult to grow: mid-mahogany, green-tinged rim; pruney and not terribly expressive on the nose; lovely fig and prune flavours, good depth and concentration, medium-sweet in style seemingly with a dryish finish (although 130gr/litre residual sugar!). A real curiosity that just falls a little bit flat amongst its peers. ***

Blandy 1954 Malmsey

Bottled 1975, from a very successful vintage, 'Bual, Malmsey and Bastardo especially good,' records Noel Cossart. He goes on to compare 1954 with the greatest Malmsey vintages of 1808 and 1880. It must have been plentiful, too, as I have tasted this wine on many occasions (most recently in 2011) and been bowled over every single time: mid-deep mahogany, thin green rim; beautiful floral aromas, very lifted and quite powerful and aromatic too, touch of coffee emerging; rich and intense, figs, raisins and marmalade, lovely depth and texture, quite complex, rich (125 g/l residual sugar) and very beautiful, very fine, combining pungency, power and elegance. Outstanding Malmsey. *****

Blandy 1948 Bual

Tasted at the Madeira Wine Company in 2011: mid-deep mahogany, thin green tinge to the rim; rich, savoury (almost cheesy) with good depth and intensity; lovely rich savoury-sweet flavours, big, full and concentrated with a lovely expansive finish, giving the impression of being savoury rather than sweet. ****

Blandy 1944 Sercial

From Blandy's Demi-john Selection, small quantities of wine from 'forgotten' demi-johns bottled specifically for a sale at Christie's, London in December 2013. All these wines have red wax capsules; this was bottled in 2013 although the date does not appear on the bottle. Tasted in December 2014: pale-to-mid amber with a reddish glint; toffee and wood smoke on the nose, quite pungent and forthright; quite rich initially with honeyed sweetness quickly offset by fresh, racy acidity, slightly savoury (hickory) with a slightly charred, barbeque finish. Austere. ***/****

Blandy 1940 Sercial

Fine wartime vintage, described by Noel Cossart as 'really noble with an almost salty and nutty finish'. I must say that I didn't find it in this wine but it is a classic Sercial, nonetheless. Three very consistent notes here, first in 1997 for a wine bottled in 1988: very fine, lifted and high toned, beautifully clean with crisp acidity, ****. In 1998: classic tea-leaf nose, delicate, gunpowder tea; fine and delicate on the palate, quite austere, almost punishing but pure Sercial. Also in 1998 at Alex Liddell's book launch: pale amber; wonderful high-toned aromas, tea leaf and spice; crisp focused and incisive with an explosive finish, very fine, ****/*****. Third note in 2013: pale amber colour; slightly singed on the nose with leafy fruit underneath; a touch savoury with fine, rapier like acidity, bitter-sweet lemon peel twist, seemingly bone dry and quite austere on the finish. Gentle yet incisive, this is a pure, prototype Sercial, very little of which is made any more. ****

Blandy 1920 Bual

A number of consistently good notes on this wine dating from Alex Liddell's book launch in 1998, 2007 (twice) and again in 2014: mid-deep mahogany; complex, powerfully concentrated honeyed aromas, floral and slightly smoky, sings from the glass; beautifully incisive on the palate, raisins and figs offset by racy acidity. Honeyed richness in near perfect balance. Magnums of this wine were bottled in 2006 and distributed to celebrate the Blandy family bicentennial in 2011. ****/*****

Blandy 1915 Malmsey

Tasted at the MWC with Francisco Albuquerque in 2005: mid-mahogany; not very expressive on the nose, quite rich but soupy and lacking in definition, tastes of caramel with a burnt finish. **

Blandy 1911 Bual

At Patrick Grubb's tasting in 2009: red-tinged mahogany; fragrant, this wine really sings from the glass, quite pungent autumnal aromas, autumn leaves, tea leaves and a hint of white pepper; light, delicate, flavours, crisp and quite dry for a Bual, clean as a whistle, long, fine and still very fresh. ****

Blandy 1908 Bual

Tasted in December 1993: deep mahogany; perfumed and pungent, a hint of Bovril; rich and sweet for a Bual, good depth balanced by brisk acidity. ***/****

Blandy 1907 Bual

Tasted in 2005: mid-deep mahogany; lovely fragrant floral aromas, herbal tea and spice, good richness and texture let down by a slightly burnt, rather rustic bitter-sweet finish. ***

Blandy 1902 Malmsey

From my own cellar, opened for my daughter's christening in 2009: deep mahogany colour, almost like a dark coffee; high-toned toffee and roasted coffee-bean aromas with a touch of molasses; very rich with lovely texture and mouthfeel, creamy toffee and fudge-like richness offset by steely acidity, long and fine with a singed finish. ****/*****

Blandy 1891 Boal Solera

A wine probably bottled in the 1970s (with a stopper cork) for the Portuguese market (hence perhaps the spelling of 'Boal') when Blandy's had an office in Lisbon on the Rua Victor Gordon in Chiado. In those days Blandy's produced the number one gin in Portugal, named 'Tower of London', at a time when imported gin was five times the price (I feel that I was brought up on it)! This bottle came from my own cellar tasted in 2015: mid-amber with a green hue to the rim; pungent, rather burnt aromas, slightly smoked; better on the palate though still singed, quite rich, tangy marmalade fruit character, some good weight mid-palate but overall rather coarse and 'thick cut' in style with a slightly peaty finish. ***

Blandy 1880 Solera Verdelho

At Patrick Grubb's tasting, 1998: complex smoky character, rich, quite sweet for Verdelho, well balanced, clean, fresh but rather lacking in depth and complexity. **/***

Blandy 1874 Malmsey

Tasted in December 1993: a tiny harvest, blighted by phylloxera: deep mahogany; rich, raisiny aromas and flavours, full and concentrated, richness offset by rising acidity and a long finish. ***/****

Blandy 1870 Solera Verdelho

Three fairly consistent notes, the first in 1997 with James Symington: complex and smoky on the nose, high toned, green and leafy, very fine, let down slightly by a coarse finish, ***. Then in 1998 at 'A Celebration of Vintage Madeiras', Chesterfield Hotel, London: slightly cloudy, rich and rather soupy, **. At Alex Liddell's book launch, also in 1998: muddy brown colour, smells of old casks, incisive, racy green flavours with a burnt finish. ***

Blandy 1870 Terrantez

Bottled 1921 and recorked in 1986, just pre-phylloxera: mid-deep amber/mahogany with a red glint and yellow green rim; very fine, lifted perfume, garden flowers with a touch of wood varnish; bitter-sweet candied peel, clean, med-dry in style, gentle but lithe, very fresh and alive. Delightful wine. ****

Blandy Cama de Lobos 1868 Boal

A rare example of a glass-aged Bual, the wine having spent just eighteen years in wood prior to being bottled in 1886. There is a tasting note on this wine in Vizetelly's *Facts about Port and Madeira* published in 1880 where he describes it as 'a powerful sub-pungent wine'. My note dates from a tasting in New York in 2014: clear and pale, unusually so, amber/orange in hue; very gentle lime and grapefruit marmalade character, a touch savoury too with a hint of almond toffee; fresh, quite dry in style with a delicate texture, dried apricots with grapefruit-like acidity although not that pronounced and a gentle ('filigree') though dryish finish more in the style of Verdelho than Bual. An unusual wine but really lovely nonetheless. ****/*****

Blandy Grand Cama de Lobos Solera 1864

Tasted in 2002 at Gambrinus restaurant in Lisbon, a bottle that may have been on ullage for some time: pale mahogany, dusty nose with a touch of *rancio*, very dry and slightly dusty and rustic in style, searing acidity and very dry on the finish. **

Blandy 1864 Sercial

Tasted December 1993 at the Portuguese Embassy, London, a wine from a small harvest: mid-mahogany; high volatility, some raisiny fruit; raging acidity. Second bottle tasting stewed.

Blandy 1863 Bual

Bottled 1913, recorked 1986: from an outstanding vintage for Boal, especially in Campanário. Tasted at the Blandy lodge in 2005 and in the Blandy Bicentennial Tasting: deep, red-tinged mahogany, thin green rim; very powerful, dense, pungent aromas – ethereal; rich candied peel, thick-cut marmalade, rich, dense, big and still very powerful, expansive bitter-sweet length, full, fine and still fresh with a lovely texture. Treacle toffee finish. Just a touch of cask on the nose and on the finish, something that Francisco Albuquerque put down to the oxidation of the alcohol. *****

Blandy 1862 Malvasia Velha

At Patrick Grubb's annual tasting in 2009: mid-amber with a green-tinged rim; delicate honeyed aromas, not very expressive but very fine, acacia honey; lovely rich, honeyed flavours (Manuka), very fine, rich but not pungent, long. Liquid honey. ****

Blandy 1860 Bual

Unlike many other Blandy vintages, this does not seem to have appeared under other MWA/MWC labels. This is a rare wine with only three bottles having been recorded as sold at auction. This one originated from the UK and was tasted in New York in 2014: mid-deep red-tinged mahogany; very strange nose, wild, funky character, slightly damp too (although this diminished in the glass), like a closed-up room, quite complex; quite rich yet gentle with lovely texture and mouthfeel, showing none of that dampness on the palate, seamlessly rich with a slight saline character on the finish. Not that sweet or intense: mellow. ****

Blandy 1826 Solera Bual

This is one of a set of *solera* wines released in the 1950s and 1960s. It was probably bottled between 1956 and 1960 and is based on the 1836 Campanário that Walter Grabham left to the Blandy family on his death in 1955 (see more information under 1811 *Solera*, below). Tasted in New York in 2014: deep mahogany colour; rich smoky nose, autumnal bonfires and a touch of forest floor; rich lemon and lime marmalade with lovely mouthfeel and texture, leading to a delicate marmalade finish. ***/****

Blandy 1811 Commemoration Solera Bual

I have long been mystified by this wine which I have tasted and greatly enjoyed on a number of occasions. It was shown for Blandy's bicentennial celebrations in 2011. I am especially grateful to Emmanuel Berk of the Rare Wine Company in Sonoma California for his research as to how the wine came to be as it is. It came to Blandy's (like the 1826 *solera* above) via Dr Michael Grabham (1840–1935) who married Anne Mary Blandy and inherited a very fine cellar. He left this to his son Walter Grabham who died in 1955, in turn leaving his wines to his cousins Graham and John Blandy. In 1960 Graham Blandy sold hundreds of bottles to the MWA, writing to managing director Horace Zino that 'they can well be made into a solera'. The 1811 is not a *solera* in the conventional sense of the word (although until relatively recently there was no Portuguese definition) but resulted from a one-off blending of various old wines belonging to Walter Grabham. The Blandy family needed a wine to celebrate John Blandy's arrival in Madeira and so the decision was made to uncork much of the Grabham collection to produce a commemorative wine. The following Blandy wines may well have gone into this historic bottling: 1826 Campanário, 1858 Sercial, 1829 Porto de Cruz, 1788 Malmsey, 1827 Bual, 1827 Old London Particular, 1830 'Cask' and the famous São Martinho Challenger which had sailed on board HMS *Challenger* in 1873. There is even a possibility that some of Grabham's 1792 so-called 'Napoleon Madeira' may have gone into the blend.

It has to be asked why such historic madeiras, already in bottle, were deemed suitable for blending? The answer to this is held by Tom Mullins, former managing director of the MWA whose task it was to taste through the Grabham wines. He opened the bottles with his wife over a series of evenings and reported back as follows: 'In my view they should be served as curiosities and preferably at the beginning of the dinner or lunch, with the soup. I do not think they will bring any credit to the name of Blandy, nor encourage people to drink madeiras.' The wines would almost certainly have been in bottle since the 1830s and 1840s and would probably have suffered from serious bottle stink. It seems likely that Mullins didn't aerate the wines properly and merely took the wines from bottle at face value, condemning them in the process.

So to the '1811' *solera* which is probably based on an 1811 Bual aged in cask blended with drier wines from the Grabham collection. I have two notes: the first in 2011 on a wine bottled in 1900 and recorked 1986: mid-amber/mahogany, red glint, thin green rim; gentle, verging on fragile, lifted smoky-savoury aromas, nuts and wood smoke; gentle, dry, lovely linear style, citrus (lime) still fresh and kept alive on the finish by searing steely acidity. A beautiful, haunting wine, *****. The second note is from 'The Beauty of Bual' tasting three years later: lovely chestnut colour with gold-green rim; wonderful aroma, heady, amontillado-like and autumnal, a blaze of autumn sunshine (a rather lovely sort of decay); rich yet quite dry in style, a touch of cinnamon, great poise and length. Not really Bual in style: too dry ****/*****. It still leaves a few questions unanswered: is this a wine that is greater than the sum of its parts? How many individually great wines were really sacrificed to make the 1811 Solera? These questions will never be answered.

Borges

The Borges family bought up wines in the second half of the nineteenth century and became *partidistas*, supplying other shippers, notably Krohn Bros (see page 190). The founder of the company, Henrique Menezes Borges, left a number of wines to his children and these have subsequently been divided among members of the family. Many of these wines are magnificent. The family is still in business as a shipper (see page 100) and many of the family's finest old wines bear the initials of the founder (HMB). Some of the wines below are not therefore known to the current generation of Borges, cousins Helena and Isabel, who now run the company.

H. M. Borges Malvasia Over 40 Years Old

A blended wine, mostly from a single year (although Borges won't admit to which one), over fifty years old in 2014. There were 1000 bottles of this wine bottled to celebrate 500 years of the city of Funchal in 2008.

A bottle from my cellar tasted in 2015: mid-amber; fine, lifted aromas, caramelised citrus, just singed around the edges; very fine on the palate, lime marmalade with a touch of quince and butterscotch underlying, well defined tough not especially rich, pure and clean all the way through with a long, gentle finish. ****/*****

H. M. Borges Verdelho Solera 'Reserve'

At Patrick Grubb's 1998 tasting: dusty dog-biscuit smell, quite sweet and rich but balanced with smoky complexity on the finish, much cleaner on the palate than on the nose (possibly bottle stink due to inadequate decanting time). ***

H. M. Borges 1979 Sercial Dry 'B'

Bottled in 2009 and tasted pre-sale at Christie's in 2013: pale-to-mid amber, slightly dusty, spirity nose like an old Cognac with a touch of vanilla too; very clean and fresh on the palate, lemon and lime marmalade, long and quite sweet on the finish for Sercial (55g/l residual sugar), lingering candied peel flavours. Perhaps rather atypical but a lovely wine, very pure in style. ****

H. M. Borges 1977 Boal

Three rather inconsistent notes here, all from the 2002 bottling. The first comes from a 2003 tasting in the *armazém* in Funchal: nut brown/ mahogany, thin green rim; very fine, gentle, ethereal high-toned aromas, floral, with a hint of green tea; delicate leafy flavours with candied and figgy richness. Wonderful length of flavour. Very fine, ****. Again in 2006: fine, lifted, high-toned aromas with a hint of green tea; delicate leafy aromas with some figgy richness mid-palate, yielding to a long fresh, persistent finish. Gentle and fine, ****. A third note from a pre-sale tasting at Christie's, London in 2013 where I expect that the wine would have been much improved by prior decanting: slightly cloudy mid-deep amber; singed on the nose, not very expressive, a hint of consommé perhaps; much better on the palate, incisive tawny marmalade flavours with crisp acidity all the way through to the finish, quite delicate and fine in style for Boal. **/***

H. M. Borges 1940 Verdelho

Tasted in 2005: Pale-mid mahogany; this wine sings from the glass and smells rather like a carpenter's workshop, but not off-putting: varnish on new wood; fine off-dry bitter-sweet orange peel, very pure and fine with a streak of acidity running all the way through. ****

H. M. Borges 1940 Solera Malmsey

Tasted in 2005: mid-mahogany, lovely high-toned aromas with a touch of butterscotch and spice, not that rich but fine tawny marmalade concentration. Great length and poise. ****

H. M. Borges 1915 Solera Verdelho

Tasted in 2008: mid-amber hue, rather stewed on the nose, touch of bonfire; fine medium-rich, spicy flavours, quite sweet for Verdelho, lovely texture and a rich warming finish. ***

H. M. Borges 1877 Terrantez

Believed to have been transferred from cask to demi-johns around 1900. Bottled May 2013 especially for auction at Christie's later that year: beautiful colour, clear, bright mid-amber; very expressive with a 'wow' of a nose, fragrant, floral and slightly wild; quite sweet initially with rich toasty, spicy savoury-sweet flavours; leading to a long austere bitter-sweet finish. Very pure and clear in its expression. *****

H. M. Borges Verdelho, believed 1875

Tasted in 2013 at the Velhissimo Verdelho tasting in New York: mid-deep amber colour; strange nose, heady, nutty but not quite clean, perhaps just bottle stink (?), slightly caramelised; fine, but quite rich and full in style for a Verdelho with a rather dusty finish, long and linear nonetheless. ***

H. M. Borges 1875 Boal

Mid-amber; fragile and high toned on the nose, varnish with spirit showing through; richer with dried apricots on the palate, spicy and spirity with good mouthfeel mid-palate, sweet and singed on the finish but tailing off to be quite lean and bony. **/***

Believed 1862 Terrantez H. M. B. (Purchased by Leacock)

H. M. B. probably stands for H. M. Borges although Helena and Isabel Borges have never seen this wine. It almost certainly originated from a single grower, Dr João Alexandrino dos Santos. Michael Broadbent is a huge fan of this wine and awards it six stars (out of a maximum of five!) in his book *Vintage Wine*. When it was shown by Patrick Grubb in 2009 I didn't get quite so excited: lovely old golden-green colour; very fine, delicate aromas akin to an old amontillado sherry, a hint of coffee; dry, delicate (bitter-sweet), very clean and focused, like a good old amontillado but without the same tang, candied peel with a touch of toffee and butterscotch with a slightly casky finish. ****

H. M. Borges 1810 Sercial

A wine labelled 'Family Reserve, Henrique Menezes Borges, established 1877' shown by Patrick Grubb MW in 2013: pale-mid amber; very strange vegetal aromas, garden lilies with a touch of cat's pee; tastes much better then it smells, quite rich for a Sercial initially though followed up by dry astringency with a characteristically austere finish. Not a very pleasant drink to my mind – though others at the tasting thought differently. **

H. M. B. 1800 Verdelho

One of several wines left by Henrique Menezes Borges to his children on his death in 1916, with instructions not to sell them. The wines ended up with one son, João Maria, who on his death in 1980 bequeathed them to his six children. On 13 February 1889 the wines were all bottled from demi-john in the presence of the Borges family and were divided equally among the family. Though the date was given by H. M. Borges, it should be considered approximate. Twenty-three bottles of 1800 Verdelho were bottled in 1989. This was tasted in New York in 2013: mid-deep amber, green rim; lovely nose, clean, gentle, delicate yet lifted and savoury; very fine, powerful toasty-savoury flavours, spice as well, dry tangy finish with the merest hint of candied citrus peel, beautifully clean and elegant, amazing for a wine at 213 years of age! *****

GREAT MADEIRA COLLECTIONS

Conde do Cannavial

João da Câmara Leme Homem de Vasconcelos, the first Conde do Cannavial (1829–1902) was a doctor, chemist, industrialist and politician. He devised a new and rather crude method of *estufagem* which involved passing wine through a coil heated in a *bain marie* of water at 70°C. Cannavial also developed a means of mixing quinine with madeira, preventing the wine from turning cloudy. There was a market for Malmsey laced with quinine in the Portuguese colonies of Angola and Mozambique, and *vinho quinado* became popular for a time in Portugal. Cossart Gordon bought the patent for Cannavial's method.

Dr Cannavial Verdelho 1870

This wine came from one of the descendants of Dr Cannavial, was bottled from cask by the Madeira Wine Company in 2013 and was tasted at Christie's in 2013: mid-deep amber/orange hue; lovely toasted aromas, savoury and seductive; wonderful flavour of toasted almonds with a fine streak of acidity cutting in mid-palate and lingering through a long semi-sweet finish. A lovely wine with great presence and poise. *****

Verdelho 1870

The last major vintage before phylloxera struck, this wine was bottled in 2013 from a cask belonging to the Conde do Cannavial, having been passed down to his relatives: mid-deep amber; lovely, savoury, seductive toasty aromas and similarly dry toasty flavours, a touch of bitter almond, backed by a streak of bracing acidity leading on to a long persistent finish. A lovely wine. I question how a wine so fresh has been kept going in cask for so long! ****

H.M.B. 1780 Bual

At Patrick Grubb's tasting in 2013, a wine presumably from Borges, heavy sediment: mid-amber, green rim; wonderful aromas, lifted and very expressive, a touch vegetal, herbal, crushed leaves; herbs and spice on the palate, quite dry in style initially, long with great persistence and poise. Remarkable for a wine of this age. ****

Boal c. 1780 (from the Borges family)

This could be exactly the same wine as the one above but I tasted it on a separate occasion in 2002 and my note is rather different. It was bought in cask and demi-john by Henrique Menezes Borges in 1900, an astute judge of fine wine: mid-amber/mahogany, thin green-tinged rim, beautiful aromas, fine open and high toned, quite floral, rose petals; quite rich and sweet in style, offset by fine acidity, finishes with a flourish, very fine, long and remarkably fresh for all its years. ****

'Pather'

A famous wine from the Borges family, c.1720 and thought to be Terrantez. The name 'Pather' originates from the Middle-English word Father. Henrique Menezes Borges bought the wine in 1915 and stated at the time that it was one of the oldest on the island and should be passed down through his family. Consequently, it is very rare. Bottled in 1989: pale mahogany with a green-tinged rim; quite subdued on the nose with a hint of treacle and molasses; very fine and delicate, sinewy and entrancing with a beautiful texture and fabulous length. *****

Companhia Vinicola da Madeira

Established in 1870, the company's lodges used to be on the Rua dos Ferreiros in the centre of Funchal. The CVM were associated with Justino Henriques but the company closed in 1984 and the stock was sold. Some was retained by Justino's and bottles labelled 'CVM' can still be found in the Madeira Wine Company lodges.

CVM 1954 Verdelho

Tasted in the MWC lodges in 2005, a wine bottled in 1986 shortly after the firm closed: mid-amber; rather soupy and lacking in definition, sweet for a Verdelho and soupy on the palate too, tawny marmalade richness on the finish. **/***

Companhia Vinicola da Madeira (CVM), Malvasia 1880

Tasted in 2002 at Gambrinus restaurant in Lisbon: very deep mahogany colour; rich and raisiny with a smell of molasses and moscatel; very rich, sweet and raisiny on the palate, molasses and burnt sugar, especially on the finish. Heavily caramelised. *

Companhia Vinicola da Madeira, Verdelho 1850

Tasted in 2008: mid-deep nut-brown to amber, rich, singed and rather lacking in definition on the nose, autumnal aromas; rich, rather soupy caramelised flavours with a slightly savoury-rancid undertone, crisp acidity and a rather treacle-like finish. Strangely unbalanced. **

Luís Gomes da Conceição

Once an important family firm, established in 1868 and subsequently absorbed into the Madeira Wine Association.

1865 Gomes RB

'RB' possibly stands for Reserva Bual, tasted in 2006: pale mahogany; not terribly expressive on the nose, slightly casky and leathery, quite dry in style, certainly drier than one would expect from a Bual, clean and sinewy, fine and focused but rather austere and astringent – doesn't give a great deal of pleasure. **

Cossart Gordon

Established in 1745, Cossart Gordon & Co. were for many years the largest shippers on Madeira until they were overtaken by the Madeira Wine Association in the 1920s. Their *armazens* were split between three sets of buildings close to the Ribeira de Santa Luzia in Funchal, named Serrado, Estufa and Pateo. Vizetelly describes it as being close to a ravine forty feet deep and says that in 1803 'the rushing torrent overflowed … carrying away a store of Cossart, Gordon & Co. which had been erected on the verge, together with several hundred pipes of wine all of which were lost'. Vizetelly goes on to describe the Serrado wine stores in bucolic detail: 'All the unoccupied ground at these Serrado stores is planted with vines trained in corridors, interspersed here and there with a mango, a fig or custard apple tree. Trellised vines moreover cover in all the walks in front of the various stores, enabling the men employed in them to always be in the shade. The first store which we visited – a long narrow building some three hundred feet in length, with square grated openings along its front to allow the free admission of air – is capable of holding six hundred pipes, in triple rows of three tiers each. It is used for receiving the "vinho em mosto" or newly made wine. Scarlet geraniums about a man's height are trained all over its front, and under the broad canopy of trellised vines – stretching from the roof of the store to that of the opposite shed – empty casks waiting to be "wined" [i.e. seasoned] are stowed away.' I quote this at length here because the pre-1950s wines below will have been aged in these *armazens* and because, sadly, this scene is now under the Rua 5 de Outubro and a block of apartments.

Cossart Gordon 1977 Terrantez

Two consistent notes, the first in 2005: cooked nose, stewed fruit, a bit rancid (cheesy), tastes fresher but rather soupy and lacking definition for Terrantez, **. In 2006, for a wine bottled in 2004: mid-amber; marred by cheesiness on the nose with a touch of Marmite; soft, medium rich but not very characteristic of Terrantez, smooth and well balanced with a savoury finish akin to sucking on a Twiglet! ***

Cossart Gordon 1977 Sercial

Tasted at a Madeira Seminar with Richard Blandy in 1999: 2,333 bottles bottled 1995: amber with a red tinge, squeaky clean high-toned aromas with an earthy-casky undertone, clean and grassy on palate, tangy fresh finish but a bit dull (48g/l sugar). **/***

THE ARMAZEM DOS VINHOS VELHISSIMOS OF MESSRS. COSSART, GORDON, & CO. AT FUNCHAL.

Cossart Gordon 1975 Verdelho

Tasted at the MWC in 2005 : pale amber; rather burnt, beefy, *rancio* nose, coarse; better on the palate, powerful, quite dry and incisive for Verdelho but then rather thin and lean on the finish. Disappointing for a wine of this calibre. **

Cossart Gordon 1973 Verdelho

Tasted at the MWC with Francisco Albuquerque in 2000: mid-amber; not very lifted (put down to low VA), rather subdued toasty aromas; soft and seemingly lacking incision initially but with acidity rising in the mouth, leading to a steely finish. **/***

Cossart Gordon 1969 Bual

At Patrick Grubb's tasting 1998 and again in 2006, the latter bottled in 1992: red-tinged colour; burnt sugar aromas and flavours with a dusting of tannic astringency, dusty finish, **. Mid-mahogany, singed, verging on burnt on the nose, autumnal leaves and a touch soupy in style; finer and more focused on the palate, rich in texture, long and finely balanced by a persistent streak of acidity. ****

Cossart Gordon 1961 Bual

I take a special interest in this wine as it is one of very few madeiras from the year of my birth. There are all too few fortified 1961s (1261 bottles of this) so when I spotted it in the *garrafeira* of the Madeira Wine Company I asked to purchase a few bottles for future birthdays. Tasted 2011, a wine bottled in March 2004 having spent forty-three years in wood: deep amber/mahogany in colour with a burnt nose, characteristic *rancio* with a touch of dried fig and prune (Francisco Albuquerque, wine maker for the Madeira Wine Company also finds 'vanilla' and 'curry' on the nose); lovely singed flavours, dried apricots and prunes with the natural richness and concentration offset by acidity. ***/****

Cossart Gordon 1958 Bual

Tasted on at least four occasions meaning that there must be lots of it. First note at MWC in 1996: gunpowder tea nose, very fine and complex, rich and smoky with rising acidity on the finish, ****. Second note at

1999 MW Madeira seminar for a wine bottled in 1985 (1500 bottles): deep amber, lovely caramelised high-toned aromas, rich and tangy, full and round with a long raisiny finish, lovely combination, ****. At an Anglo-Portuguese Society tasting with Richard Blandy in 2001 (where I met my future wife for the first time), bottled in 1995 (1500 bottles): mid-deep mahogany, green, *rancio* (forest floor, decomposing leaves); rich and searing, perfectly balanced. Analysis: residual sugar 105.5 g/l (4.2° Baumé), VA 1.2g/l, dry extract 35.10 g/l, ****. On the 2006 bottling noted in October 2006: mid-deep mahogany; rich, pungent but rather soupy aromas; very rich and powerfully concentrated, raisins, walnuts and figs but with a slightly hard edge on the finish, ***. A final note from 2011 on the same 2006 bottling: deep mahogany; rather soupy aromas, burnt, perhaps appealing to some (but not to me); caramelised toffee, rich toffee-apple flavours, better than on the nose, more definition with a surprisingly dry and rather burnt finish. Could it be that this wine has been left too long in wood? ***

Cossart Gordon 1954 Sercial

A fine year, mostly for the sweeter wines, notes Noel Cossart; this wine tasted in 2005 at the Madeira Wine Company: pale amber; lovely, gentle crystallised citrus fruit aromas, savoury, slightly smoky and singed. Very fine. Remarkably fresh, lemon and lime flavours, fine racy acidity yet gentle and not as austere as most Sercial with a singed finish. Very elegant, ethereal wine. ****/*****

Cossart Gordon 1954 Malmsey

At Patrick Grubb's 1998 tasting: rich smoky-raisiny character, rich but rather soupy and muddy in style, sweet and raisiny but lacking in definition. **/***

Cossart Gordon 1950 Sercial

A bottle from my cellar tasted in 2014: pale-to-mid amber with a golden glint; lifted but gentle leafy aromas, green tea and a touch of apple; very fresh, clean with searing acidity rather overpowering the toffee-apple fruit, dry and forceful with a long rather piercing finish. Very typical if slightly punishing Sercial. ****

Bual 1941 'C. D. G. C.'

The late Noel Cossart set aside a pipe of this wine to mark the birth of his son David, whose initials appear on the bottle. The Bual grapes come from the vineyard of Francisco Filhimino in Campanário. Fortified with grape spirit, rather than spirit derived from sugar cane, this wine was aged in a pipe that had previously held the 1862 Terrantez (see below). After annual loss due to evaporation in wood the total number of bottles would amount to twenty-seven dozen but very few turn up now. Bottled in July 1976. The last bottles were sold at Christie's, London in 1994. This one came from Patrick Grubb in 2011: mid-amber with a green tinge to the rim; beautiful fragrance, slightly lifted and singed, lemon barley sugar, heavenly aroma; fine, pure and delicate, lime marmalade flavours with just a hint of cask on the finish, long and linear. **** / *****

Cossart Gordon 1934 Verdelho

'All wines excellent' according to Noel Cossart; this was bottled in March 2006 and tasted in 2005: mid-mahogany, thin yellow rim; lovely smoky, nutty aromas, hazelnuts, gentle and delicate; similarly gentle toasty flavours, almonds, lemon and lime acidity, vibrant finish, very fine balance and poise. Salted nuts on the finish. *****

Cossart Gordon 1916 Malmsey

Tasted in 2011: mid-deep reddish amber colour; very expressive on the nose, soily, touch of cat's pee on a doormat, cinnamon too (Noel Cossart in his 1984 book asserts 'cloves'), an unusual mix but surprisingly attractive and beguiling; lovely gentle greengage fruit, spiked with richness and sweetness but delicate on the finish and overall. ****/*****

Cossart Gordon 1915 Bual

Tasted in December 1993 at a Madeira Wine Company tasting at the Portuguese Embassy in London: First World War vintage, generally very good, Bual especially: mid-amber/mahogany; extraordinary, pungent smoked tea leaf aromas; very powerful with raging acidity and a green leafy finish, very unusual for a Bual and not to everyone's taste, but I rather liked it. ***/****

Cossart Gordon 1910 Sercial

At the same tasting as the wine above in December 1993: All wine excellent, 'especially Sercial': mid-amber; high toned, smoked and floral on the nose, an unusual mix; very dry and austere, with nervy acidity right the way through, long, clean and incisive. ***/****

Cossart Gordon 1910 Bual

Tasted in 1997 with James Symington: high toned, very concentrated, everything there, lost for words! ****/*****

Cossart Gordon 1908 Bual

Two very consistent notes on the same bottling (1984, with seventy-seven years in cask), first in 1999 at MW seminar with Richard Blandy: deep mahogany, thin green rim, heavenly aromas, open and singing from the glass; very rich and concentrated (130 g/l residual sugar), raisiny, a touch burnt around the edges but very, very fine, *****. Second note from 2004, a tasting at the MWC: deep mahogany with a thin olive-green rim; incredibly pungent, powerful and concentrated on the nose. Balsamic. Ethereal. Wonderfully rich, prunes and figs with a hint of chocolate. Beautiful texture, the very essence of Madeira. So fine and complex that it leaves me lost for words, *****. Third, slightly less effusive, note from 2005: mid-deep mahogany; fine, fragrant high-toned aromas; rich with a touch of molasses, powerful concentration of figgy sweetness offset by racy acidity. Waxy length. ****/*****

Cossart Gordon 1899 Terrantez

Tasted December 1993 at the Portuguese Embassy in London: dark mahogany; tea-leaf aromas (some bottle variation) but rather hefty and ponderous in style, almost overweight, acidity rising in the mouth which just about redeems the rather pruney cloying fruit. Not at all typical of Terrantez. ***

Cossart Gordon 1893 Malmsey

At the same tasting in December 1993: a fine vintage for Malmsey, probably the best since phylloxera: deep amber/mahogany; enjoyably fragrant and high toned; lovely concentration, dried fruit (apricots and prunes), rich and full with depth and length. ****

Cossart Gordon 1875 Bastardo

From a vintage in the midst of phylloxera. At Patrick Grubb's 1998 tasting: singed and high toned on the nose, powerful acidity, quite dry and nervy in style with a finish that is rather like sucking on a piece of old wood. **

Cossart Gordon 1868 Very Old Boal 'EBH'

The 1868 'EBH' has appeared under several brand names including Cossart Gordon (see also 'EBH' Bual on page 211). Tasted in 2009: deep amber with a red tinge and thin green rim, a touch of sediment; slightly burnt on the nose (charred), heavy smoke; rich and quite caramelised, again quite forceful on the palate, rich and powerful, tawny marmalade offset by acidity and a bitter-sweet finish. ***

Cossart Gordon, 1868 Solera

An island-bottled wine shipped to one of Denmark's best wine merchants and tasted at Patrick Grubb's annual tasting in 2009. Grapes from Câmara de Lobos where it was an excellent year for Bual: pale amber with a green tinge; very toasty and appealing, savoury aperitif style, toast and peanut butter on the nose; fine delicate, saline flavours akin to a bowl of mixed salted nuts, almost no sweetness but with lovely poise and gentle length. A crème brûlée finish. Very impressive. *****

Malvazia 1865 Solera, Cossart Gordon

At Patrick Grubb's tasting in 2008: amber centre, olive-green rim; high toned and varnishy on the nose, hint of boiled sweets (which would be a major fault in any other wine) and a caramelised tang; wonderfully soft, rich and figgy with a powerful tang. Sweetness and acidity in near perfect counterpoint. Fine but seemingly confected on the finish. ***

Cossart Gordon 1864 Verdelho

Apparently this is the only 1864 wine labelled 'Verdelho' in existence and fairly rare. Tasted in New York in 2013: mid-deep amber, green-tinged rim; lovely candied-peel aromas, not especially expressive, very clean and gentle; fine and delicate, beautifully taut flavours, orange peel and spice balanced by near-perfect acidity, long and lithe on the finish with a touch of bitter orange. Very fine and focused. *****

Cossart Cordon 1862 Terrantez

A very small harvest due to oidium, supposedly outstanding for Terrantez. Tasted in December 1993: reddish colour; strangely dumb and rustic on the nose, rather undistinguished with characteristic bitter sweet austerity and a lean finish. **/***

Cossart Gordon 1860 Solera

Noel Cossart says of 1860 that production was 'very small but generally very good, especially Sercial'. The wine from this *solera* was matured in wood for sixty-five years before being put into demi-johns. Tasted in 1997 with James Symington: wonderfully scented, high toned, floral; thrilling, very complex flavours, spicy, quite lean but very elegant. ****/*****

Cossart Gordon Bual Solera 1845

At a madeira seminar with Richard Blandy in 1999: 7,000 bottles, bottled in 1988 after eighty-five years in wood: deep blackish brown, burnt on the nose, peaty undertones with raisins and molasses, very rich and concentrated (107 g/l residual sugar) long searing finish. ***/****

Newton, Gordon, Cossart & Co 1840 'The Rebel' (bottled February 1889)

A rare surviving example of the glass-aged madeiras popular in the US in the nineteenth century. It came from the Goelet collection sold at Morrell & Co. in New York in 1999 (see page 177). The wine presumably arrived at New York on the ship called *The Rebel*. It is not clear if 1840 is the date of bottling or the vintage. The label also bears the name of William F. Fearing, a wine merchant who for decades sold madeiras to wealthy New Yorkers on behalf of William Neyle Habersham of Savannah. The February 1889 date on the label is presumably when Fearing transferred the wine from demi-john to bottle. The bottle was recorked on April 16 1919, only a few months before the start of prohibition: pale-mid amber, green-tinged rim; odd nose, smelling of mothballs and butterscotch, syrup too (others noted glue, shoe polish, rubber); similarly odd taste, malty flavours, smooth, quite soft, falling away on the finish, is this why it is called 'The Rebel'? I have never tasted a wine quite like this before! Sadly this wine does not live up to its distinguished history.

Cossart Gordon 1822 Verdelho

Tasted December 1993 at the Portuguese Embassy in London: mid-golden amber colour; fabulous bouquet, high toned, floral (rose petals), singing beautifully from the glass; soft and mellow initially with racy acidity rising towards the finish. Very fine, fresh and upright. *****

Donaldson

An English shipper described by Vizetelly and noted for its 'high-class wines matured by natural in preference to artificial heat'. He goes on to describe their delicate wines and concludes that 'on the whole the wines of this firm were exceedingly interesting'. Donaldson became part of the Madeira Wine Association so I assume that the wines were subsequently bottled under other labels.

F. F. Ferraz

The Ferraz family were sugar producers and distillers who also became wine shippers in 1880. They owned impressive *armazens* on the Rua dos Netos in the centre of Funchal. The company was absorbed into the Madeira Wine Association in 1937 but the Ferraz  label continues to be used in the French market. The Ferraz family continue to have important shipping interests in Funchal.

Ferraz 1880 Velhissimo Reserva

Billed as 'a legendary wine' by Patrick Grubb who showed it at his annual tasting in 2011, and this did not disappoint: deep-green-tinged amber; exuberant perfumed nose, touch of *rancio*, powerful but not aggressive; figgy richness mid-palate, crystallised fruits, powerful, rich and to be enjoyed. Long and fine with great poise. ****/*****

Favila

The Favila family, descendants of Bartholomew Perestrelo, were owners of vineyards in Câmara de Lobos. During the reign of Luís I (1838–89) the Favila wines displayed the royal insignia and a wine produced by the family won the very first gold medal awarded to a madeira, from the Paris International Exhibition in 1889. Some of the best wines came from the Ribeira Real estate in Câmara de Lobos, a name that has recently been revived by Barbeito. The Favila family still keep stocks of old wine in their *garrafeira* in the Rua da Carreira, Funchal.

R.R. 1882 Malvasia

'R.R.' stands for 'Ribeiro Real', a wine aged in pipe for around a century when the wine went into demi-johns in the 1980s. It was returned to pipe by Ricardo Diogo of Barbeito for bottling in February 2015. This note is taken from a cask sample tasted shortly prior to bottling – there will be around 180 bottles in total: lovely, iridescent mid-deep green-tinged mahogany; wonderfully lifted (1.92g/l volatile acidity), ethereal aromas that left me speechless, so pungent and with the underlying concentration of syrup of figs; rich, mellifluous and intense (4.5° Baumé), the very essence of madeira, singed, caramelised syrup of figs, slightly roasted with a beautiful bitter-sweet finish that goes on and on. *****

GREAT MADEIRA COLLECTIONS

Dr Frederico de Freitas

Dr Frederico de Freitas was a Funchal lawyer who left his home and collection of antique furniture to the people of Madeira; this can be seen in the Casa-Museu Frederico de Freitas on the Calçada de Santa Clara. During his working life he was given many old bottles of madeira in gratitude for his work. Many of the bottles are unidentifiable apart from a vintage date, the initials of the grower or district of production.

Tinta Velha, Freitas e Irmão

From the de Freitas collection, a wine bottled around 1890 and tasted in 2005, at Patrick Grubb's annual tasting: mid-amber, beautiful aroma, toffee and caramel with a hint of torrefaction; dry but not austerely so with lovely concentration of flavour, dried apricots and allspice, racy acidity picking up on the finish. ****

1847

Tasted in 2007 at Patrick Grubb's tasting: mid-amber, wild, herbal aromas, varnish too; very dry and austere with the tang of an old amontillado sherry and a burnt finish. **/***

Vinho Velhissimo 1825

Bottled in an old burgundy-shaped bottle and tasted in 2005: bright amber with a green tinge; lovely toasted aromas, almonds and biscuits with a touch of lemon both on the nose and in the mouth; remarkably fresh and bright with olive and citrus fruit and tawny marmalade on the finish. Unusual (I actually pondered if this was madeira or something else) but very fine nonetheless. ****/*****

W. W. Casa dos Leilos

From the family of Dr Frederico de Freitas, tasted in 2009: mid-pale amber; lovely gentle, savoury aromas, hint of butterscotch with casky overtones; fine, dry, delicate in style, dried fruit (figs) with fresh acidity, gentle length. ***

GREAT MADEIRA COLLECTIONS

Sir Stephen Gaselee

Sir Stephen Gaselee (1882–1943) worked at the Foreign Office in London and visited Madeira every winter between 1919 and 1939. He befriended both Portuguese and British families on the island and was sold or given wines that few others could access. Among Sir Stephen's friends on the island were Harry Hinton, the Bishop of Funchal and Charles Cossart who were commissioned to find parcels of old wine for him. Sir Stephen was also a friend of Dr Michael Grabham (see page 178) and many of the same wines could be found in his cellar, housed at Magdalene College, Cambridge. He often imported madeira wines in pipe and hogshead and bottled them in Cambridge. Sir Stephen had an experimental approach to food and wine but loved nothing more than serving a madeira wine with turtle soup. Among the wines in his collection were bottles purchased from the Henriques, Bianchi and Borges families. See Avery's Verdelho 1838.

GREAT MADEIRA COLLECTIONS

The Goelet Family

Originally of French Huguenot stock, the Goelets arrived in New Amsterdam (later New York) in the mid-seventeenth century. The Goelets set up as retail merchants and diversified into wine, shipping and property, becoming a wealthy New York family second only to the Astors in their real-estate holdings. The collection began with Peter P. Goelet (1764–1828) and was passed down through the family until it was sold at Morrell & Company, New York in 1999.

'Brig Twins' 1806

The *Brig Twins* was a ship that sailed from Funchal, probably via South America, to Charleston, New York or Boston to include two crossings of the equator. This wine was in a whisky bottle, imported January 1810, bottled September 1816, recorked 1919 and 2002. Probably Rainwater in style when shipped. Tasted at Patrick Grubb's tasting in 2002: pale/mid-amber;

extraordinary smell of musty cupboards and mothballs, very austere and dry, searing acidity and a taste of old casks, possibly not fortified?

Murdock Yuille, Wardrop & Co.

In an amber whisky bottle, imported 1824, bottled in 1825, recorked 1919 and 2002. Tasted in 2002 as above, probably Verdelho/Rainwater in style: very pale amber in colour; gentle ethereal aromas, hint of fresh peaches and apricot; very, very dry and austere, not offering a great deal of pleasure to taste, vaguely nutty and quite delicate on the finish. A curiosity.

'Victoria Wine'

Imported in October 1841 by March & Benson, bottled in 1843 and decanted into demi-johns in 1883. Bottled December 1889 by William H. Fearing. Sold in New York from the Goelet family collection. Tasted in 2002, a wine ullaged to the bottom shoulder: the palest amber in colour; odd mothball nose (bottle stink?) with overtones of boiled sweets; tastes much finer, bone dry with an amontillado-like pungency and a bone dry earthy finish. Very unusual. **

Isidro Gonçalves

Founded in 1870 by António Izidro (Isidoro) Gonçalves, this family shipper used to occupy Consul Veitch's house on the Rua 5 de Outubro. The company's wines were sold almost exclusively to Brazil until it was taken over by the Companhia Vinicola de Madeira (CVM) in 1919.

GREAT MADEIRA COLLECTIONS

Dr Michael Grabham

Dr Michael Grabham (1840–1935) came from Rochford, Essex, England. He studied at St. Thomas's Hospital, London where he qualified in 1861 and served as house surgeon. In 1865 he married Mary Anne Blandy, daughter of Charles Ridpath Blandy, and took up permanent residence as a practitioner on the island of Madeira. Grabham was an observer and writer on botany and other scientific subjects, including the island's climate. A lover of wine, over his long professional life he assembled one of the finest cellars on the island. The core of his collection came directly from Charles Ridpath Blandy (see page 15) who left his most-prized wines to his daughter. Thus Michael Grabham acquired the remains of the legendary 1792 Napoleon Pipe which had been bottled by John Blandy in 1840. Aged 93, Grabham was persuaded to sell two dozen bottles of this wine to the Saintsbury Club in London. Grabham's cellar included many other treasures including the Challenger Madeira which enjoyed a round trip on HMS *Challenger* between 1862 and 1876. In 1952, Michael Grabham's son, Walter, gave his father's cellar to John and Graham Blandy. (See the story on Blandy's 1811 Solera Bual for more information on the Grabham wines.) Bottles from the Grabham collection can still be found in private cellars and occasionally come up for auction.

São Martinho 1879

Blandy embossed on the capsule, bottled 1893, recorked January 1953, 1960, rebottled and recorked July 1996. A bottle from my late father-in-law's cellar, produced during the phylloxera decade and almost certainly from the Grabham collection: mid-amber orange colour, broad green rim; gentle, delicate ethereal aromas, dried apricots with a hint of blossom, very pure and clean; quite dry in style (Verdelho in style), long and lithe, lovely texture and purity on the palate, apricots with a touch of honey and a long dry finish. Gentle and expressive. Tasted twice: in Seattle 2003 and again in New York in 2013. *****

Verdelho 1822 – part of the Grabham collection

Bottled in 1900, and recorked 1986. Tasted in 2011: Mid-mahogany, olive-green rim; fine, lifted, high-toned aromas, ethereal, delicate leafy, floral; fine, linear and sinewy on the palate, gentle but still wonderfully fresh with a tea-leaf and candied-peel character and a lovely, long linear finish. Supremely delicate but in no way fragile. ****/*****

A. C. Pacheco

Pacheco was a *partidista* in Funchal. This wine, bottled in 1927, was probably from the Grabham Collection. I tasted this rather wonderful pre-phylloxera wine in 2006 at Patrick Grubb's tasting: mid-amber/mahogany; lovely scented floral aromas, rose petals; linseed and beeswax, very unusual with explosive acidity towards the finish. Like licking a highly polished antique table and rather lovely for that. ****

Bual Barbosa c.1820

The label rather usefully explains: 'Owing to the absence of the owner, grapes were picked almost as raisins. Grown at Quinta Stanford. Vintage about 1820, in wood for 65 years, demi-johns for 50 years, bottled around 1935'. Quinta Stanford was located just to the west of Funchal immediately above Quinta Perestrelo and the modern-day Pestana Miramar hotel. It was also known as Quinta Pitta, the name of which lives on in the Rua Dr Pitta, and the property is now known as Quinta da Vista Alegre. The name Quinta Stanford has recently been revived for some holiday cottages behind Vista Alegre. 'Bual Barbosa' is clearly a reference to the grape variety although this is the only reference that I have seen to a grape of this name, Malvasia Barbosa being the better-known variety. The label of this wine, observes Patrick Grubb, is reminiscent of the late Dr Grabham's collection. Tasted in 2009: mid-amber/mahogany, olive-green rim; delicate, high-toned aromas with a touch of varnish and polish; powerful, thick-cut marmalade and barley sugar flavours, long, rich and gripping, very powerful with fine concentration and a big finish. ****/*****

A. E. Henriques

The son of João Joaquim Gonçalves Henriques, the founder of Henriques & Henriques, António Eduardo Henriques established his own firm, A. E. Henriques Succrs. The company was bought by H&H soon after his death.

Bual 1907 Solera

Tasted in 2002: mid-deep mahogany, rich slightly soupy, raisiny aromas, similarly rich on the palate, fruit cake and *bolo de mel* (honey cake) with a touch of molasses on the finish. **/***

Henriques & Henriques

Established in 1850 and now based in Câmara de Lobos, H&H are profiled at length in Chapter 5. Until 1974 the family owned some of the finest vineyards on Madeira (see Quinta do Serrado, below) and many of these wines will have been produced from the company's own grapes. This is an outstanding range of wines.

Henriques & Henriques Extra Reserve

A blend of wines at least thirty years old, bottled to commemorate the opening of the new *adega* and *armazens* in Câmara de Lobos on 4 June 1994, tasted with John Cossart in 2004: very deep mahogany colour, thin olive-green rim; rich, pungent aromas, raisins, *bolo de mel* (parkin); incredible richness and intensity, molasses mid-palate followed up by a wonderfully incisive finish. Very sweet and unctuous but saved from cloying by ravishing acidity. This has it all. *****

Henriques & Henriques Boal 1980

Tasted at H&H in 2004: mid-deep mahogany, green tinge; beautiful floral aroma, rose petals; lovely medium-rich flavour, fine and expressive with the concentration of fruit cake and a tang of marmalade towards the finish. ****

Henriques & Henriques 1976 Terrantez

Tasted at H&H in 2004: deep amber; rather subdued floral character; lovely clean incisive flavour, bitter-sweet marmalade fruit lingering onto the finish. ***/****

Henriques & Henriques 1971 Sercial

Tasted in London, 2007: lovely scented wine, floral with toasty undertones; dry but not austerely so, clean as a whistle with steely acidity, fine and delicate with a bone-dry finish. ***/****

Henriques & Henriques 1964 Sercial

A wine rebottled in November 2005 and tasted with Humberto Jardim in 2015: mid-deep orange/amber; powerful, pungent, savoury aromas with a touch of Marmite; wonderfully austere in style, almost to the point of being punishing, with the rapier-like power of Sercial's nervy acidity cutting in mid-palate, very long with a fine *salgadinho* finish. ****/*****

Henriques & Henriques Boal 1957

Tasted at the Portuguese Embassy, London in 2007: mid-mahogany; lovely savoury, meaty nose; rich (92 g/l residual sugar), savoury-sweet, full, honeyed and slightly toasty with concentrated rather pruney length. ****

Henriques & Henriques Boal 1954

From a fine vintage, 'especially for Bual, Malvasia and Bastardo', notes Noel Cossart. This wine tasted at H&H in 2004 and again in 2015, bottled in June 1993: deep burnt umber; soft, rich and floral on the nose, just a touch soupy and lacking definition; tangy, medium-rich style with dried apricot concentration and allspice, dryish finish. Well balanced, ***/****. Rich *rancio* aromas, floral with a touch of carpenter's workshop; mellifluous and honeyed initially with *bolo de mel* offset by a slightly astringent finish. ****

Henriques & Henriques Malvasia 1954

Tasted at H&H in 2004: very deep, dark mahogany, thin olive-green rim; big, rich but slightly ponderous on the nose, slightly burnt and smoky; very fine, incisive bitter-sweet flavour, candied orange peel, with a beautifully poised finish. ****

Henriques & Henriques 1954 Terrantez

Tasted with John Cossart in 2004 and again (a long-opened bottle from my own cellar) in 2014: mid-red tinged mahogany, thin olive-green rim; ethereal aromas, gloriously focused and concentrated; tawny marmalade and allspice with a fine thread of bitterness running all the way through to the finish. Just verging on unctuous but then perfectly offset by racy acidity. Fine, delicate, bitter-sweet finish. Fantastic! ****/*****

Henriques & Henriques 1944 Sercial

Tasted at 'A Celebration of Vintage Madeira', London, 1998: deep colour for Sercial, squeaky clean, high-toned aromas, quite rich in style smoky flavours, a touch too caramelised for my liking but with lovely texture and a long nervy finish, ***/**** . Tasted again at H&H in 2004: mid-mahogany; fine, ethereal leafy nose, smoky with a touch of lapsang suchong tea; dry yet full and concentrated with tangy flavours of lime marmalade and a fine, racy finish. ****/*****

Henriques & Henriques 1934 Verdelho

Tasted at H&H in 2004: very deep mahogany, lovely, autumnal bonfire of a nose, tea-leaf character, dry but rich and concentrated at the same time, orange peel, powerful with kick to the finish. ****

Henriques & Henriques, Ribeira Real Reserva

A wine that belonged to the late John Cossart, this was bottled in 1957 and is thought to have been around fifty years old at the time. Presumably from the famous vineyard of Ribeira Real in Câmara de Lobos: mid-deep orange/amber; very fine, smoked aromas, very complex with a touch of green hedgerow underlying; bitter-sweet orange peel and honey, fabulous richness and concentration with a hint of peat and malt towards an effusive finish. ****/*****

Henriques & Henriques, Century Malmsey

From a *solera* laid down in 1899 but not bottled until 1999, tasted on three occasions with three very similar notes: mid-deep mahogany, thin green rim; pungent high-toned aromas, redolent of green leaves and flowers, a hedgerow of a nose; incredibly rich (123g/l of residual sugar), unctuous dried fig and prune-like fruit offset by powerful yet ravishing acidity which keeps the wine fresh and alive. Long, powerful sinewy length. Great poise. ****/*****

Henriques & Henriques 1898 Solera Verdelho

A wine greatly treasured by John Cossart, this was only bottled in 2009, a year after his death. Tasted in 2015; very fine, gentle complexity, beautifully restrained with a touch of vanilla and malt; fine, gentle, toasted hazelnut complexity with a long savoury finish. Very elegant Verdelho. ****

Henriques & Henriques 1898 Solera Boal

At Patrick Grubb's tasting in 1998: lovely nervy high-toned character; not that rich but fine and balanced with a long, dry toasty finish. ***/****

Henriques & Henriques 1894 Founder's Solera

A wine made from Malvasia, tasted in 2015; deep-green-tinged mahogany; ethereal bouquet, beautifully lifted and singing from the glass, butterscotch and the merest hint of molasses; torrefaction with a hint of dark chocolate concentration and toffeed richness, acidity rising to yield a toffee-apple finish. ****/*****

Henriques & Henriques Reserva Sercial

Thought to be 200 years old, a wine rebottled in 1965. Tasted at H&H in 2004: mid-mahogany; lovely smoky aromas, delicate lapsang suchong character; similarly fine and delicate on the palate, savoury-dry, pure and quite austere in style, long and elegant. ****/*****

Henriques & Henriques Special Reserve

Another wine reputed to be about 200 years old in 2002, this was bought into H&H at its foundation and rebottled in 1965 and 1992: mid-deep amber, green-tinged rim; wonderfully fresh aromas, dried figs and dried apricots, very fine and beautifully poised, searing acidity with great power and depth and a rapier-like finish. Powerful, pungent and focused. ****/*****

Henriques & Henriques Velho Verdelho

One of a number of wines dating back to before the founding of H&H in 1850. This wine belonged to Peter Cossart who worked at H&H for fifty-three vintages between 1938 and 1991, was inherited by his son John and sold by his children to the Rare Wine Company in the US. John Cossart believed that this wine was already considered 'old' when the company was founded and may well date back to the late eighteenth century. This wine was aired for about six months in demi-john before being recorked in late 2011: mid-deep amber, thin green rim; soft, clean, gentle aromas, not especially expressive; smooth, soft toasty flavours, hazelnut, savoury with a touch of cask on the finish and a saline edge, very elegant. *****

Henriques & Henriques W. S. Boal

One of the so-called 'Heavenly Quartet' of ancient yet undated madeiras produced by Henriques & Henriques (alongside Grand Old Boal, Malvazia and Reserva Sercial). Bottled in 1927 and recorked in 1957, 1975 and 2000, this wine was thought to be fifty years old when it was inherited by João de Belém in 1850. Some wines in the blend may date from the eighteenth century. Three positive but rather different notes on this: pale to mid-mahogany with a thin olive-green rim; very fine, elegant if slightly subdued aroma; quite dry yet fine, beautifully poised, bitter-sweet flavours and fantastic rapier-like concentration and depth. Captivating wine, *****. In 2002: mid-amber/mahogany, green-tinged rim; rather woody-peaty aromas, some nuttiness; rich on the palate, brazil nuts, very fine and intense with great depth and persistence. Savoury length, ****. Tasted again at 'The Beauty of Bual' tasting in New York in 2014; a bottle that was acquired by the Rare Wine Company from John Cossart's own cellar following his death in 2011 (it was aired for six months in demi-john before being rebottled and re-corked): mid-deep amber; still rich on the nose, a touch of honey with *bolo de mel* (Madeira 'honey cake') or parkin (its Yorkshire equivalent) on the nose; wonderful texture and intensity, not especially sweet or rich but with a marmalade tang and above all wonderful balance and poise, almost delicate on the finish. Very fine. ****/*****

Henriques & Henriques Grand Old Bual

Another member of the 'Heavenly Quartet' (see above), this probably originates from the 1820s and was already old when H&H was founded in 1850. It was held in wood then demi-johns, and bottled off bit by bit between 1920s and 1960s. Two notes, the first from 2006: orange/amber in colour; very fine, intense floral bouquet of a nose with a hint of Irish whiskey; fine and focused, leathery and savoury, not *that* sweet yet rich and very powerful. Tight knit and very fine, *****. The second, not quite so heavenly, note comes from 'The Beauty of Bual' tasting in 2014: slightly deeper in colour than the WS (see above) with a rather dank nose and some varnish; richer and fatter than the WS, powerful and vibrant on the palate, concentrated with a full finish but lacking a little in freshness. ***/****

Boal Velho, Miguel Jardim, Henriques & Henriques

This wine dates from the first half of the nineteenth century. It was bought by H&H in 1906 and bottled in 1927, recorked in 1955, 1969 and 1991. There were 890 bottles and this one, tasted in 2011 is number 96: mid-deep red-tinged amber; an autumnal bonfire on the nose with a slightly sour note; nothing sour on the palate, rich autumnal flavours, clean, gentle with lovely weight and the texture of age, savoury dry finish akin to brazil nuts falling away quite fast. A fascinating wine. ****

Henriques & Henriques Reserva Malvasia

Dating from the first quarter of the nineteenth century and bottled in 1964, my note is from a tasting at H&H in 2005: mid-deep mahogany; delicate though not particularly expressive on the nose, high toned and a touch singed; very graceful and elegant on the palate with fine, racy acidity offsetting the richness to perfection, beautifully poised and fine. **** / *****

Quinta do Serrado 1835 Boal

Quinta do Serrado at Câmara de Lobos was the family estate of the Henriques family. A huge parcel of nineteenth-century madeira was sold at Christie's in London in 1989 and 1990 (about 2,000 bottles) but the Henriques family retained some bottles including this one (tasted in New York in 2014), purchased by the Rare Wine Company, Sonoma in 1997: mid-deep, red-tinged mahogany and light sediment; gentle toffeed fruit, slightly honeyed on the nose but not giving a great deal away; quite rich with lovely sweetness backed by limey acidity. Good depth and length. There is a touch of old cognac about this. ****

Quinta do Serrado 1827 Boal

From the same Henriques family estate. This was put into demi-john in 1935 and bottled in 1988 for shipment to London where nearly 1,000 bottles were sold at auction over two years from 1990. Tasted in 2013: deep mahogany; not a great deal happening on the nose, slightly dank but with an underlying tang; very rich, spicy and intense, thick-cut marmalade, offset by lovely acidity and a fabulous finish which really wakes you up. Full and very satisfying. ****

Vinhos Justino Henriques (Justino's)

Justino's have sometimes been looked down on rather unfairly for the quality of their 'vintage' wines. Some show a slightly earthy rusticity but they have the depth and concentration of age. Older vintages originated from the Companhia Vinicola da Madeira (CVM) which used to own Vinhos Justino Henriques (VJH). Since 1996 some of these wines have also been bottled under the Broadbent label and shipped to the US. (See page 108 for an extensive profile of Justino's.)

VJH Terrantez 1978 (bottled 2004)

Three notes on the same wine, two under Justino's and the other under the Broadbent label. Justino's, tasted in 2007: high toned, quite delicate with lovely lemony acidity, finishes well. Recognisably Terrantez in style, ***. Broadbent's: amber-tawny; subdued, slightly dusty, savoury-sweet aromas; fine bitter-sweet orange marmalade tang balanced by fresh acidity and a dusting of tannin. Slightly rustic in character but good nonetheless, ***/****. Tasted blind at the *Decanter* World Wine Awards in 2014 where this wine won a gold medal: not very expressive on the nose, clean slight toastiness with a hint of old cognac; lovely rich seamless flavour, candied peel and crystalised fruit, lovely off-dry finish. ****

VJH 1978 Boal

Tasted in 2004 and again in 2015 (2014 bottling): mid-deep amber with an olive-green tinge to the rim; vegetal aromas, wild sorrel; quite full, rich and well-defined flavours with a lovely thick-cut marmalade character, brisk acidity with a slightly dusty finish. ***

VJH 1964 Boal

Tasted in 2004 in Justino's *armazém* and again in 2015 (bottled 2014): mid-mahogany, olive-green-tinged rim; singed nose, perhaps lacking a little definition but with a lovely hint of lapsang suchong tea; rich and rather soupy on the palate but full and satisfying with a fine tang to the finish, ***/****. Beef tea aromas, rich, sweet apricot flavours with a racy, astringent savoury-sweet finish. ***

VJH 1964 Malvazia

Tasted in 2015: deep mahogany; rich, singed and distinctly caramelised on the nose; similar on the palate, thick-cut marmalade offset by zesty acidity though rather astringent and rustic in style on the finish. ***

VJH 1954 Verdelho

From a fine year in general, this wine is also bottled under the Broadbent label. Tasted in 2004: pale-mid mahogany, olive-green tinge; subdued and slightly dusty caramelised nose; much more expressive on the palate with a fine tang of lime and orange marmalade followed by a bitter-sweet finish, ***. Tasted again in 2015, a bottling from November 2014: glossy, polished aromas, quite delicate in style with lemon and lime marmalade, fine nervy acidity with a rather astringent finish. ***

VJH 1940 Sercial

A fine year with Sercial being 'especially good' according to Noel Cossart. This wine was bottled in January 2005 and tasted shortly afterwards: amber verging on mahogany; fine if slightly subdued on the nose, toasted almonds and a hint of peat; very fine, dry toasty flavour, classic in style with wonderful searing acidity heading towards a racy finish. Lovely texture and concentration for a dry wine, ****. Another positive note from 2014 on the November 2014 bottling: lovely lifted, aromas, lemon and lime marmalade, grapefruit freshness, very pure and racy with wonderful nervy length. A very fine Sercial. ****/*****

VJH 1934 Verdelho

Two very positive notes on this wine, the first from a tasting at Justino's in 2000: mid-deep amber; lovely high-toned leafy aromas, apricots and crisp citrus acidity, well balanced with lovely poise, ****+. Tasted blind at the *Decanter* World Wine Awards in 2014 where this wine won a gold medal and again at Justino's in 2015: mid-deep mahogany colour; beef tea aromas with a touch of figgy richness underlying; similarly rich but very elegant on the palate, savoury with dried fig concentration and a long dryish, astringent finish. Great poise. ****/*****

VJH 1934 Boal

Tasted in 2015, a wine bottled in November 2014: mid-deep amber/mahogany; fine, lifted aromas, just stopping short of high-toned, crystalised fruits and citrus; grapefruit and tangerine marmalade with butterscotch richness and depth, at the same time complex and elegant on the finish. ****

VJH 1934 Malvasia

Tasted in 2015, bottled November 2014: deep mahogany, distinctly high-toned, furniture polish aromas; torrefaction (mocha) with wonderful texture and depth. A very beautiful wine. ****

VJH 1933 Malvasia

Three quite positive notes, first at Patrick Grubb's 1998 tasting: burnt and slightly rancid on the nose (possibly due to inadequate decanting time); much better on the palate, rich and balanced, focused with a touch of all-spice, ***. In 2000 at Justino's: mid-deep mahogany, high toned and singing from the glass (1.5 g/l of VA), rich, figs and dates with a touch of coffee, lovely texture and balance, crisp acidity on savoury-sweet finish, ***/****. In October 2006 at a *World of Fine Wine* comparative tasting, bottled January 2006: pungent high-toned aromas with cinnamon and allspice; powerful tawny marmalade richness with wonderful concentration and texture from long ageing in cask. Richness balanced by lingering, steely acidity. ****

Justino Henriques Verdelho 1748 Solera

This wine was shipped to the US in the mid-1960s and sold by Sherry Wines and Spirits on Madison Avenue (predecessor of Sherry-Lehman). According to Justino Henriques, the wine had been acquired from João Alfredo Faria, 'an important land owner in Funchal'. In 1967 an advertisement claimed that the entire contents of one 1748 cask were bottled, totalling 700 bottles. This bottle, tasted in New York in 2013 is number 38: slightly cloudy mid-mahogany, green-tinged rim; a really soupy, beefy nose, Bovril character both on the nose and on the palate, very meaty and coarse in style, attenuated without any power, pungency or depth. Proof that not all old Madeira is great!

Hinton

At the end of the nineteenth century the Hintons were one of the most successful families in Madeira. William Hinton was born in Naples in 1817, the son of a landowner from Wiltshire, England. He arrived in Madeira in 1838 and married the daughter of Robert Wallas, a wine shipper and the owner of a flour mill on the island. William Hinton started a sugar factory which his son Harry expanded into a sugar monopoly (including the supply of *aguardente de cana* which was used for the fortification of madeira wine until 1967). Harry Hinton joined forces with Welsh & Cunha and Henriques & Câmara in 1913 to form the embryonic Madeira Wine Association but was forced to leave four years later. The Hinton sugar mill was at Torreão in the centre of Funchal (now the site of a municipal park called the *Jardim de Santa Luzia* although the tall brick factory chimney still stands).

GREAT MADEIRA COLLECTIONS

Braheem Kassab

Braheem (sometimes Brahim) Kassab was a Syrian embroidery merchant who amassed a fine collection of old madeiras in the early twentieth century, marking each bottle with his personal seal: B. A. K. A large part of his cellar was auctioned by Christie's, London in 1986. His cellar included the oldest dated bottle thought to be in existence: a 1715 Terrantez stencilled with the initials 'JCA & CA' (presumably João Carlos Aguiar).

1820 Verdelho

Embossed with the Kassab seal in wax, no indication of any shipper, stencilled hand-blown bottle from my own cellar tasted in 2015: pale orange-tinged amber, pale green rim; very fine, caramelised orange and candied peel aromas, pure and restrained with the spirit just showing through; bitter-sweet candied citrus flavours, still with orange and grapefruit freshness and a touch of quince, seamless on the palate all the way through to a dry tang on the finish. A fascinating old wine. ****/*****

Krohn

Founded in 1858, John and Nicholas Krohn came from Russia where the family lived for two generations, having originated in Denmark. One member of the family had been food taster to the Tzar, so they had all the right connections. Krohn Bros. & Co. had its headquarters in the Carmo district of Funchal where they would both *estufa* and sun their wines for months at a time. They were the last company to have an *estufa do sol*. There were so many members of the Krohn family in Funchal that the city was known jokingly as Krohnstadt. At the end of the nineteenth century Krohn were the second largest shippers after Cossart Gordon, selling mostly to Germany and Russia; some wines were labelled in Cyrillic.

INTERIOR OF THE ARMAZEM OF MESSRS. KROHN BROTHERS AT FUNCHAL, MADEIRA.

When sales to these markets collapsed during the First World War the company went out of business and the last member of the family left the island in 1953. Krohn became part of the Madeira Wine Association and was used for a time as a minor brand. In their heyday Krohn had an excellent reputation (Vizetelly writes well of them after his visit in 1877), but I have only knowingly ever tasted one of their wines.

Old Reserve Cama de Lobos

With a label in Cyrillic, tasted in 2006 at Patrick Grubb's tasting: mid-amber, rather an earthy-peaty nose, akin to an Irish whiskey (more Paddy than Bushmills), soft, rather rustic flavours, full but dry in style, still offset by steely acidity on the finish. **

Leacock

John Leacock came to Madeira in 1741 and the family story is told in Chapter 5. The late William Leacock's private cellar was sold at auction in London in December 2008.

Leacock 1978 Malvasia

Tasted at the MWC in 2000: pale mahogany, green-tinged rim; savoury-sweet with a hint of cigar box on the nose; soft raisin and dried fig flavours, lovely richness offset by spicy acidity. ***/****

Leacock 1969 Sercial

Tasted in 2005 and again at the *Decanter* World Wine Awards in 2013 where it won a gold medal: pale amber; open, fragrant, aromatic yet delicate and perfumed; very fine, pure, lime marmalade flavours, typically austere with searing acidity on the finish, ****. Walnuts and old furniture polish on the nose, wonderful intensity with rapier-like grapefruit acidity. ****/*****

Leacock 1963 Sercial

Tasted in 2014, a bottle from my own cellar: mid-amber; fine, supremely delicate, high-toned aromas, slightly smoky, leafy and slightly peaty; searing and very finely poised yet delicate toffee-apple character, clean as a whistle with a lovely steely, citrusy finish. A difficult wine for some, an acquired taste but a very beautiful nevertheless. ****/*****

Leacock 1954 Verdelho

Shown at Patrick Grubb's tasting in 1998: singed and smoky on the nose; quite sweet in style for Verdelho but balanced and delicious with smoky tea-leaf length and complexity ***/****

Leacock Bual 1954

At Patrick Grubb's tasting in 2008: deep amber/mahogany; fine and expressive, high-toned, thick-cut marmalade aromas and flavours, fine richness, texture and weight with a lovely tang on the finish. Good balance and depth. ****

Leacock's Verdelho 1952 Jubilee Selection

'All wines fine' according to Cossart; 'Verdelho excellent'. This note comes from a tasting in 2011: deep mahogany, unusually deep for Verdelho; lovely lifted green-tea aromas with some pungency and intensity; quite rich in style for Verdelho, slightly smoky flavours, lovely intensity offset by lemon and lime acidity, beautiful, almost explosive finish leaving a hint of chocolate orange. ****

Leacock's Sercial 1950

'Generally very fine, Sercial especially,' wrote Noel Cossart about the 1950 harvest. Two very consistent notes, first at Patrick Grubb's tasting, 1998: wonderful floral scent; characteristically nervy and steely, perfect balance with great persistence, ****. Second note from a tasting at the MWC 2011: mid-amber/orange, green rim; lovely lifted, floral aromas, green and leafy too, freshly crushed leaves, gunpowder tea; quite delicate; very clean yet gentle grassy character, off-dry with a powerful savoury finish (salted nuts) but not too punishing or austere. Very fine Sercial. ****/*****

Leacock 1934 'SJ'

From an outstanding vintage, the grapes for this wine came from the Leacock's own São João vineyard where Thomas Slapp Leacock experimented with ways to control phylloxera (see page 41). Tasted in 2011: mid-green-tinged amber; lifted liquorous aromas, perfumed too, like an apricot liqueur (if there is such a thing); bitter sweet (actually more bitter than sweet), dried apricots and figs, slightly singed with a touch of chocolate towards a dry finish. Complex, very unusual and rather lovely. ****

'HFS' 1896 (from the Leacock family)

Tasted in 2011: mid-deep amber/mahogany; curiously closed and sullen, very uncommon in a madeira of this age (could it be that this wine will open up more on ullage?), touch of quince jelly richness on the nose; quince again on the palate, medium sweet and gentle in style, almost elegant on the finish, not rich but beautifully poised yet restrained. ****+?

Leacock 1882 Verdelho AO - SM

Produced by D'Oliveira who were *partidistas* until the 1970s and sold wine to the Madeira Wine Association (now the Madeira Wine Company). This was bottled under a variety of labels including Blandy, Cossart Gordon and Lomelino. António Oliveira (AO) was a producer with vineyards in São Martinho (SM). Tasted in New York at the Velhissimo Verdelho tasting in 2013: very deep mahogany colour with a thin yellow-green rim; rather a soupy nose, lacking in definition, caramelised fruit, rich and sweet in style, soupy, raisiny fruit with a burnt edge. The colour and the character of this wine suggest the addition of caramel or *calda* at some stage. **

Leacock 1863 Boal

The 1863 Boal appeared under a number of different MWA /MWC labels and presumably all the bottlings share a common origin. Tasted in New York in 2014, this was only bottled in 1978 and imported into the US by World Shippers of Philadelphia: very deep, dark, reddish mahogany colour with a heavy sediment; rich, verging on soupy on the nose, burnt pruney fruit with a touch of coffee bean and molasses; very forceful with a pronounced tang, rich and raisiny with a pruney finish. Just a bit too heavy and ponderous to score more highly. **/***

Leacock 1860 Sercial Solera

Tasted in 1999 at a Master of Wine Madeira Seminar with Richard Blandy: 1000 bottles, bottled 1988 (with sixty-five years in wood) deep browning colour, marmite on nose and Bovril flavour, very powerful but lacking in finesse. **

Leacock 1856 Bual

From a vintage in the midst of oidium, wines from 1856 are rare. This bottle (tasted in New York in April 2014) was imported into the USA in the 1960s by Leacock's erstwhile agent, Julius Wile. Mid-deep amber/ mahogany; slightly floral with a honeyed character and a touch of furniture polish too (menthol and mint tea also noted); rich with lovely texture and intensity, full, heady and figgy, quite powerful and well integrated with wonderful depth but not that much noticeable acidity to keep it alive on the finish. ***/****

Lomelino

I have always had a big soft spot for Lomelino, and the name has been imprinted on my brain ever since I tasted some lovely old wines from them early in my wine trade career when they were represented in London by Russell & McIver. The company was named after Tarquino Torquarto de Câmara Lomelino who took over the firm of Roberto Leal in 1820 and began shipping wines under his own name. On Tarquino Lomelinos's death the firm was inherited by his sister Anna who was married to Carlo de Bianchi, a ship owner of Genoese origin. 'C. de B.', as his bottles were marked, amassed a fine stock of old bottled wine. The Bianchis owned a vineyard and were also *partidistas,* holding stock to sell to other shippers. Lomelino supplied wines to the Swedish Royal Family. The company became part of the Madeira Wine Association alongside Power Drury in 1934

and António de Bianchi was the first technical director at the MWA. His son Ferdinando Bianchi, who died in 2006, was General Manager of the MWA in the 1960s and 1970s. Until recently the Lomelino family house on the Rua das Mercês served as the administrative headquarters for the Madeira Wine Company.

Lomelino 1914 Bual

Tasted in 2014, a bottle from my cellar which I opened to commemorate the anniversary of the outbreak of the First World War: deep amber with slight reddish glint, considerable sediment in the bottle; pungent, lifted with a touch of butterscotch and toffee; savoury, almost amontillado, character to underlying, lightly toasted and singed around the edges; caramelised orange freshness accompanied by quince marmalade richness, smooth and seamless, the richness extends all the way through a long, lithe finish. ****/*****

Lomelino 1906 Malvazia

A bottle from my own cellar, purchased from Patrick Grubb and drunk over Christmas 2014: mid-deep amber/mahogany; ethereal, pungent, lifted aromas; beautifully focused toffeed richness rapidly offset by rapier-like acidity with caramel toffee reappearing on the finish. Long and rich, but not that rich for a Malmsey due to the high acidity, indubitably fine. ****/*****

Lomelino 1885 Verdelho

This wine is a rarity with only two bottles having appeared at auction. Tasted in New York in 2013: mid-amber to pale mahogany, green-tinged rim; gentle, savoury smoked aromas, hickory, nuts too; rather rich in style for Verdelho, savoury flavours, hazelnuts, slightly salted towards the finish, lovely savoury length. ****

Lomelino 1869 Boal

Tasted in New York in 2014, one of the finest wines in 'The Beauty of Bual' tasting: mid-deep amber colour, orange-green rim; lovely open floral aromas, a touch of carpentry workshop but clean, fragrant and wonderfully fresh, just a touch roasted at the edges; quite sweet initially, apricots, and mandarin orange, lovely weight and orange marmalade richness offset by a beautiful streak of acidity that runs all the way through to the finish. Perfect balance and poise. *****

Lomelino 1862 Verdelho

From a vintage known for Terrantez, this wine has appeared under at least three different labels: Lomelino, Blandy's and Avery's. A rare wine, nonetheless, with only five bottles seen at auction under the three brands. Tasted in New York in 2013: pale mahogany, thin green rim; pungent and powerful on the nose, expressive tawny marmalade character, rich and powerful, quite sweet with lovely limey acidity to offset the tang of tawny marmalade. A touch meaty. The acidity goes all the way through to the finish, giving this wine great poise. *****

Campanário 1846

Tasted in 2013 at Patrick Grubb's London tasting, this wine is labelled 'Herdade do Dr. Tarquino T. C. Lomelino, Eugenia de B. Henriques. Metal capsule embossed 'Camara de Lobos. F. Eduardo Henriques Succr'. (See also 1868 Very Old Boal 'EBH' on page 211.) Companário is one of the best areas of vineyard to the west of Funchal (see page 57). Lovely orange/amber colour, green rim; open, expressive crystalised fruit, apricots and a hint of spring flowers; lovely texture, fine, quite delicate with dried apricots on the palate, long and lithe, a very beautiful wine with the merest touch of cask on the finish: fine, focused and linear. *****

Lomelino, Quinta da Paz, 1840

Quinta de Paz was an estate belonging to Joseph Phelps which was on the Ilheus, just to the west of Funchal. When Phelps left the island at the end of the nineteenth century the property passed to the Bianchi family, owners of Lomelino. The stock then came into the possession of the Leacock and Blandy families when Lomelino joined the MWA in the 1930s. The wine had been rebottled by Lomelino in 1926. In 1971 Graham Blandy gave each of his children two bottles, calling them 'museum pieces'. He noted that the wine was probably Verdelho. This bottle belonged to the late William Leacock whose wines were sold at Christie's in London in 2008 and was included in the 'Velhissimo Verdelho' tasting in New York in 2013: mid-mahogany, green-tinged rim; unusual and somewhat disjointed initially on the nose, slightly scented, floral, leafy; bitter-sweet twist, lovely candied peel character, cinnamon too, complex with a beautiful texture, leafy finish with a green edge. ****/*****

NAPOLEON'S MADEIRA, BOAL 1792

This legendary wine accompanied Napoleon when he called in at Funchal en route to St. Helena in 1815. It was never drunk by the exiled Emperor, nor was it officially paid for, but the British Consul Henry Veitch was apparently given some gold coins by Napoleon in exchange. These were buried beneath the foundation stone of the Anglican Church (Church of the Holy Trinity) in Funchal, the building of which was supervised by Veitch. Two years after Napoleon's death the wine was returned to Veitch, who sold it on to Charles Ridpath Blandy (see page 15). The wine was left to Dr Michael Grabham (see page 178) who was born in the year the wine was bottled (1840) and whose father was born in 1792. Two dozen bottles were bought by the Saintsbury Club in London. The following poem by Martin Armstrong, one of the founding members of the Saintsbury Club in London, describes the episode:

On a Certain Madeira Boal 1792

The doomed and broken Bonaparte
To thaw the ice that bound his heart
Bore from Madeira to his jail
Islanded twixt sea and gale
The barreled juice of grapes that grew
Twenty-three years ere Waterloo.
But Death was urging to his bed
Him who so richly Death had fed;
Aye, that more grim Napoleon
Was closing icy fingers on
The little body and great brain,
Bidding the haughty lip abstain
From comfort of the anodyne.
The weakening hand put by the wine,
And when at last the hand fell slack,
Homeward the cask was carried back
Unbroached, and when the wine had stood
Nigh half a century in wood,
They bottled it and duly laid Cellared in its native shade.
The heart that hoped the world to gain
A century in dust has lain.
Yet we of these late times may sip
The wine forbid his dying lip.

Pereira D'Oliveira

The D'Oliveira family were vineyard owners in São Martinho and essentially *partidistas* until they began shipping wine in their own right in the 1980s. The company is very well stocked with old wine dating back to 1850, the year of their foundation. Their only gap comes in the 1940s and 1950s when there was very little wine set aside for long-term ageing. Some of their dated wines were rather confusingly stencilled '*reserva*' until this designation was abolished for dated wines in 2010. A full profile of the company can be found on page 124.

D'Oliveira 1988 Verdelho

A wine tasted shortly after bottling in January 2015: mid-deep amber with a glint of red; savoury with a touch of *rancio* on the nose, though still not very expressive; soft, toast, savoury-nutty flavours backed by a touch of spicy marmalade. Needs time to settle. *** +?

D'Oliveira 1982 Boal

Also bottled in 2015: mid-deep amber; gentle, perfumed aromas, quite exotic (sub-tropical fruit) with a touch of curry; rich, sweet and slightly burnt on the palate, bitter-sweet and astringent on the finish. ***

D'Oliveira 1981 Verdelho

Tasted shortly after bottling in 2004: deep amber, rather soupy in style, yet leafy and recognisably Verdelho, open and fragrant; quite rich and sweet in style for Verdelho with more than a hint of caramel/toffee, just about offset by crisp acidity. Long bitter-sweet finish. **/*** +?

D'Oliveira 1977 Sercial

Tasted shortly after bottling in 2015: mid-deep amber, dark for Sercial; fine, high-toned crème brûlée aromas with a touch of *rancio*; powerful, tangy citrus character (just 30g/l residual sugar), orange peel with black pepper and allspice, nervy grapefruit-like acidity, uncompromising in style and very expressive of Sercial. ****

D'Oliveira 1977 Terrantez

Three rather different notes from 1998, 2002 and 2007 respectively: mid-deep mahogany colour, rich but dull and not very expressive on the nose, full, spicy with nervy acidity and a rather soupy-woody finish. Not much in the way of varietal expression here, **. Complex and high toned, dry and rather searing in style, bitter sweet, nutty complexity with a hint of roasted coffee, **/***. A 2007 bottling: high toned, sings from the glass with bitter-sweet citrus fruit and a very powerful seemingly dry, tangy finish that goes on and on. ***/****

D'Oliveira 1973 Verdelho

Tasted at the *World of Fine Wine* magazine in London in 2006, a bottling from 2002: mid-mahogany; lovely high-toned caramelised aromas with a touch of Demerara; full, rich and concentrated with a powerful tawny marmalade tang and a slightly rustic, woody-casky finish, ***. Another note made in 2007: leathery aromas, quite rich and savoury, good weight but a bit wild and slightly medicinal on the finish. ***

D'Oliveira 1973 Boal

At the same tasting (above) in 2006, a wine bottled in 2002: mid-mahogany; pungent high-toned aromas, dried fruits, slightly singed; big, powerful flavour, dried fruit compote with racy acidity and a powerfully astringent finish. Makes up in power for what it lacks in finesse. ****

D'Oliveira 1971 Terrantez

Tasted at the Portuguese Embassy in London in 2014: high-toned aromas, quite delicate in style, barley-sugar sweetness with a typical bitter-sweet twist. A rather lovely wine. ****

D'Oliveira 1968 Bual

Tasted in 2002: mid-mahogany, clean, high-toned aromas, lovely mature flavour, candied fruit offset by a lovely searing finish. ****

D'Oliveira 1937 Sercial

Two notes, one from Patrick Grubb's tasting 1998 and another in the same year from a 'Celebration of Vintage Madeira': very deep colour for Sercial; strange nose, rather burnt aromas combined with grass and compost; rather muddy style, lacking definition, raging acidity with a burnt finish, **. Lifted if slightly caramelised orangey aromas, bitter-sweet citrus, allspice and savoury richness, very complex if rather rustic towards the finish, ***. Most recent and very similar note from 2015, a wine bottled in 2003: very deep mahogany; rich caramelised aromas, oranges and citrus peel, vanilla, a touch burnt around the edges, lovely texture, bitter-sweet with a rather rustic, peaty finish. **/***

D'Oliveira 1927 Bastardo

A wine acquired from the purchase of Adegas do Torreão in 2001. Very rare grape variety, bottled 2005 with two notes from 2005 and 2006 respectively: deep amber/mahogany; fine high-toned aromas with butterscotch and coffee; rich, concentrated fudge-like fruit offset by bracing acidity and a long, rather singed finish. Not without charm but very unusual, ***/****; burnt nose, rather peaty but not without considerable charm, singed flavours, off-dry, rather astringent and coarse on the finish. ***

D'Oliveira 1922 Reserva Boal

Tasted in 2002: a rather short note as I was conducting a tutored tasting at the time: pronounced smoky-peaty aromas; rich and complex with nervy acidity on the finish. ***/****

D'Oliveira Boal 1908

Tasted in 2010, a bottling from 2008: very deep, dark mahogany colour, thin green rim; powerful, pungent, high toned, rather soupy and old fashioned in style; powerful bitter-sweet flavours with the concentration of age but without much elegance. Singed flavours. Molasses. Long, rich and leathery. A wine to respect more than a wine to enjoy. ***

D'Oliveira 1907 Malvazia Reserva

Bottled 2003, tasted in 2007: deep mahogany, lovely rich, lifted, dried fruit with a touch of resin and eucalyptus; rich and powerful, fine concentration but rather rustic on the finish. Fine but curious. ***

D'Oliveira 1905 Verdelho Reserva

Four quite consistent notes on this, at Patrick Grubb's tasting 1998, again at the Portuguese Embassy in London in 2005 and again with Patrick Grubb in 2008, then again in 2011: deep in colour for Verdelho; very rich in style, soft, balanced but lacking in complexity with a rather coarse, dusty finish ** / ***; deep mahogany; rather burnt autumnal aromas, quite rich in style but rather rustic and burnt towards the finish, ***. Mid-deep mahogany, green-tinged rim; a rather coarse, meaty *rancio* nose, verging on rancid; quite rich for a Verdelho, fresher on the palate than on the nose with good weight and texture and a thick cut marmalade tang, ***. 2011: slightly muddy mahogany colour; typically soupy nose, baked and lacking definition; quite rich in style for a Verdelho, akin to caramelised oranges with a thick topping of brown sugar, rich but clumsy on the finish. ***

D'Oliveira 1901 Malvazia

Tasted shortly after bottling in 2015: mid-deep mahogany; rich curried, spicy aromas, still needs to settle down; very sweet and liquorous with wonderful texture and concentration, thick-cut orange marmalade with a slightly astringent bitter-sweet, peaty finish. ***/**** +?

D'Oliveira 1900 Reserva Malmsey

I celebrated the turn of the millennium with this wine but, needless to say I didn't take notes. Two earlier notes, first at 'A Celebration of Vintage Madeira', London 1998: deep mahogany, pungent, slightly casky *rancio* aromas, rich, sweet, cooked raisins, long and sweet offset by brisk acidity, ***. At Patrick Grubb's tasting also in 1998: deep mahogany, concentrated but lacks pungency and poise, very rich and sweet with burnt Demerara sugar flavours. **/***

D'Oliveira 1890 Verdelho

Almost certainly from the family's vineyards in São Martinho, D'Oliveira still have stock of this wine in wood at their *armazens* in Funchal. Tasted in New York in 2013: mid-mahogany colour, thin yellow-green rim; torrefaction aromas, singed leaves with a touch of cask but lifted and aromatic; fine, nervy marmalade style, rich with lovely texture and mouthfeel. Caramelised with the torrefaction character re-appearing on the finish. ***

D'Oliveira 1850 Verdelho

At the time of writing this is the oldest Verdelho still available from D'Oliveira, coinciding with the year of company's foundation. This wine from the family's private collection was bottled in the 1960s or 1970s, tasted at the Velhissimo Verdelho tasting in New York in 2013: very deep red mahogany colour, thin green rim; rich but not soupy, lifted figgy aromas, a touch burnt around the edges, D'Oliveira in style but not overtly so; big and rich against a slightly casky backdrop, tawny marmalade character and roasted coffee. Very rich and long with lovely acidity. ****

Phelps

J. & W. Phelps were established as wine shippers in 1786, the family originating from Gloucestershire, England. They became a large family with vineyards all over the island. The company became Phelps & Page in 1804 and continued trading under the same name until the Phelps family moved back to England at the end of the nineteenth century. Their assets were bought by the Bianchi family who owned Lomelino. The Phelps were great philanthropists. Elizabeth Phelps led a programme of reforestation of the island, planting European oak, beech and chestnut. She also introduced the women of the island to embroidery, still a signature industry in Madeira today. In recognition of the family's contribution there is a square named Largo do Phelps near to the Rua do Carmo in Funchal where the family firm was based. The Phelps had a country estate named Quinta da Paz (see page 197).

Rutherford, Drury & Co. / Henry Dru Drury / Power, Drury & Co.

James Rutherford, partner in a firm named Rutherford & Grant, was joined by Dr Dru Drury who then traded on his own from the 1870s onwards. Henry Vizetelly describes a visit to the firm's *armazens* in 1877; this was adjacent to a convent on the western side of Funchal, with its own small vineyard. Dru Drury's son Henry Dru Drury formed a partnership with Charles Power who

INTERIOR OF THE ARMAZEM OF MR. H. DRU DRURY AT FUNCHAL, MADEIRA.

lived at Quinta Deão where he was known as a great horticulturalist. The property, with its magnificent gardens and arboretum, was located by the Ribeira de Santa Luzia and had been the official residence of the Dean of Funchal. When the last Charles Power died in 1953 the Quinta Deão was abandoned and became a high-rise housing estate in 1980. The name lives on in the Rua Nova da Quinta Deão. Power, Drury became part of the Madeira Wine Association and the name continued to be used until the 1980s.

Power Drury 1954 Terrantez

At Patrick Grubb's tasting in 1998: quite complex on the nose, a touch floral, singed but also slightly rancid with a hint of cheese, burnt toast, a rather unusual set of aromas and flavours. ***

Rutherford & Miles

Rutherford & Miles was the name of the London shipper based at Old Trinity House in Water Lane, supplied with madeira by H. P. Miles & Co after the Rutherford family left Madeira due to phylloxera in 1872. It later became Rutherford, Osborne & Perkin and was taken over by Martini Rossi in the 1960s. The Miles family history is recounted in Chapter 5.

Rutherford & Miles 1920 Bual

From a great year, 'Bual excellent' according to Noel Cossart; two notes first at Patrick Grubb's 1998 tasting: deep amber colour; lovely high-toned aromas, raisiny, wonderful concentration and complexity, a touch of molasses, long and lovely, ****. Second note in 2005: mid-deep mahogany; classic, lifted high-toned aromas, spiced tea leaf; slightly burnt, sweet-spicy marmalade character, well balanced and still fresh and expressive. ****

Rutherford & Miles 1901 Malmsey

Tasted in December 1993 at the Portuguese Embassy in London: deep mahogany colour; pungent and powerful, incredibly fresh and clean tasting, long and beautifully balanced with bitter lemon acidity offsetting the richness on the finish. A lovely wine. ****

Rutherford & Miles 1881 Bual

Tasted at Patrick Grubb's tasting in 2006, a wine with a heavy crust: mid-deep mahogany, powerful, pungent high-toned aromas; rich, intense, almost unctuous intensity, amazingly balanced by brisk acidity and a wonderfully fresh citrus peel finish. ****

Shortridge Lawton

This was still a name to be reckoned with when I joined the wine trade in 1984, the company having joined the Madeira Wine Association. The brand name continued to be used until the 1990s. Shortridge, Lawton & Co. was established in 1757 and John Shortridge was the first president of the Funchal Chamber of Commerce in 1835. Shortridge Lawton also claimed to be one of the last shippers to send casks of wine round the globe and back by sea (*vinho da roda*).

Torre Bella

The Torre Bella estate dates right back to the discovery of the island by João Goncalves Zarco in the early fifteenth century. Shortly afterwards João Afonso Correa, one of Zarco's companions, was granted a huge tract of land. A direct descendent, Fernando José Brandão Bettencourt de Noronha Henriques, born in 1768, became the largest landowner on the island with an estimated 45 per cent of the vineyards. These included some of the best sites on the south coast at Câmara de Lobos, Ribeira Brava and Campanário. Noronha Henriques was a career diplomat and in 1812 was made the Visconde de Torre Bella. As ambassador to various European countries, Torre Bella required a considerable private income. In order to supplement this he sold off parts of the estate in 1821 including the Fajã das Padres at Câmara de Lobos and the Quinta da Achada in Funchal. The latter eventually came into the ownership of the Blandys. In the nineteenth century the estate passed through a female line of the family to Russell Manners Gordon, grandson of Thomas Gordon, who had established himself as a merchant on the island in 1758 (subsequently Cossart Gordon & Co.). Manners Gordon was allowed to inherit the Torre Bella title on condition that he became a Portuguese national and he consequently had to relinquish his partnership in Newton, Gordon Cossart & Co. (see page 120). The estate again passed down a female line until it was inherited by Dermot Bolger. On his death in 1974 the estate was inherited by the two great-granddaughters of Russell Manners Gordon, Mrs Anne Fairlie and Mrs Susan Seldon. At the time it was estimated that the family estate comprised 10.6 per cent of the entire island with 1,200 tenants. With the abolition of *contracto de colónia* after the 1974 revolution (see page 23) the estate was broken up. When Mrs Fairlie died in 1986, the wines from the estate were transferred to Scotland (inadvertently via the Panama Canal and San Francisco). The wines were sold at Christie's in London by Captain David Ogilvy Fairlie of Myers Castle in Scotland in 1988 and again in 2001. Unusually for madeira, they are often bottled in old champagne bottles. These were recycled from the hotels in Madeira (most probably Reid's).

Torre Bella 1930 Boal

Tasted in 2008: deep amber; powerful nose, high toned, floral with just a hint of mothballs on the nose; fine rich concentration of flavour, lime marmalade with citrus-like acidity, slightly burnt on the finish but fine nonetheless. ***

Torre Bella 1887 Verdelho 'São Filipe'

Two notes from 2005 and 2013: pale amber, strange nose, redolent of mothballs, possibly bottle stink; much better on the palate with oriental spice and toasted almonds, off dry – a spice shop of a finish! ***/****. In New York in 2013: pale mahogany–amber with a red glint and a yellow-green rim, perfumed, seductive, lifted and very beautiful on the nose, floral (honeysuckle); soft initially, gentle and almost mellifluous until the acidity cuts in, toasted character, multi-layered and quite complex with a rich yet bitter edge to the finish. Dry for a Verdelho and quite funky! ****

Torre Bella 1879 Verdelho 'Santo António'

A wine from the Santo António district of Funchal, an area of vineyard which has now largely given way to houses. Tasted in New York in 2013: mid-orange/amber with a broad green-tinged rim; singed nose, quite delicate and high toned, smoky, not so funky as the 1887 but there is a family resemblance; toasty flavours, touch of apricot with good weight and mouthfeel, lovely length, quite well defined with just a hint of cask on the finish. ****

Torre Bella 1877 Verdelho

At Patrick Grubb's annual tasting in 2002: slightly cloudy mahogany, thin green rim; lovely perfumed, floral, high-toned character; beautifully fresh, crisp and crystalline, dried apricot fruit with a fairly dry, rapier-like finish. Very fine. **** / *****

Torre Bella Sercial 1865

Bottled in the 1930s and recorked in 1974 and 2013, specifically for a sale at Christie's: pale mahogany, deep in colour for a Sercial; strange savoury – peppery aromas, redolent of beef gravy initially with some dried fruit character underlying; very dry in style (20–25 g/l residual sugar), again peppery, austere with a slight soily-peaty character on the finish which spoils it. Intense but very austere, ***?. Second bottle tasted at Patrick Grubb's tasting in 2013, having been recently recorked before shipment: mid-amber with a green tinge; perfumed, floral aromas, orange blossom; a touch of sweetness initially, bitter-sweet marmalade character, lovely texture, a touch soily – casky on the finish, long and bone dry. A lovely old wine. ****

Adegas do Torreão

This old established *partidista* had *armazens* at Torreão close to the centre of Funchal. Some good vintage wines were released in 1994 on the death of the owner, Vasco Loja. Adegas de Torreão was bought by Pereira D'Oliveira in 2001 and the premises are currently being revamped having been damaged in the floods of 2010.

Adegas do Torreão, Malvasia 1875

Tasted in 2002 at Gambrinus restaurant in Lisbon: Deep mahogany, clean, fresh raisiny, high-toned aromas; deliciously rich, figs and prunes, cut by acidity leading to a clear, pure finish. ****

Veiga França

A family-owned shipper established in 1944, Veiga França operated from premises on the Estrada Monumental until the mid-1990s. Most of their business was low-quality bulk wine. I visited the company's *armazens* in 1991 when the business was clearly on its last legs. Wines were produced for the company by the *partidista* P. E. Gonçalves who currently supply J. Faria. The Veiga França brand now belongs to Henriques & Henriques and members of the Veiga França family still live on the island.

Veiga França 1930 Solera Boal

Two notes, the first at the company's *armazens* in 1990: high-toned, rich and spicy but not exceptional, *. At Patrick Grubb's tasting in 1998: stewed, rancid, cheesy nose; the wine tastes cleaner but lacks finesse and has a flat finish. No mark awarded.

Val Pariso

The Visconde Val Pariso owned land at Porto Moniz on the north-west corner of the island, an area traditionally famous for its Sercial and Verdelho. The family were related to the Bianchis who owned Lomelino (see above).

Val Pariso Reserve Velhissima

No date on this bottle, acquired by Patrick Grubb from a director of Cossart Gordon's London importer. Tasted in 2013 at the Velhissimo Verdelho tasting in New York: amber mahogany, green-tinged rim; lovely gentle, savoury-nutty aromas; fine, rich and quite powerful on the palate, a lovely pungent tang, great intensity and depth. This may be the same wine as the Avery's bottle on page 139. ***/****

Welsh & Cunha (subsequently Welsh Bros.)

Established in 1794 and once important suppliers to the Russian and Swedish courts; John F. Welsh was appointed the Russian Consul in 1893. Prior to the outbreak of oidium in the 1850s, Welsh were the largest madeira shippers in terms of volume, their focus being on cheaper wines. In the second half of the nineteenth century they came to focus on better quality wines, shipping bottled wines to the United States. Vizetelly notes that they preferred to mature their wines in *estufas do sol* rather than artificially heated *estufas*. Part of the Madeira Wine Company since 1913, the Welsh family continue to have a number of interests on the island, including those formerly belonging to the Hinton family. The Welsh family own Quinta das Vinhas (formerly Quinta do Lombo dos Serrões) at Estreito de Calheta above Jardim do Mar.

Wines not attached to a Shipper

Malvazia, Fajã dos Padres n/v

Tasted at Patrick Grubb's annual tasting in 2013, this wine was recorked prior to shipment in 2012. Fajã dos Padres at the foot of Cabo Girão is the source of some of Madeira's best Malvasia Candida (see page 56). It is thought that this wine was produced in the late 1800s: cloudy amber/mahogany colour; savoury, rather rancid cheesy aromas (possible residual bottle stink?); rich figgy fruit, pungent and powerful with dried figs and spice on an expansive finish, lovely breadth and depth, just let down by the aromas on the nose. ****

Very Old Madeira, Fearon, Block and Smith

Bought by Patrick Grubb from a fellow wine merchant around 1990. The wine came from a deceased customer's reserves after the Second World War when proof of ownership was impossible because so many of the firm's records had been destroyed in the blitz. Tasted in 2009: pale amber with a green tinge; slightly burnt, singed grapey fruit on the nose; dry attenuated, savoury-nutty flavours, rather earthy and soily on the finish. Rustic. */**

E. L. R. 1940 Sercial

E. L. R. stands for Eduardo Luís Rodrigues. This wine was bottled in 1986, and tasted at the Madeira Wine Company with Francisco Albuquerque in 2005: mid-amber; savoury, beefy nose; gentle and quite soft for a Sercial, racy acidity on the finish but overall not very complex for a wine of this age. **/***

Torre Vineyard, Cama de Lobos, 1936 Sercial

A wine from the late Noel Cossart, tasted at Patrick Grubb's annual tasting in 2007: mid-deep in colour; quite subdued and slightly singed both on the nose and palate, fine and focused, clean and quite austere with grassy flavours matched by searing acidity and great length. ***/****

'FV' 1920 Malvasia

Dr Favila Vieira's family owned vineyards in Calheta, Ponta do Sol and Jardim do Mar on the south side of the island. He was related to the Henriques, Bianchis and Perestrelos. This bottle is stencilled in the

Barbeito old style. Tasted in 2011: mid-red-tinged mahogany; rich yet subdued thick-cut orange marmalade character; full, very rich, classic Malvasia style, thick-cut marmalade richness cut through by crystalline acidity, long and explosive on the finish. Very fine, a classic. *****

LMR 1915 Bual

LMR stands for L. M. Rodrigues and from the information I can find this wine was bottled in 1978. From my own cellar, tasted in 2007: deep nut brown/mahogany; fine, high-toned, caramelised aromas, nuts and toffee; intense and beautifully poised, quite dry and focused for a Bual with a tawny marmalade tang and citrus acidity leading to a relatively dry finish. ****

AO-SM 1908 Boal

António Oliveira (AO) was a producer with vineyards in São Martinho (SM). Tasted with Francisco Albuquerque at the MWC in 2005: very deep burnished chestnut/mahogany colour; smoky-savoury character on the nose, a touch meaty; very rich and concentrated, tawny marmalade backed by toffee and spice, beautifully balanced with racy acidity and a peacock's tail of a finish. ****/*****

Moscatel Roxa 1902

Possibly a tasting sample from a shipper's lodge: mid-deep mahogany; very unusual aromas, savoury, meaty overtones with garden mint underlying; relatively sweet and unctuous yet delicate with a wonderful texture and mouth feel, a touch bitter-sweet then with a toffee finish. Very unusual. ****

AO–SM 1882 Verdelho

Classic Verdelho from São Martinho, tasted with Francisco Albuquerque at the MWC in 2005: mid-deep amber/mahogany; very fine, aromatic candied orange and lime peel, slightly caramelised; rich in style for Verdelho, toffee apple with lovely limey acidity through to the finish. ****/*****

1880 Reserva

Thought to be from Blandy's with the words 'Muito Especial' hand written on the bottle. I purchased this at auction at Christie's, London in 2013. The bottles were ullaged to low shoulder but the wine did not seem to have suffered greatly, such is the resilience of madeira: surprisingly pale red-tinged mahogany (heavy sediment); lifted, waxy aromas, highly polished furniture; soft and wonderfully mellifluous on the palate, slightly medicinal (in a warming way), malt and Manuka honey with a touch of roasted coffee leaving a delicate, slightly bitter-sweet finish. A rather fine curio. ****

V. M. V. 1877

Shown at Patrick Grubb's tasting in April 2013: producer unknown, re-corked and rewaxed prior to shipment. Heavy sediment. Mid-amber/orange with a green tinge; lovely thick-cut tawny marmalade character with a touch of blossom on the nose; medium-rich, lovely spicy, citrus character with good weight mid-palate, retaining wonderful purity of fruit after all this time. A lovely wine in near perfect condition that goes on and on! *****

1868 Very Old Boal 'EBH'

The initials stand for Eugenia de Bianchi Henriques who had two famous grandfathers: Tarquino Lomelino (qv) and Carlo de Bianchi. She was Noel Cossart's aunt and the wife of Tiburcio Henriques. These connections explain why a number of wines appeared under the EBH initials from years like 1869, 1870 and 1893. The year 1868 happened to be a very good vintage for Boal although this wine did not quite live up to its billing: deep amber with a red tinge and thin green rim; not that expressive on the nose with a lifted toffee-apple character; much more powerful on the palate, tangy tawny marmalade, quite forceful with richness offset by crisp Cox's apple acidity on the finish. It is probably the same wine as the Cossart Gordon 'EBH' on page 172 but may have been bottled at a different time. ***

Teixeira 1863 Boal 'JRT'

The back label on this wine tasted in New York in 2014 says it all: 'This old madeira formed part of the private reserve of João Romão Teixeira (1864–1933), a prominent wine producer at Lugar de Baixo in south-west Madeira. In the 1950s, the wine was transferred to glass demi-johns from the oak casks in which it had been matured, and was bottled, unrefreshed, in 1987. Of a total of 320 bottles, this is no. 0066.' Deep amber/mahogany; rich and pronounced, on the nose, a touch floral and a hint of wood smoke; very rich and intense, bitter-sweet mid-palate with pruney depth of flavour. Quite a lot going on but lacking poise with a very slightly soily finish, although this disappeared slowly in the glass. **/***

1815 Boal

A wine from a fine vintage, the same year as Napoleon called at Funchal en route to St Helena. Shipper unknown but the stencilling suggests a British source whereas the spelling of 'Boal' suggests a Portuguese one. Tasted at 'The Beauty of Bual' tasting in 2014: mid-deep amber, thin green rim; gentle leafy aromas, not especially expressive (almost closed) but fresh and spring-like; smooth, intense, not that sweet but very powerful, apricots with a touch of orange peel, long and full. ****

7

BUYING, KEEPING, SERVING AND TASTING MADEIRA

Madeira wine is no longer the everyday drink that it was a century ago. As a result most wine drinkers no longer have the same understanding and are deterred from buying it, afraid of the unknown. In fact madeira is one of the most undemanding of wines and is far more versatile than it is given credit for. This chapter is a short and straightforward guide to getting the most from madeira wine.

WHERE TO BUY MADEIRA WINE

Most wine retailers worth the name list at least one madeira, generally a three- or five-year-old blend from one of the main shippers. But, as this book makes clear, there is a big gap between these and the much more exciting ten- or fifteen-year-old blends and *colheitas* and again between these and some truly thrilling vintage madeiras or *frasqueiras*. One of the best places to buy these wines is on the island and all the shippers have retail outlets with their latest releases, as well as a selection of older wines. (Mainland Portugal is not a good place to find madeira wine, although interesting bottles may be found at the Garrafeira Nacional in Lisbon.) But with the stringent security restrictions that accompany air travel it is difficult to bring more than a couple of bottles back from Madeira at a time[4]. Added to which, some of the really great madeiras have long since left the island and languish, sometimes forgotten, in private cellars all over world. These wines still turn up at auction and can be bought from the main houses in London, Europe and the USA.

Traditional wine merchants usually list a number of madeira wines but there are a number of specialist madeira merchants who will mail bottles worldwide (subject to local legislation). For anyone pursuing an enthusiastic interest in madeira wine I would strongly recommend the following:

Patrick Grubb Selections

Orchard Lea House, Steeple Aston, Bicester, OX25 4RT, United Kingdom.
Tel. (44) 1869 340229
Email: patrickgrubbselctions@dsl.pipex.com

Patrick Grubb MW, former head of Sotheby's Wine Department, has built up an extraordinary collection of madeira wine, many of the bottles sourced directly from families on the island. His annual list has around 200 different wines, from recent *colheitas* to wines dating back to the late eighteenth century. Some bottles on the list are almost certainly unique. Subject to regulations, he will ship wines all over the world.

The Madeira Collection

Kaaistraat 62a, 8800 Roeselare, Belgium
Tel. +32 (0)477 527 946.
Website: www.themadeiracollection.be
Email: info@themadeiracollection.be

'It started as a passion after drinking two glasses of Boal 1968 Madeira at a refined restaurant in Belgium. It resulted in the biggest collection of old, available madeira wines on Earth.' So reads the introduction to this evocative and well-organised website which lists wines from the major shippers dating back to the early nineteenth century. The man behind it, Bert Jeuris, has a passion for madeira wine and has developed a series of own-label wines (from Barbeito), helpfully designated numbers 1, 2 and 3. The Jeuris brothers also import a good selection of wines from mainland Portugal.

---

4   The Madeira Wine Company have a facility where the wines can be delivered directly to your plane.

The Rare Wine Company

21468, Eighth Street East, Sonoma, California 95475
Tel. (1) 800 999 4342 / (1) 707 996 4484.
Website: www.rarewineco.com

Emanuel 'Mannie' Berk began importing madeira into the United States in 1989. He turned the Rare Wine Company into the largest importer of madeira and represents Barbeito and D'Oliveira in the US. His range includes exclusive wines known as The Historic Series with wines named after the US cities where madeira was most popular in the eighteenth and nineteenth centuries: New York Malmsey, Boston Bual, Savannah Verdelho, Charleston Sercial, Baltimore Rainwater and New Orleans Special Reserve. Produced by Barbeito, these and the other blended wines in the series represent madeira at its best. The Rare Wine Company also lists wines from the Leacock Collection and the John Cossart Collection. The website is a mine of information on madeira wine. Mannie Berk republished Noel Cossart's book *Madeira, the Island Vineyard* with new introductory and postscript material in 2011. The appendix covering madeira sold at auction from 1971 to 2010 is an encyclopedic labour of love.

STORING AND KEEPING MADEIRA

Madeira is one of the easiest of all wines to store. Having been exposed to both heat and oxygen during the wine-making process, madeira is not nearly as demanding as other wines. There is no need to lay down a bottle of madeira in a cool cellar. It can be stored at room temperature though it should be kept in the dark, avoiding extreme heat or cold. Bottles should be left standing upright (although Patrick Grubb suggests that wines that have been recorked and recapsuled should be stored horizontally). Three-, five-, ten- and fifteen-year-old blends (as well as some *colheitas*) are generally bottled with stopper corks, which can be easily replaced once a bottle has been opened. These wines will keep on ullage but are made to be drunk young and are not as indestructible as older vintage wines.

Frasqueira or vintage madeiras have driven corks and are sealed either by a metal capsule or with wax. Until recently the driven corks used in the finest of wines were usually short in length and provide a relatively poor barrier between the wine in the bottle and the outside world. Any wine being kept for any length of time should be recorked, perhaps once every twenty or thirty years. Occasionally the date(s) of recorking are affixed to the bottle. A representative of IVBAM must be present when any bottles are recorked by a shipper on the island. Unless the cork fails and the wine starts to evaporate from the bottle, madeira wine can be kept almost indefinitely.

SERVING MADEIRA

With the exception of an old dated madeira, all madeira wine can be served directly from the bottle into the glass. Vintage or *frasqueira* wines often throw a light sediment and if the bottle is in any way disturbed the wine can appear muddy or cloudy. Some very old wines will have a heavy crust which sticks to the side of the bottle, and care should be taken not to dislodge this when decanting. All wines with considerable bottle age (and there may of course be no date to indicate how long the wine has been in bottle) should be decanted well in advance, ideally a day before serving. This gives sufficient time for any reductive aromas or 'bottle stink' to disseminate before drinking. You can gauge from some of my notes in the previous chapter just how much this can detract from a potentially great wine.

It is common practice to double decant madeira from the bottle to a decanter and back into the original, carefully rinsed bottle (being careful to remove any crust). All that is generally needed is a funnel, a keen eye and a steady hand, but a fine filter can also be used to catch the sediment or bits of cork. Let the sediment settle and you may get another glass of precious wine; otherwise keep it back and use it in cooking.

Unlike a bottle of venerable claret or vintage port, there is absolutely no need to drink a bottle of madeira at one sitting. Any remaining wine can be returned to the bottle and revisited weeks, months or even years later if well stoppered. The Madeira shippers advise drinking a *colheita* within six months of opening. A venerable *frasqueira* or vintage will keep on ullage for considerably longer. I was recently served a glass of Barbeito's 1795 Terrantez from an open bottle that had been forgotten and had been open for twenty years. (It had been left, standing up in a wardrobe in Madeira!) Although the wine had obviously evolved on ullage it was still, thankfully, in a very drinkable condition

Consequently madeira is the perfect wine for drinking with confidence in restaurants (unlike a fino or amontillado sherry) but few seem to value its versatility or keeping ability. The idea that you can have a number of 'goes' at the same bottle of wine takes the pain out of paying a high price of a distinguished or venerable madeira. No other wine behaves the same way and gives quite the same amount of pleasure. With this in mind, the English wine writer Jancis Robinson selected a bottle of vintage madeira as the ultimate luxury to take to a desert island.

Many wines are impaired by being served at the wrong temperature. 'Room temperature' has increased over the past few decades and nowadays few centrally heated houses are heated to less than 20°C. Warm ambient temperatures bring out the alcohol, especially in fortified wines, and this tends to mask the subtlety and complexity in the wine. Most madeira, like red wine, should be served at 'old fashioned' room temperature: 14–16°C. Only the driest of madeira benefits from being served any cooler and Sercial can benefit from being served chilled for a short time in the fridge: do not overchill. On the island of Madeira during the summer months a young dry wine may occasionally be served over ice but it would be an appalling crime to dilute a wine other than a three or five year old.

The pleasure to be gained from a fine wine is marred by the use of an inappropriate glass. The classic fortified wines – port, sherry and madeira – are all too often served brimful in tiny glasses, sometimes at leading establishments that should know better. Although fortified wines are generally consumed in smaller quantities than the average red or white wine, they should still be served in reasonably sized glasses. Like sherry and port, madeira has its own glass; a tulip-shaped glass with a short stem and a small but bulbous bowl which tapers towards the rim. These are difficult to obtain anywhere but on the island, and they are not necessarily the best type of glass in which to appreciate a madeira wine. A fine white wine glass, filled as little as an eighth to a quarter full, is ideal for madeira. Cognac glasses, on the other hand, are best avoided as the wine will tend to warm up too quickly.

Hotels on Madeira frequently compete with one another to produce the most exotic cocktail from a madeira wine base. With names like 'Columbus', 'Madeira Forever', '*Estufa*' and '*Ilha do Sonho*', I find that these drinks do nothing to enhance madeira wine – in fact, usually the effect is quite the opposite (although they may of course be used to cover up a poor base wine). Although I am the first to enjoy a well-made cocktail I am something of a purist when it comes to enjoying the aromas and flavours of wine.

TASTING MADEIRA

Madeira wine requires a completely different tasting vocabulary from those used to describe other wines. Volatile (vinegary) and oxidative characteristics, which would be described as faults in most other wines, are positive facets in madeira provided they are in proportion and under control.

There is a three-stage procedure in appreciating any wine, starting with its appearance. In a well-lit room, tilt the glass back against a white background. A menu card or napkin will do. Madeira should be clear and bright with a range of colours from straw yellow for a young dry wine made from white grapes through gold, orange and amber to chestnut brown and deep mahogany for the oldest and richest of wines. In some cases an abnormally deep colour, especially in a younger wine, may denote the addition of caramel. Wines made from the Tinta Negra grape (see page 43) may show a glint of red that tends to subside with age. Older madeiras display an olive-green hue which is most evident on the rim. I am no 'legs man' but the viscosity of the wine can be seen from the 'legs', 'tears' or 'arches' that the wine forms on the side of the glass.

The second stage in appreciating a wine is to swirl the glass around gently in order to release the aromas. The range of aromas found in madeira is vast and generally gains in breadth, depth, complexity and pungency with the age of the wine. Do not expect the primary fruit character of a young red and white wine. Most of madeira's characteristics are secondary or tertiary, resulting from either *estufagem* and/or ageing in *canteiro* (see pages 77–81). Rather than being fresh or 'primary' the fruit character in a young madeira tends to be dried, candied or crystallised in style: apricots, dates, figs, raisins, lime, orange peel or marmalade. On top of this there may be a savoury, toasty or nutty character from the ageing process in cask. However, sometimes this can be an earthy, fungus-like aroma, either due to dirty wood or bottle stink where a wine has been inadequately decanted. Because of the heating process (either natural or artificial), expect to find a slightly singed element, but to my mind a good wine should not smell burnt, cooked, stewed or soupy. In some madeiras the spirit can be evident, especially in three-year-old wines when the alcohol may not have had time to meld into the blend. The volatile element in a madeira helps to lift the aromas from the glass and terms like 'lifted' and 'high toned' (the latter a favourite expression of Michael Broadbent) are commonplace in my notes. Floral aromas, resin and occasionally varnish or carpenter's shop or furniture polish can be found, especially in older wines. This is not necessarily a pejorative expression if the wine is stable and in balance.

Tasting the wine on the palate is the third stage, which usually serves to confirm much of the information gleaned from the appearance and aroma. Take a sip rather than a gulp, taking in a little air at the same time. Leave the wine in your mouth for a few seconds to appreciate the texture (mouthfeel) as well as the flavour. After swallowing (or spitting at a professional tasting), breathe out gently through the nose. One of the defining characteristics of nearly all madeira is the high level of natural acidity. It is this that gives madeira its freshness and provides the counterpoint to the natural richness in the wine. Some dry wines can appear lean and overwhelmingly acidic but, at the opposite end of the spectrum, a rich or sweet madeira should never be flat or cloying. A wine made from one of the classic white grapes (Sercial, Verdelho, Bual, Malvasia, Terrantez) should reflect generally the variety from which it is made. The variety normally manifests itself in terms of sweetness (although it is possible to find a relatively sweet Verdelho or a dry Malvasia) as well as in terms of the integrity and individuality of the grape itself (see pages 44–53 for more on the characteristics of Madeira's grape varieties). The longer a wine has spent in wood before bottling, the more powerful and concentrated it becomes. This manifests itself on the palate in terms of mouthfeel/texture and length of flavour. The older and more distinguished the wine the greater the intensity of flavour, which will continue on the palate long after the wine has been consumed. It is not uncommon to be able to taste the vestige of a great madeira a day after having drunk the last drop!

As with all wine, a truly great madeira is denoted by its balance: between alcohol, acidity, concentration and richness. This can sometimes be summed up in one word: poise. There is much more to a great madeira wine than this, some of which is quite impossible to describe. I tend to keep my notes concise and to the point, without lapsing into the purple prose to which wine writers are prone. But there are wines that occasionally leave me speechless (see also Chapter 6 for a personal perspective on serving and tasting old madeira wine).

The following lexicon, grouped into category, is far from exhaustive but includes the words most commonly used as descriptors for the aroma and flavour components of madeira. By no means all of the expressions below are flattering. There is a big difference between '*rancio*' and 'rancid' and I am always suspicious of wines that are over-caramelised, so this is a word I use with care.

Floral

scented
herbaceous
leafy/grassy
tea leaf (green tea, earl grey –
    bergamot, gunpowder, lapsang
    suchong)
rose petals
violets
pot-pourri

Fruit

apricots
greengage
lemon
lime
orange
grapefruit
quince (*marmelada*)
dried fruit: apricots, dates, raisins,
    figs, prunes
crystalised fruits: Elvas plums
marmalade: tawny, thick cut

Nut

almond
walnut
hazelnut
brazil nut

Spice

allspice
curry (see also soloton
    on page 77)
pepper
cinnamon
clove
nutmeg

Sweetness

caramel/caramelised
malt/malty
toffee
chocolate
honey/mellifluous
molasses/treacle
vanilla
cake: fruit cake, *bolo de mel*
    (Madeiran honey cake), parkin

Savoury

nutty
meaty
gamey
vegetal: cabbage, sorrel
cheese
rancid

Acidity

brisk
crisp
ravishing/rapier-like
racy
zesty
tangy
searing/swinging/piercing
sharp
bitter

Volatile acidity

high toned
lifted
balsamic
varnish
vinagrinho (little vinegar)
vinegar

Body/alcohol

concentration
full
power(ful)
pungent
hot/curry
spirity

Texture

smooth
creamy
rich
unctuous
fat
soupy (lacking in definition)

Maderised

singed
toasted
crème brûlée
coffee/mocha
baked/baked alaska
caramelised
rancio
roasted
smoky/wood smoke
cooked
tar
burnt

Microbiological

fungus/mushroom
rancid
lactic: butter, cheese

MADEIRA: WINE AND FOOD

Madeira is often pigeon-holed, along with port, as an after-dinner wine. There is no denying that a glass of Bual or Malmsey after a meal is immensely satisfying but there is so much more to madeira than this. In the nineteenth century madeira used to be the focus of an entire party with five or six different styles consumed over two or three hours. As late as 1933, when cocktails were in vogue, Elizabeth Craig (writing in André Simon's book *Madeira*), gives detailed instructions on how to give

THE MADEIRA PARTY

Until the end of the nineteenth century, madeira was the most prestigious wine in North America. Collectors held madeira parties to share their knowledge and show off their wines. These were common among high society, whose members lived on the eastern seaboard in cities from Boston to New Orleans including Philadelphia, Baltimore, Savannah and Charleston. Madeira parties generally took place in the late afternoon with eight to a dozen men sharing and discussing perhaps half a dozen wines over a period of two or three hours. One of the most lavish madeira parties was hosted in Baltimore by David Thomas in 1899 when twenty-six madeiras ranging in date from 1805 to 1854 were served in one sitting. This is recorded in detail by Emanuel Berk in a self-published pamphlet entitled *A Century Past, A Celebration of the Madeira Party in America.* The madeira party died out, along with the popularity of madeira wine, as the cocktail took over in the early years of the twentieth century. It lives on in name only, with a range of wines produced by Barbeito for the US market named after the cities where the parties took place (see page 95). However, since 2012 a group of international madeira *aficionados* have been assembling annually in New York to taste and discuss twenty rare and venerable wines, some of them from old American collections. Many of these wines are described in Chapter 6.

a madeira party along with over thirty different recipes to accompany the wines. For better or for worse, the madeira party has died out but there is no reason why madeira should not be given more leeway to be drunk at different times of the day, with or without food. Harking back to tradition before looking forward, I see every reason to revive the slightly decadent practice of serving a glass of Bual or Malmsey with a slice of fruit cake for elevenses (particularly over Christmas) and/or in the afternoon, with or without a cup of tea and biscuits.

Ricardo Diogo Freitas of the firm Barbeito (see page 96) is a passionate advocate of matching madeira wine with food and has undertaken 'road shows' around the world to demonstrate this. In general terms, madeira can cope with strong, spicy or piquant flavours better than most other wines. My late father-in-law, Richard Blandy, always recommended drinking Bual with curry. Most wines are massacred by coffee or chocolate, but richer styles of madeira stand up fairly well to puddings flavoured with coffee and/or chocolate as I found many years ago, when selecting wines to accompany *Leith's Book of Desserts*, written by Brazilian author Valeria V. Sisti.

The following food and madeira pairings are by no means exhaustive (and those marked with an asterisk have worked particularly well for me):

With Sercial

Roasted, salted almonds* and
   olives
Prawns with garlic/*gambas 'al ajillo'*
Mushrooms with smoked ham
   and garlic
Sushi*
Tuna fish sashimi*

With Verdelho

Soups: consommé or clear soup*,
   oxtail, shellfish, asparagus,
   French onion, mushroom
Roasted pimento peppers
Welsh Rarebit
Confit of duck
Espetada (traditional Madeiran
   kebab)

With Boal

Curry*
Blue cheese
Apple pie
Panna cotta
Caramelised oranges*
Dried fruit compote*
Fruit cake/Christmas cake*
Bolo de Mel (Madeiran honey cake)*
Ginger cake/Parkin*
As a digestif with nuts and dates*

With Malvasia

Foie gras terrine*
Mature cheddar
Crème caramel/crème brûlée*
Treacle tart* or pecan pie
Sticky toffee pudding
Christmas pudding*
*Bolo de mel**
Ginger cake/Parkin
As a digestif with nuts, dried figs
   and dates*

Cooking with madeira

It is impossible to be certain of just how much madeira is used in cooking. The sales figures in Appendix IV give a clue to this but if you include the bottled wine kept in the kitchen, it must still add up to well over half the island's total annual production. The pronounced and distinctive character of madeira has long been appreciated in that French culinary staple *sauce madère*. In fact, there are a number of classic sauces that benefit from a measure of madeira being added just before serving, especially a cream sauce served with veal, and gravy to accompany beef, venison or game. Likewise the flavours in a consommé or clear soup are sharpened by the addition of a glass of madeira. I favour the use of drier wines in savoury dishes and the richer styles for sweet sauces and puddings: chestnut cream, sabayon, caramelised fruits and sweet soufflés. In all cases it pays to use a good three- or five-year-old madeira rather than a more distinguished wine.

There are a number of different recipes for *sauce madère* but this is one of the most straightforward that I have found:

1 tablespoon of butter
1 tablespoonful of flour
145 ml meat or vegetable stock
145 ml of madeira wine
Melt the butter gently in a saucepan. Stir in the flour. Once froth has formed, stir in the stock and madeira, and heat until boiling. Add salt and pepper to taste. Continue to cook for a few seconds. Serve over baked ham.

8

VISITING THE ISLANDS

Most visits to Madeira begin and end in the capital, Funchal. Much the largest town on the island, the city centre is compact, if congested, and can be visited easily on foot (sightseeing buses are also available). A good place to start is the *Zona Velha* (**old town**) with its old houses and black-cobbled streets. **The Madeira Story Centre** on the edge of the old town tells the story of the island through audio-visual exhibits and has an interesting section on the history of the wine trade. To take in the local colour and culture be sure to visit the fish and vegetable market (*Mercado dos Lavradores*) when it is at its most active on a Friday or Saturday morning. The sixteenth century *Sé* **or cathedral** marks the centre of the city, which extends westwards along the elegant Avenida Arriaga with its open-air cafés. Overlooking the Praça do Município, the *Museu de Arte Sacra* (**Museum of Sacred Art**), housed in a former bishop's palace, has a good collection of Flemish paintings bought by local merchants in the sixteenth century when the sugar trade was at its height. As well as taking in at least one of the wine producers (the Madeira Wine Company, Pereira D'Oliveira and H. M. Borges and are located close to the city centre), it is worth ambling along the narrow cobbled back streets. The Rua da Carreira, Rua dos Netos and Rua dos Ferreiros are lined with prosperous mercantile houses. Look upwards for the *torres avista-navios*, look-out towers built by merchants to keep watch over the port. The steep Calçada da Santa Clara leads past the **Casa-Museu Frederico de Freitas** (a collection of English and Portuguese furniture and paintings) to the **Convento de Santa Clara**. Founded by João Gonçalves Zarco in 1497, the interior walls are adorned with magnificent seventeenth century *azulejos.* Zarco, who discovered Madeira for the Portuguese (see page 1), is buried under the altar. Many of the larger houses around Santa Clara and nearby São Pedro and Santa Luzia have so-called *casas de prazer* ('pleasure houses'), ornate little summer-houses which were used to keep an eye on the streets below. Immediately above Funchal lies the community of **Monte**, a pilgrimage site which comes to life with a religious festival on 15 August. A railway used to climb the hill to Monte and its course is still marked by the Rua do Comboio ('train street'). Nowadays Monte can be reached by cable car (*teleférico*) starting from the old town in Funchal. Visit the subtropical gardens at Monte Palace and return to the city by the traditional Madeiran *corsa* or toboggan.

Outside Funchal, new roads have brought even the most remote part of the island to within half a day's drive of the capital. Most of these roads burrow through deep tunnels, so to see the island to full advantage it is still better to take the old switch-back roads, painfully slow as they are. A road leads up from Funchal through **Poiso** (past the Abrigo da Montanha bar and restaurant) to **Pico de Arieiro**, at 1818 metres above sea level. There is now a giant radar station at the top. A path (not for those who suffer vertigo) leads 4 kilometres north to **Pico Ruivo**, the highest point on the island at 1862 metres. Take the road down through the ancient laurel forest and past the trout farms at **Ribeiro Frio**. With UNESCO World Heritage status, the *laurisilva* of Madeira is the vestige of a previously widespread laurel forest type. It is the largest surviving area of laurel forest and is believed to be 90 per cent primary forest.

The road descends to **Penha da Águia** (Eagle's Rock) between **Faial** and **São Roque de Faial** on the spectacular north coast. Head west towards **Santana** and **São Jorge**; Santana is known for its emblematic and much-photographed A-frame houses. Stay at Quinta do Furão at Achada do Gramacho west of Santana or Quinta do Arco, **Arco de São Jorge** (see below). Arco de São Jorge also has one of the largest rose gardens in Europe as well as a small museum of wine.

The coast road along the north side of the island is steadily being improved. Part of the old road between São Vicente and Seixal used to be single track, following a ledge along the cliff. Tunnels now bypass this famously picturesque but dangerous stretch and it is worth stopping the car and walking along the old road to take in the drama of the scenery. Make a detour to the restaurant at **Chão da Ribeira** above Seixal to eat *espetada* (beef barbequed on laurel skewers) accompanied by *milho frito* (fried maize). Ask for a glass of *poncha* or punch made from *aguardente de cana* (sugarcane brandy). The town of **Porto Moniz** is famous for its natural rock swimming pools and is also home to an aquarium. From Porto Moniz there are two routes back to Funchal, either over the **Paúl da Serra** or along the winding coast road past **Ponta do Pargo**, the island's most westerly point. At 1500 metres above sea level, the Paúl is flat like no other part of the island; a high plateau stretching for 10 kilometres on which sheep graze. A track leads down from the Paúl to **Rabaçal** where a well-marked footpath follows the ravine under waterfalls to **25 Fontes** ('25 springs').

On the southwest coast, Paúl do Mar, Jardim do Mar, Calheta and Madalena do Mar were isolated coastal communities that are now becoming small resorts in their own right. Despite lacking a beach, **Jardim do Mar** is a mecca for surfers. **Calheta** has one of the few beaches on the island, made up from sand shipped in from North Africa and the Portuguese mainland. Above the coast, **Estreito de Calheta** has a delightful hotel, Quinta das Vinhas (see below), situated next to one of the government's experimental vineyards. Travelling east, the new coast road takes you to **Ponta do Sol** where there is a fine new museum of contemporary art (*Casa das Artes*), ingeniously built into the cliff above the town. On the opposite side of the town there is an ultra-modern *estalagem* (see below), perfectly positioned to take in the sunset. A new highway leads from Ribeira Brava straight back to Funchal. If time is on your side, it is worth taking the old main road through **Campanário**, **Quinta Grande**, past vineyards belonging to Henriques & Henriques and Barbeito's wine lodge to **Estreito de Câmara de Lobos**. This is the main area of vineyard on the island (see page 56–7). From here a road winds up to **Jardim da Serra** ('Mountain Garden'), known for the production of Sercial grapes and cherries. There is a cherry festival here in June and a vintage festival at Estreito in September. Most visitors to Madeira take a detour to the top of **Cabo Girão**, the second highest cliff face in the world. A lift plunges down the 630-metre cliff face to **Fajã dos Padres** where there is a restaurant and good sea bathing from the stony beach. Alternatively you can get there from Funchal by boat.

Câmara de Lobos, just to the east, is now a large fishing village that has been over-promoted to the rank of *cidade* ('city'). The centre retains much of its traditional charm with women embroidering in the streets and bright fishing boats sheltering in the bay and on the beach. Henriques & Henriques have their wine lodge here, just above the main square at Sitío de Belém. From Câmara de Lobos, the Estrada Monumental leads through the main area of hotels on the island and back to the centre of Funchal.

Many of the villages immediately east of Funchal have lost their individuality as the city has expanded but, despite its proximity to the airport, the coastal town of Santa Cruz has retained its identity and charm. **Machico**, just to the east of the much extended airport runway, was Madeira's first capital and is supposedly named after Englishman Robert Machim who was shipwrecked there in the fourteenth century (see page 2). There is a small artificial beach there. Above Machico is the little town of **Camacha** which is best known for wickerwork and the town square is the site of the first ever football match to be played on Portuguese soil, in 1875. Madeira's two golf courses can be found east of Funchal, at **Palheiro** just above the city and at **Santo da Serra**. Further east, the little fishing harbour of **Caniçal** has expanded greatly in recent years to become the island's principal cargo port and is now the site of Madeira's *Zona Franca* or Freeport. There is also a large new vineyard here. From Caniçal to the end of the island the landscape is barren, windswept and treeless. The easternmost point is the long, narrow **Ponta de São Lourenço**, named after the ship on which João Gonçalves Zarco first reached the island.

Porto Santo, 75 kilometres northwest of Madeira, can be reached by the Lobo Marinho car ferry from Funchal, a journey that takes two hours, or by plane (fifteen minutes). The chief attraction is the long sandy beach, backed by sand dunes, which extends for nearly 9 kilometres along the island's south coast. The island's tiny capital, **Vila Baleira**, is growing rapidly with the construction of holiday villas and hotels, but the centre has a number of historic buildings including the sixteenth-century parish church and a small museum dedicated to Christopher Columbus. Just outside the town is a huge golf course which was built in 2003 to attract ever greater numbers of tourists to the island. Vineyards, which once occupied the centre of the island and the coastal dunes, are now hard to find.

HOTELS

With the rapid growth of tourism on Madeira there is no shortage of places to stay. Most of the hotels are on the western outskirts of Funchal where the equivalent of an entire new city has been built over the past thirty years. Built overlooking the sea, many of the larger establishments are short on character. The following hotels both in Funchal and elsewhere on the island combine comfort and character in roughly equal measure and/or have links to wine:

Funchal

Quinta Bela Vista,

Caminho do Avista Navios, 4, 9000-129 Funchal
Tel. + 351 291 706400
www.belavistamadeira.com

Small five-star hotel in an old colonial-style quinta above Funchal, furnished with antiques. Luxuriant gardens.

Quinta da Casa Branca,

Rua da Casa Branca, 7, 9000-088 Funchal
Tel. +351 291 700 770
www.quintacasabranca.pt

A quinta belonging to the Leacock family, centred on the old family house with ultra-modern buildings in the garden. Good restaurant open to non-residents.

Hotel Choupana Hills,

Travessa do Largo da Choupana, 9060-348 Funchal
Tel. +351 291 206 020
www.choupanahills.com

French-designed hotel with the feeling of a luxurious jungle lodge. Restaurant, called Xoupana, is open to non-residents, serves fusion cooking and has a good wine list.

Cliff Bay Hotel,

Estrada Monumental, 147, 9004-532 Funchal
Tel. + 351 291 708 750
www.cliffbay.com

Large, sympathetically designed five-star hotel on a promontory just west of the centre of Funchal, partly belonging to the Blandy family. Private sea access. Ideal for families. The restaurant, Il Gallo d'Oro, has Madeira's only Michelin star.

Estalagem Jardins do Lago,

Rua Dr. João Lemos Gomes, 29, 9000-208 Funchal.
Tel. + 351 291 750 100
www.jardins-lago.pt

An old house belonging to the Blandy family, now restored and converted into a small five-star hotel. Quiet location yet close to the centre of Funchal.

Quinta da Penha de França,

Rua Imperatriz D. Amelia , 85, Se, 9000-018 Funchal.
Tel. +351 291 204 650
www.penhafrancahotels.com

Historic family-owned *quinta* set in gardens, converted into a small hotel. Very well located, with access to the sea.

Hotel Porto Santa Maria,

Avenida do Mar, 50, Funchal
Tel. + 351 291 206 700
www.portobay.com/en/hotels/portugal/madeira-island-portugal/porto-santa-maria/

Very comfortable four-star hotel, well located close to the old town in the centre of Funchal with good views over the harbour. Belongs to the same hotel group as the Cliff Bay (above).

Reid's Palace Hotel,

Estrada Monumental, 139, 9000-098 Funchal.
Tel. +351 291 71 71 71
www.reidspalace.com

Still *the* place to stay in Madeira, with a magnificent cliff-top location overlooking the bay of Funchal. Old-fashioned charm. Recently refurbished with the addition of a spa. The restaurant alongside the hotel, Villa Cipriani, is one of the most romantic places to eat.

Casa Velha do Palheiro,

Palheiro Golf, São Gonçalo, 9060- 415 Funchal.
Tel. +351 291 790 350
www.casa-velha.com

On an estate belonging to the Blandy family, with its own golf course above the city of Funchal. Relais & Château. Elegant five-star accommodation and fine food.

The Wine Lodges,

Rua de São Francisco, 8, 9000-050 Funchal
Tel: (+351) 963 022 060
www.thewinelodges.com

Four apartments, named Sercial, Verdelho, Bual and Malmsey, in the centre of town and adjacent to the Blandy Wine Lodge.

Arco de São Jorge

Quinta do Arco,

Sítio da Lagoa, 9280- 018 Arco de São Jorge.
Tel. +351 291 570 270

Self-contained cottages in a dramatic setting on the north side of the island, set amongst vineyards with a huge rose garden featuring over seventeen thousand roses and a thousand different varieties.

Câmara de Lobos

Quinta do Estreito,

Rua José Joaquim da Costa, 9325-034 Estreito de Câmara de Lobos.
Tel. + 351 291 910 530
www.charminghotelsmadeira.com

An old house, peacefully situated amidst the vineyards, with maginificent stunning views of the mountains and sea. Good restaurant, called 'Bacchus'.

Estreito da Calheta

Quinta das Vinhas,

Lombo dos Serrões, 9370-223 Estreito da Calheta.
Tel. +351 291 824 086
www.qdvmadeira.com

Belonging to the Welsh family, six rooms in the old house and self-catering cottages in the grounds, surrounded by vineyards – as the name suggests.

Jardim da Serra

Quinta Jardim da Serra,

Sítio da Fonte Frade, 9325-134 Jardim da Serra
Tel. + 351 291 911 500
www.hotelquintadaserra.com

The former country residence of British Consul Henry Veitch, now a five-star hotel.

Ponta do Sol

Estalagem da Ponta do Sol,

Caminho Do Passo, 6, 9360-529 Ponta do Sol
Tel. + 351 291 970 200
www.pontadosol.com

Situated immediately above the town of Ponta do Sol, an ultra-modern hotel that makes the most of the magnificent views and the sunset.

Santana

Quinta do Furão,

Achada do Gramacho, 9230-082 Santana.
Tel. +351 291 570 100
www.quintadofurao.com

Atmospheric four-star hotel on Madeira's dramatic north coast, situated in the middle of a vineyard overlooking the sea.

Porto Santo

Hotel Porto Santo,

Campo de Baixo, 9400-051 Porto Santo.
Tel. +351 291 980 149
www.hotelportosanto.com

The original hotel on the island, situated right on the beach. The new annexe has some beautiful bedroom suites and houses a spa.

POSTSCRIPT: THE FUTURE FOR MADEIRA WINE

In January 2015 there was a mild air of optimism in Madeira. It might have been helped by the warm winter sunshine – the temperature is 20°C in Funchal and the vines are not getting their winter downtime this year – but in 2014 madeira wine had a successful year. Global sales of 3.37 million litres were not spectacular, but they were up by 5.8 per cent on the previous year and in line with the ten year average. With a total value of 18 million euros (up 6.5 per cent) there was a clear move towards so-called 'premium' quality wines in the two markets that matter most to the shippers: the UK and US.

Just over a decade ago, a madeira shipper described the 'bulk' market to me as 'worthless', yet wine classed as 'denatured' or 'modified and disqualified from bottling' still accounts for nearly 25 per cent of all madeira's sales. For today's shippers this represents valuable cash flow while the premium wines (those aged five years and above) tie up capital. *Canteiro* wines (aged in wood and not subject to *estufagem*) have been greatly aided by the POSEIMA/POSEI campaign (see page 81), which began in 1992 and is set to continue for the foreseeable future. Without this long-running subsidy it is clear that some of the smaller shippers would not have been able to survive.

The *colheita* category has brought a new level of interest to madeira in the way that LBV did to Port in the 1970s. These early-bottled wines have drawn some criticism from madeira *aficionados* in that they are no substitute for the real thing i.e. 'vintage' madeira that has aged for twenty or more years in pipe. There is of course the longer-term risk that in the interests of maintaining cash flow, the shippers will throw the baby out with the bath water and bottle too much too young. But, in my opinion and provided the category is well managed and the wines are not over-priced, *colheita* brings small quantities of dated madeira to a wider audience. With improved wine making showing up in many of the more recent *lotes, colheita* looks set to develop into a category which might take madeira wine a step closer to the island's unique *terroir*.

The 'super-premium' market is booming and has been gathering momentum for some years. This is a small but vital niche for madeira with prices rising steeply for 'vintage' wines, many still dating back to the nineteenth century and beyond (see Chapter 6). But unlike port, where shippers have been falling over themselves to bottle rare nineteenth-century *colheitas* in super-duper packaging, vintage madeira continues to be presented in demure stencilled bottles accompanied by the minimum of information, sometimes not even the all-important bottling date. There are winds of change here and it is important that madeira does not overdo it, putting the wines out of reach of genuine *aficionados,* but it is clear that more value could be added to *frasqueira* wines by improving presentation.

In the meantime it seems that a gap is opening up with three-year-old madeira becoming harder to sell. There may be a good reason for this. The modernisation and thorough cleaning up of *estufagem* (the heating process) has had unintended consequences in that many of the wines, admirably clean though they may be, are now just bland. This applies especially to the three-year-old dry and medium dry categories which don't really have a unique selling point. To my mind it only serves to reinforce the point made in the preface, and again in Chapter 4, that with madeira, there really is no substitute for age.

But the madeira wine shippers are a resourceful bunch and, with the tacit indifference of IVBAM, there is currently a considerable amount of experimentation with new or at least 'newer' oak. For some shippers this may become a panacea, as others have already turned their back on wines that have the vanilla and coconut character of oak, especially higher up the age scale. It is tempting to dismiss these wines as 'atypical' but it is hard to ignore the fact that a slug of new wood lends much-needed character to a three- and even a five-year-old blend at the drier end of the spectrum.

The financial crisis of 2008–9 has shaken Madeira's economy to its core. The impact is plainly visible with abandoned projects both in the public and private sectors. On the north side of the island the *via expresso* is unfinished with unconnected tunnels and at Câmara de Lobos a new viaduct, supposedly heading up to Jardim da Serra, ends abruptly and leads nowhere. There are similar vanity projects in the private sector with a number of hotels in the hands of the banks and high-profile unfinished developments like the Savoy and Madeira Palácio hotels. But fortunately the wine industry did not over-extended itself in the same way. In fact, the general move towards modern, purpose-built out-of-town facilities has brought new efficiency to the industry. Justino's, for example, functions with just twenty employees. The same cannot be said for the state sector, which is still top heavy with a bloated bureaucracy. At the time of writing the island has a public sector debt totalling €6.5 billion (a considerable sum of money for two small islands with a population of not much over 250,000). The President of the Regional Government for the last thirty-seven years, Dr Alberto João Jardim, is stepping down and a new regime will pick up the tab and impose the necessary austerity, which will be severe.

IVBAM has done much to bring itself into line with the rest of Portugal, especially the *Instituto dos Vinhos do Douro e do Porto* (IVDP) and it is clearly a much more transparent organisation than it was a decade ago. But budget cuts have already meant that the experimental vineyards, repositories of so many unique grape varieties, are suffering from neglect. At the time of writing there is a serious lack of plant material on the island, so much that it is hampering the continued improvement of Madeira's vineyards. There remains, as always, a shortage of traditional white grapes so it is easy to see why the increasingly quality-conscious Madeira Wine Company is buying and leasing vineyards to secure more of its own supply.

Organic cultivation is clearly a challenge on Madeira with its warm, damp climate and disease-susceptible grapes. But since 2008 a number of small growers have risen to the challenge and come up with small quantities of organically produced wine. The barrier to producing an organic madeira wine has been a lack of organic fortifying alcohol but from 2014 this has been overcome. Expect to find organic *colheitas* on the market from 2020 onwards.

Vineyards go hand in hand with tourism (so-called *enoturismo* as it is known in Portugal). There are some spectacular examples of this on the Portuguese mainland, taking advantage of the scenery in the

Douro and Alentejo. Madeira has scenery like no other wine region in the world and yet, at present, relatively few tourists venture outside the cosseted world of Funchal and its handful of historic wine *armazens* or lodges. The companies that have these lodges are undoubtedly at an advantage for tourism and it should be a matter for regret that so many old *armazens* have been demolished. But with the new road system making the vineyards ever more accessible, there must be potential for more high-quality wine-associated tourism outside Funchal. So far only Henriques & Henriques have a detailed *enoturismo* project planned (at Quinta Grande) but I am certain that others will follow.

One of the most refreshing characteristics about twenty-first-century Madeira (other than some of the nineteenth-century wines) is the increased openness and transparency to be found among the island's wine producers. There is, thankfully, much less to cover up than in the past, and at the start of 2015 there is more to be optimistic about than there has been for fifty or more years. Madeira's eighteenth-century glory days are not coming back but a slim, trim madeira wine industry has much to be confident about, not least its heritage of truly remarkable wines.

GLOSSARY OF PORTUGUESE AND TECHNICAL TERMS

Abafado: (as in *vinho abafado*): a general term for a fortified wine where the fermentation has been arrested by the addition of *aguardente* (q.v.) leaving residual sugar. From the verb *abafar*, meaning to choke, smother or stifle.

ABV: alcohol by volume, expressed as a percentage.

Adega: winery, and sometimes by extension a building where wine is aged and stored.

Aguardente: brandy. It is also the name of the grape spirit (98% abv) used to fortify madeira (see page 74–5).

Aguardente de cana: brandy made from cane sugar, once used to fortify madeira.

Americanos: native American vines (not *Vitis vinifera*).

Armazém: (plural *armazens*): a building where wine is aged and stored.

Armazém de calor: a wine store that is artificially heated.

Arrobo: boiled-down must, used for sweetening.

Bagaço: skins, stalks and pips left over after fermentation and pressing.

Baumé: a measure of dissolved compounds in grape juice and therefore its approximate concentration of sugars. The number of degrees Baumé is a rough indicator of percentage of alcohol by volume (i.e. grape juice with 12° Baumé will produce a wine with about 12% abv). Its inventor was Antoine Baumé (1728–1804), a French pharmacist.

Bica aberta: fermentation off the skins.

Borracha: a sack made from goatskin, once used to carry grape must or wine from outlying vineyards.

Borracheiro: the man who carries a *borracha* (qv).

Cadastro: register of vineyards.

Caderna: a card used to record the grapes sold by growers to the producers.

Calda: a syrup used in sweetening.

Canteiro: the scantling racks used to support barrels of wine. A *vinho do canteiro* is a wine that has not been subject to *estufagem*.

Casta: a grape variety.

Casta Nobre: a noble grape variety (now 'recommended')/ **Casta Boa:** a good grape variety (now 'authorised').

Cepa: an individual vine (see also *pé*).

Colheita: literally 'harvest', it also signifies a style of madeira (see page 87).

Corda do lagar: the rope that used to be wound round the *bagaço* (qv) in a *lagar* to extract more grape must.

Cuba: vat (as in *cuba de inox*, stainless-steel vat; *cuba de cimento*, cement vat).

Cuba de calor: a vat used to heat wine.

Demi-john: a large glass bottle, usually holding 25 litres of wine.

Direct producers: ungrafted vines (i.e. planted on their own roots), either hybrid or of American origin.

Desavinho: uneven development of individual berries within a bunch of grapes provoked by cold, wet weather at the time of flowering. Known as 'hen and chickens' in English or *millerandage* in French.

Dôce: sweet.

Dry extract: the sum of non-volatile solids in a wine, namely sugars, non-volatile acids, minerals, phenolic, glycerol, glycols, proteins, pectins and gums. Levels of dry extract rise with the concentration brought about by evaporation and cask age. Measured in grams/litre, a madeira may have between 22g/l for a three year old to as much as 40g/l for an old Malmsey.

Engaço: stalks, stems.

Espaldeira: vines trained vertically on wines between posts.

Estágio: a period of rest for the wine after *estufagem* (qv).

Estufa: literally a 'hot house' and, by extension, the tanks where madeira is artificially heated.

Estufa do sol: a glass house where madeira may be heated by the sun.

Estufado: (as in *vinho estufado*): a wine that has been subject to *estufagem*.

Estufagem: the process of artificially heating madeira wine.

Fining: the process where microscopic particles are removed from a wine by the addition of a fining agent. The most commonly used fining agents are bentonite, casein, egg white, or gelatine, which absorb or coagulate with potentially unstable colloidal material suspended in the wine, causing it to precipitate more quickly.

Frasqueira: a bottle store or cellar, officially used to denote a vintage madeira.

Garrafão: a glass demi-john.

Garrafeira: a private wine cellar, sometimes used to denote a vintage madeira.

Generoso: literally 'generous', also meaning fortified, as in *vinho generoso*, fortified wine.

Granel: bulk (as in *vinho de granel*, bulk wine).

Grau: degree of temperature, sugar or alcohol.

Inox: the colloquial word for stainless steel (from *aço inoxidável*).

Lagar: a wooden apparatus for treading and pressing grapes (plural *lagares*).

Latada: a horizontal trellis for training vines.

Levada: an irrigation channel (see page 37).

Lodge: a store for wine, a term that has been recently adopted in Madeira from the port wine industry on the mainland.

Lote: a 'lot' or parcel of wine, the basis or part of a blend.

Mosto: grape juice, must.

Partidista: a stockholder of wine who sells to other shippers.

Patamar(es): a modern vineyard terrace with an earth bank instead of a retaining wall. This is a concept developed in the Douro, Portugal and brought to Madeira. The terraces will be interconnected allowing for some mechanisation.

Pé: literally 'foot' but often used to refer to an individual vine or cepa (q.v.). *Pisa a pé* means to tread by foot.

Pé de Cuba: the lees at the bottom of a vat.

Pintor: literally 'painter', meaning *veraison* or the colouring of the grapes during ripening.

Pipa: a 'pipe' or cask used for ageing wine. A shipping pipe is also a unit of measurement: 418 litres in Madeira. There is no standard measure for a lodge pipe, which can contain anything up to 650 litres.

Poda: pruning.

Poio: a traditional terrace, support in vines and/or other crops.

pH: hydrogen power; a measure of the concentration of the acidity. Low pH indicates high concentrations of acidity and vice versa. All grape must is acidic, usually registering pH values between three and four. The lower the pH the more acidic the wine. The scale is logarithmic so a wine with a pH of three has ten times as much hydrogen ion activity as one whose pH is 4. Most madeiras will have a pH between 3.3 and 3.6 depending on the grape variety and age. See also total acidity.

Prensa: press (as in *vinho da prensa*, press wine).

Produtores direitos: direct producers (qv).

Prova: tasting.

Quinta: literally a farm, estate or landed property.

Racking: the process of separating the wine from its lees.

Rectified concentrated grape must (RCGM): preserved grape juice that has been processed to reduce the concentration of solids other than sugars. Used to sweeten wines in place of sugar.

Reduction: effectively the opposite of oxidation which occurs when wine is stored in the absence of oxygen in tank, cask or bottle. A madeira wine held for a long period in a full, well-stoppered bottle may become subject to reduction leading to unpleasant aromas collectively described as 'bottle stink'. Aeration by decanting helps these aromas to dissipate (see Chapter 7).

Residual sugar: the total quantity of sugar remaining unfermented in a finished wine, usually measured in grams/litre but also by the Baumé scale (qv). Residual sugar in a madeira may vary from as little as 15 g/l in a dry wine to as much as 130 g/l in the very sweetest wines.

Remontagem: pumping over during fermentation to increase extraction.

Repisa: a second or third treading of the grapes.

Ribeiro/a: a small river.

Rolha: a cork.

Saca-rolhas: corkscrew.

Seco: dry.

Surdo: literally 'deaf'; a *vinho surdo* is a must that has not been allowed to ferment due to the addition of *aguardente* (qv). Used to adjust sweetness.

Tanoaria: cooperage.

Tanoeiro: cooper, barrel maker.

Tinto: red (as in *vinho tinto*, red wine).

Tonel: a large wooden cask for storage (plural *toneis*).

Torna viagem: a wine that has completed a return journey by sea. See also *vinho da roda*.

Total acidity: a measure of both fixed and volatile acids in wine usually expressed in Portugal as grams per litre tartaric. The ideal range for grape musts is between 7 g/l and 10 g/l with wines varying between 5.5 g/l and 10 g/l for a *frasqueira*. A Sercial, the most naturally acidic of all the madeira grapes, may sometimes register as high as 12g/l in total acidity.

Turismo de habitação: guest accommodation in private houses, sometimes attached to a vineyard.

Ullage: depletion of a wine from cask or bottle leaving space for air.

Velho/velha: old.

Velhissima: very old.

Vinho da roda: wine that has completed a round trip by sea.

Vinho claro: wine that has been separated from its lees after fermentation, prior to fortification, *estufagem* (qv) or ageing.

Uva: grape.

Volatile acidity (VA): a measure of the naturally occurring organic acids in a wine that are separable by distillation. The most common volatile acid in wine is acetic acid (96%), which imparts a vinegary character if present in excessive concentrations. Low concentrations of acetic acid (below 0.2g/l) are barely noticeable in a wine whereas high concentrations of VA (above about 0.8g/l) make a wine smell and taste acetic or vinegary. A three- to fifteen-year-old madeira will have a VA of between 0.25–0.6 g/l. *Colheitas* will have levels of VA ranging from 0.3–0.75 g/l. *Frasqueira* (vintage) madeiras may have levels of VA in excess of 1.5g/l and up to 2.5 g/l in some very old wines, but still appear balanced given their concentration and level of alcohol. Such wines may be described as 'lifted' or 'high toned'. The Portuguese use the term *vinagrinho* ('little vinegar') to describe a wine with noticeable but not detrimental levels of volatile acidity (usually a term applied to old *colheita* and tawny port rather than to madeira).

Vindima: vintage or harvest.

Vinha: vineyard or plot of vines.

GLOSSARY OF ACRONYMS

Portugal has a bewildering number of different acronyms. These are the initials of organisations, institutions and projects most closely involved in the day-to-day life of the madeira wine trade:

ACIF: Associação Comercial e Industrial de Funchal.

IVBAM: Instituto do Vinho, Bordado e Artesanato da Madeira (see Appendix 1 for a description of its powers and functions).

IVM: Instituto do Vinho da Madeira (now IVBAM, above).

IVV: Instituto do Vinho e da Vinha (Institute of Vines and Wine) formerly the Junta Nacional do Vinho (JNV).

POSEIMA: Programa de Opções Específicas para fazer face ao Afastamento e a Insularidade da Madeira e os Açores.

PODERAM: Programa de Desenvolvimento Rural da Região Autónoma da Madeira.

BIBLIOGRAPHY

Binney. M., *The Blandys of Madeira 1811–2011*, London (2011)

Blandy, G., (ed.) *The Bolton Letters*, reproduced in Funchal for the English Church, Madeira (1976 and 1980)

Broadbent, M*., Vintage Wine*, London (2002)

Campo, E., Ferreira, V., Escudero, A., Marqués, J. C., Cacho. J., *Quantitative Gas Chromatography – Olfactory and Chemical Quantitative Study of the Aroma of Four Madeira Wines*, Elsevier (2005)

Cann, J. P., 'The Madeira Heritage in Colonial Madeira', from *The Thirtieth Annual Report and Review 2003* of the British Historical Society of Portugal.

Cossart, N., *Madeira, the Island Vineyard*, expanded second edition with new material by Emanuel Berk, Sonoma (2011)

Costa, B. C. Cincinato da, *O Portugal Vinicola*, Lisbon (1900)

Croft-Cooke, R., *Madeira*, London (1961)

Elliot, T., *The Wines of Madeira*, Gosport (2010)

Farrow, J. & S., *Madeira*, London (1994)

Freitas, B. K. O*., A Região Demarcada da Madeira – Characteristicas e Património Vitícola*, Funchal (2014)

Hancock, D., *Oceans of Wine*, New Haven and London (2009)

Hoare, M*, The Quintas of Madeira*, Funchal (2004)

Huetz de Lemps, A., *Le Vin de Madère*, Grenoble (1989)

Jeffs, J., *Sherry*, sixth edition, Oxford (2014)

Leitão, C., *Madeira & Porto Santo*, Funchal (2004)

Liddell, A., *Madeira, the Mid-Atlantic Wine*, London (second edition, 2014)

Mayson, R. J., *Port and the Douro*, Oxford (2013)

Mayson, R. J., *The Wine and Vineyards of Portugal*, London (2003)

Mayson R. J., 'Does Anyone Know How to Make Madeira?', *Decanter*, London (1991)

Oliveira e Silva, H., Guedes de Pinho, P., Machado, B. P., Hogg, T., Marqués, J. C., Câmara, J. S., Albuquerque, F. and Silva Ferreira A. C., 'Impact of Forced-Ageing Process on Madeira Wine', *Journal of Agricultural and Food Chemistry* (2008)

Ornelas, P., *Madeira, A Short Illustrated History*, Funchal (2007)

Redding, C., *History and Description of Modern Wines*, London (1833)

Robinson, J., Harding, J., Vouillamoz, J., *Wine Grapes*, London (2012)

Simon, A. L., (ed.) *The Bolton Letters 1695–1714*, London (1928)

Vieira, A, *A Vinha e O Vinho na Historia da Madeira*, Funchal (2003)

Vieira, A., *Breviário da Vinha e do Vinho da Madeira*, Ponta Delgada (1991)

Vizetelly, H., *Facts about Port and Madeira*, London (1880)

White R., *Madeira, Its Climate and Scenery, A Handbook for Invalids and Other Visitors,* London & Madeira, (1851)

OTHER MANUSCRIPT SOURCES:

Bazenga A., Ribeiro, J. A., Sequeira, M., *The British presence in Madeira Island: historical overview and linguistic outcomes.* A paper presented at the British Scholar Society Conference, University of Edinburgh 2012 and published online

Christie's Auction Catalogues from 1986 to 2013

The Saintsbury Club: a Scrap-Book by 'The Cellarer' [i.e. André Simon], privately printed, 1943

Vineyard reports from the Madeira Wine Company and Quinta de Santa Luzia

Vintage reports from the Madeira Wine Company, 2014–1994 and 1984–1988

Statistics from the former Instituto do Vinho da Madeira (IVM), and the Instituto do Vinho, do Bordado e do Artesanato da Madeira (IVBAM)

APPENDIX 1: IVBAM – *THE INSTITUTO DO VINHO, DO BORDADO E DO ARTESANATO DA MADEIRA*

Successor to the *Junta Nacional do Vinho* in 1979, the *Instituto do Vinho da Madeira* was formed to regulate the production and sale of madeira wine as well as to coordinate viticultural activity in the Autonomous Region of Madeira (RAM). One of the institute's early priorities was to bring administration and legislation into line with European Union law prior to and following Portugal's accession to the then EEC in 1986.

In June 2006, embroidery and handicrafts were brought in alongside wine to create the *Instituto do Vinho, do Bordado e do Artesanato da Madeira* – IVBAM.

The current statutes of IVBAM, published in 2012, run to eleven closely typed pages. In summary there are three 'pillars' to the Institute's current role on the island with the Institute's main wine-orientated responsibilities listed below:

Viticulture
• The compilation and maintenance of the *cadastro* or register of vineyards.
• Technical support and help for growers.
• Experimental vineyards.
• Viticultural laboratory.

Regulation and certification of wine

- The registration of fermentation, distilling and rectification.
- Establishing current accounts (*conta corrente*) for inputs, outputs and stocks of wine.
- Storage of surplus wine.
- Laboratory for wine analysis.
- Tasting panel (*câmara de provadores*).
- Issuing seals and certificates of origin (*selo de origem*) for all DOP fortified wine and IGP unfortified wine.

Promotion

The promotion of madeira wine at a local, national and international level.

APPENDIX II: SALES OF MADEIRA, 1976–2014[1]

Year	Quantity (litres)	Value (Euros)
1976 [2]	4 117 270	637 904
1977 [2]	4 566 990	969 812
1978	4 673 253	1 402 182
1979	5 060 575	2 111 258
1980	3 521 442	2 021 671
1981	3 796 811	2 279 643
1982	3 288 379	2 363 450
1983	3 551 154	3 198 412
1984	3 538 226	4 306 694
1985	3 347 929	4 775 064
1986	3 869 501	6 642 232
1987	3 516 251	7 548 561
1988	4 048 311	9 593 199
1989	3 836 996	9 234 543
1990	3 682 074	9 466 832
1991	3 795 033	10 624 081
1992	3 570 476	10 101 282
1993	3 543 749	10 143 312
1994	3 472 284	11 557 654
1995	3 752 875	13 499 251
1996	3 647 644	13 997 533
1997	3 709 957	14 874 268
1998	3 875 241	15 716 465
1999	3 627 257	15 706 980
2000	4 017 646	17 066 882
2001	4 707 425	18 650 968
2002	2 818 298	12 038 642
2003	3 355 238	13 598 724
2004	3 591 524	14 193 671
2005	3 398 364	14 342 804
2006	3 356 775	14 598 978
2007	3 777 142	16 623 210
2008	3 415 054	15 621 158
2009	3 273 407	14 535 224
2010	3 277 615	14 975 315
2011	3 012 266	15 274 343
2012	3 407 343	16 487 228
2013	3 187 681	16 815 757
2014	3 372 160	17 904 794

1. Source: IVBAM
2. In 1976 and 1977 figures do not include sales for the domestic market.

APPENDIX III: SALES OF MADEIRA – MAIN MARKETS, 2010–2014[1]

Market	Quantity (litres)				
	2010	**2011**	**2012**	**2013**	**2014**
Germany	340 671.00	289 613.00	253 580.25	235 244.10	268 982.15
Australia	3 553.50	5 898.00	2 760.00	3 660.00	3 372.00
Austria	26 428.50	27 411.50	43 071.00	17 806.51	35 899.50
Belgium	171 550.00	181 833.50	217 684.50	159 823.00	181 670.00
Brazil	13 552.00	22 608.00	15 351.00	22 756.50	11 238.00
Canada	44 365.50	32 791.50	42 439.50	27 577.50	40 323.90
China	765.00	486.00	742.50	2 245.20	1 485.00
Denmark	61 072.50	55 284.50	48 952.50	41 668.50	51 798.75
USA	145 823.25	186 463.25	160 355.50	185 019.25	213 915.25
Spain	7 036.50	7 798.50	6 171.00	7 437.00	8 424.50
Finland	27 072.00	26 406.00	23 985.00	17 161.20	15 411.90
France	1 121 397.00	835 323.00	1 148 650.00	1 022 317.50	1 014 741.95
Netherlands	84 457.60	51 352.95	68 807.70	54 509.40	61 118.85
Ireland	1 870.50	1 401.00	1 330.50	6 816.00	2 096.00
Italy	3 982.50	3 583.50	4 626.00	4 362.75	4 512.75
Japan	217 779.40	219 485.25	280 239.00	273 428.50	282 011.00
Luxembourg	3 496.80	3 489.30	5 710.80	3 801.30	3 538.80
Madeira	396 118.59	479 010.25	444 578.70	520 984.97	525 596.16
Norway	15 505.50	11 874.00	11 589.75	13 860.75	12 460.50
Poland	5 845.50	7 782.00	33 448.50	8 208.00	50 829.75
Portugal (continental)	60 422.30	47 625.30	50 308.20	46 258.50	68 781.10
UK	270 472.50	306 122.27	355 464.27	296 849.75	314 166.30
Russia	6 084.00	5 805.00	1 678.50	7 830.00	11 499.00
Sweden	117 721.50	95 589.00	94 885.50	94 809.00	71 398.50
Switzerland	114 274.00	83 856.00	71 672.00	87 186.55	87 597.50
TOTAL	**3 277 614.94**	**3 012 265.82**	**3 407 343.17**	**3 187 680.98**	**3 372 160.11**

1. Source: IVBAM

APPENDIX IV: SALES OF MADEIRA BY GRAPE VARIETY AND AGE 2010–2014[1]

Grape variety		Quantity (litres)				
		2010	2011	2012	2013	2014
Authorised and recommended varieties	Madeira without additives	180 050.00	204 860.00	193 840.00	172 850.00	216 310.00
	Modified wine	729 750.00	362 900.00	791 350.00	638 510.00	618 200.00
	Corrente	2 002 428.33	2 018 338.37	2 014 647.79	1 918 392.94	2 067 937.17
	5 years	156 564.61	173 316.74	174 557.02	180 233.00	187 231.95
	10 years	11 127.25	17 456.57	17 451.10	16 986.89	20 196.01
	15 years	646.50	177.00	1 820.25	1 300.25	1 090.50
	Colheita	4 644.25	7 763.00	4 951.50	7 964.75	7 607.75
	Frasqueira	143.25	228.75	12.00	18.75	88.50
Malvasia	Corrente	3 600.00				588.00
	5 years	34 197.00	34 009.75	34 584.75	47 675.50	47 502.00
	10 years	25 035.25	29 234.25	28 076.25	29 793.38	30 250.60
	15 years	3 543.75	7 426.50	4 659.75	6 853.50	2 753.25
	20 years	281.25	1 077.00	957.00	1 412.25	821.25
	30 years	15.00	18.00	42.75	3.75	567.75
	+ 40 years	211.50	42.45	267.10	751.50	397.20
	Colheita	10 822.25	10 497.50	8 974.50	8 842.25	6 123.00
	Frasqueira	1 188.75	1 443.50	1 224.75	1 827.75	1 938.75
Boal	Madeira without additives		215.00			
	Corrente			2.25	9.75	0.75
	5 years	24 711.00	29 493.50	25 956.25	33 259.75	33 851.25
	10 years	14 891.25	19 359.00	19 636.00	18 655.63	23 135.25
	15 years	3 318.75	4 153.50	5 194.50	4 009.50	2 657.25
	20 years					363.00
	+ 40 years	3.00	7.20	9.60	162.00	1.20
	Colheita	5 315.75	2 293.50	2 317.00	3 283.50	2 251.75
	Frasqueira		3 727.50	3 902.25	4 462.88	3 627.00

1. Source: IVBAM

Verdelho	5 years	13 128.25	17 393.25	14 143.50	19 021.50	21 278.25
	10 years	11 033.25	13 593.38	11 160.25	14 491.13	16 749.00
	15 years	1 561.50	3 083.25	2 475.00	940.50	1 792.25
	20 years	150.00	459.00	130.50	569.25	592.50
	+ 40 years		7.20	9.60	162.00	1.20
	Colheita	1 022.00	811.50	1 454.50	1 250.25	1 452.00
	Frasqueira	1 203.00	1 372.88	2 356.00	2 283.75	2 174.63
Sercial	5 years	21 643.50	27 294.75	18 459.00	25 663.50	26 424.00
	10 years	11 298.75	13 435.13	17 307.00	17 531.63	18 191.25
	15 years	735.00	1 320.75	636.00	1 356.00	1 085.25
	+ 40 years		7.20	9.60	162.00	1.20
	Colheita	636.00	550.00	852.00	837.00	1 237.50
	Frasqueira	1 614.00	1 895.75	1 285.50	1 471.50	2 031.00
Terrantez	10 years		81.00	189.00	140.25	140.25
	20 years	45.00	1 619.00	847.00	1 746.00	1 602.75
	+ 40 years		7.20	9.60	162.00	1.20
	Frasqueira	1 051.50	1 196.25	1 500.76	2 532.75	1 809.75
Bastardo	Frasqueira	4.50	99.75	84.00	100.50	105.00
TOTAL		**3 277 614.94**	**3 012 265.82**	**3 407 343.17**	**3 187 680.98**	**3 372 160.11**

INDEX